MARGUERITE BENNETT

RAFAEL DE LATORRE

ANIM(O)SITY ™

VOLUME 1

THE WAKE

ROB SCHWAGER

MARSHALL DILLON

JUAN DOE

AFTERSHOCK™

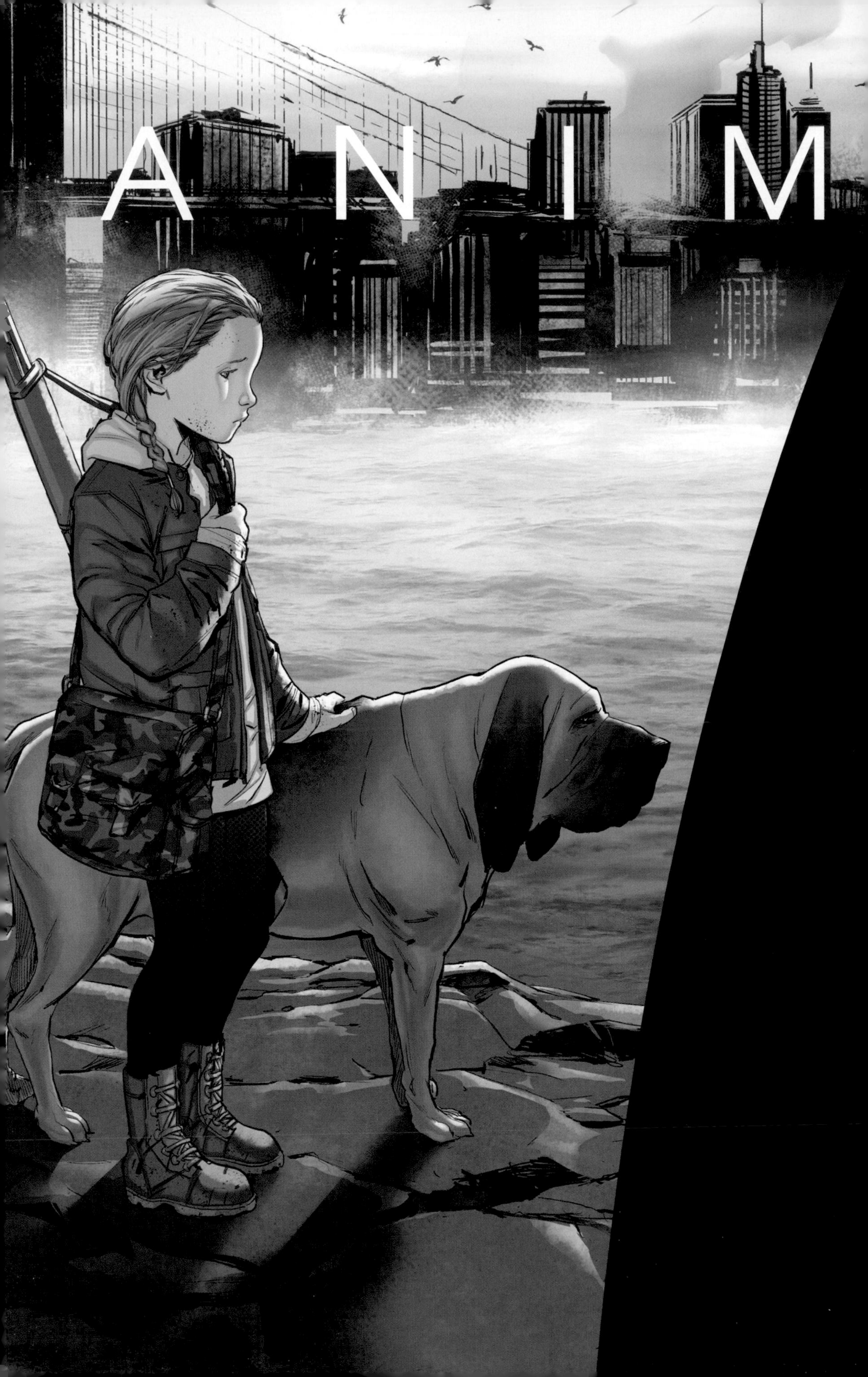
A N I M

OSITY
VOLUME 1
THE WAKE

MARGUERITE BENNETT creator & writer

RAFAEL DE LATORRE artist

ROB SCHWAGER colorist

MARSHALL DILLON letterer

JUAN DOE artist, "The Rise"

RAFAEL DE LATORRE w/ MARCELO MAIOLO front & original series covers

JUAN DOE variant front cover

JOHN J. HILL book & logo designer

MIKE MARTS editor

GARRY BROWN, REILLY BROWN, RAFAEL DE LATORRE, FRANCESCO FRANCAVILLA, MICHAEL GAYDOS, TONY HARRIS, SZYMON KUDRANSKI, JOHN McCREA, MIKE ROOTH, KELSEY SHANNON, HOYT SILVA, BRIAN STELFREEZE & KYLE STRAHM variant covers

AFTERSHOCK™

MIKE MARTS - Editor-in-Chief • JOE PRUETT - Publisher/ Chief Creative Officer
LEE KRAMER - President • JAWAD QURESHI - SVP, Investor Relations • JON KRAMER - Chief Executive Officer
MIKE ZAGARI - SVP Digital/Creative • JAY BEHLING - Chief Financial Officer
STEPHAN NILSON - Publishing Operations Manager • LISA Y. WU - Social Media Coordinator

AfterShock Trade Dress and Interior Design by JOHN J. HILL
AfterShock Logo Design by COMICRAFT
Proofreading by J. HARBORE & DOCTOR Z.
Publicity: contact AARON MARION (aaron@fifteenminutes.com) &
RYAN CROY (ryan@fifteenminutes.com) at 15 MINUTES

ANIMOSITY VOLUME 1: THE WAKE Published by AfterShock Comics, LLC, 15300 Ventura Boulevard Suite 507, Sherman Oaks, CA 91403. Originally published as Animosity #1-4 & Animosity: The Rise #1. PRINTED IN KOREA.
Second Printing: May 2017. 10 9 8 7 6 5 4 3 2

AFTERSHOCKCOMICS.COM Follow us on social media

I N T R O D U C T I O N

It's like waking from a dream.

You held me and you carried me. You fed me, washed me, nursed me, warmed me. You cradled me against your chest when you slept, until I was too big to cradle. You gave me a bed of my own, brushed my hair, read to me, taught me, played with me, comforted me, kissed me goodnight.

You loved me.

I was yours, and you were the world and everything in it.

And when I woke, and grew, and understood everything that you had done—everything that you had given me, all tenderness and all patience and all love—

I fucking wept.

We can't understand, when we're children. Only when we're grown.

Only when we wake from that dream.

And now I have to carry you. Now I get to carry you.

And I know one day I will have to leave you—live long, oh God, I hope you live so long—and that all my life is going to be about protecting yours. About making the world safe for you. About giving you up.

I love you more than anything that has ever been seen on Earth or dreamed of in Heaven or forgotten in Hell. God never made a fucking thing worth keeping—except for you.

And every day, until the day I die, will be about making you happy, and keeping you safe, and knowing, knowing in whatever passes for my fucking soul, that I will have to let you go.

That in turn, you will have to grow up, and wake from this dream.

Oh, God.

What if I just wasn't meant to have children?

MARGUERITE BENNETT
January 4th, 2016
Los Angeles

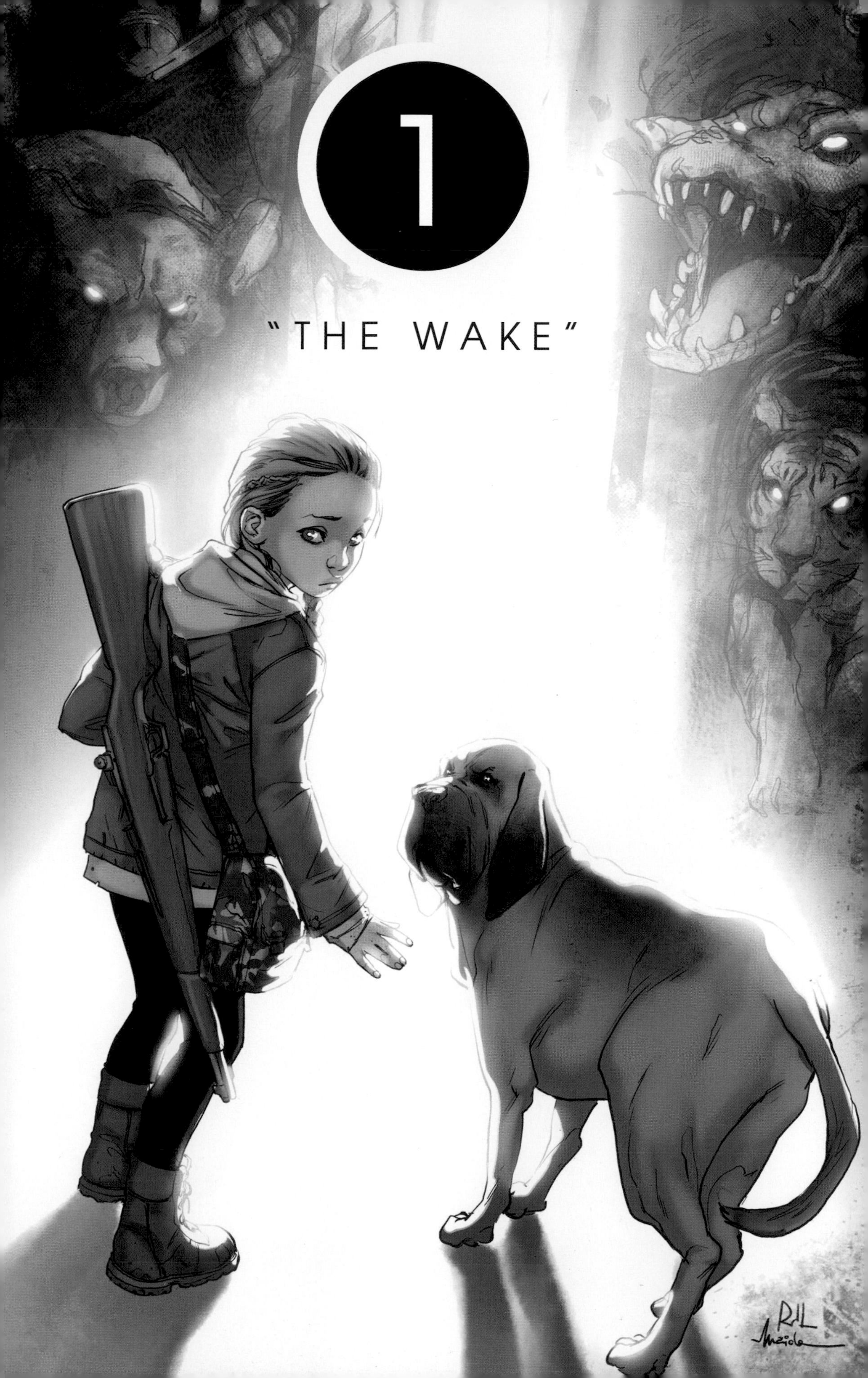
1
"THE WAKE"

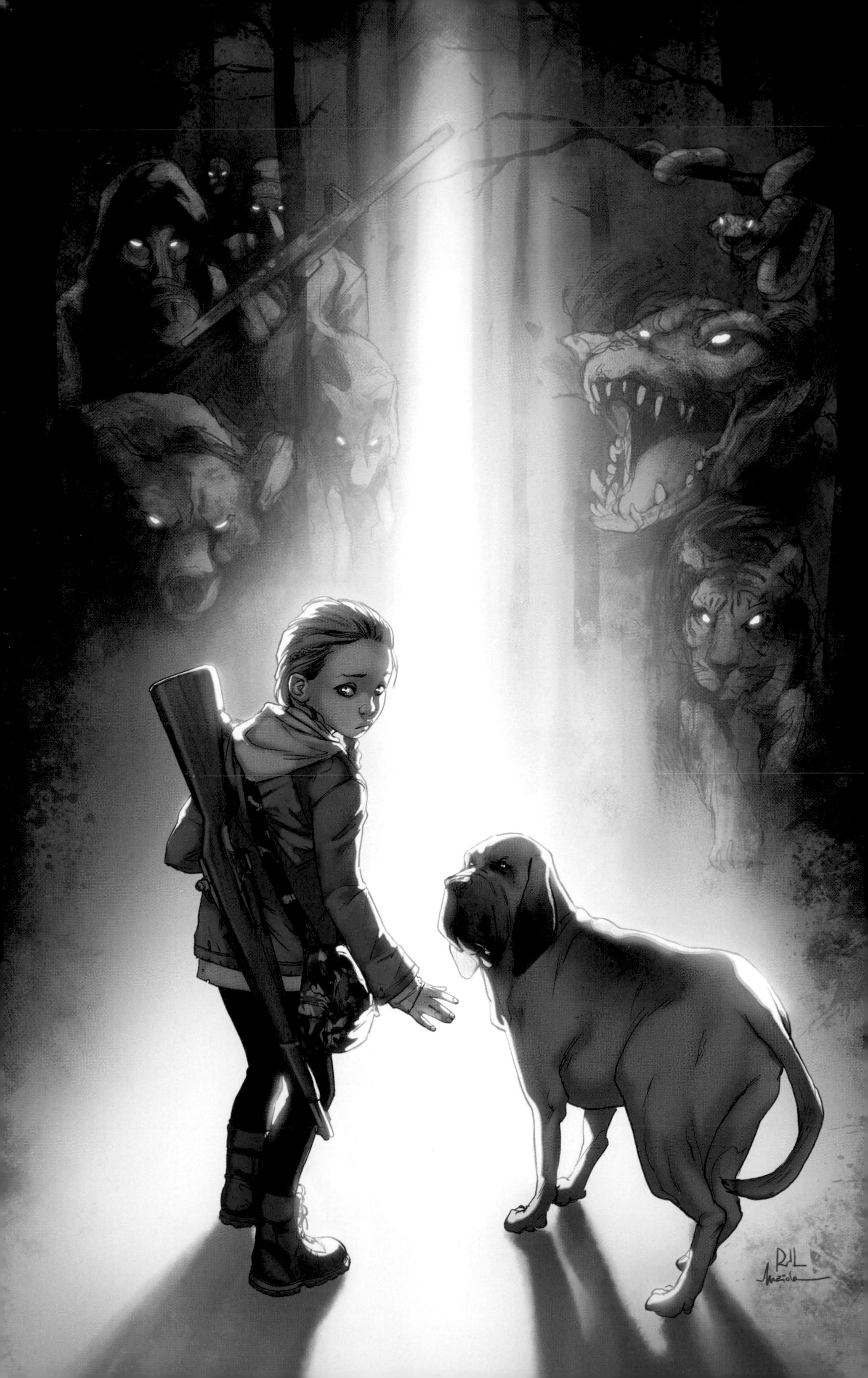

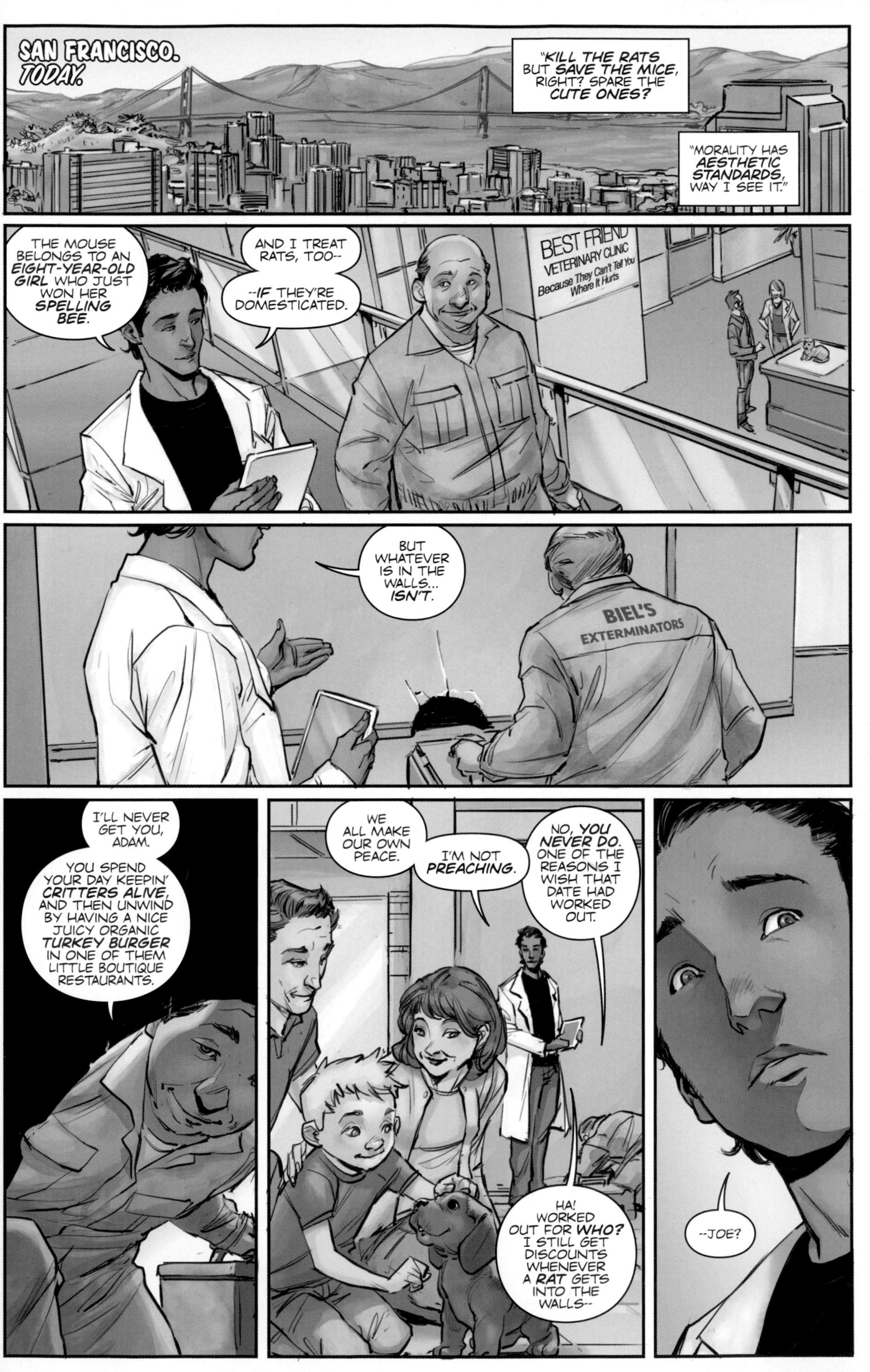
SAN FRANCISCO. TODAY.
"KILL THE RATS BUT SAVE THE MICE, RIGHT? SPARE THE CUTE ONES?
"MORALITY HAS AESTHETIC STANDARDS, WAY I SEE IT."
THE MOUSE BELONGS TO AN EIGHT-YEAR-OLD GIRL WHO JUST WON HER SPELLING BEE.
AND I TREAT RATS, TOO--
--IF THEY'RE DOMESTICATED.
BEST FRIEND VETERINARY CLINIC Because They Can't Tell You Where It Hurts
BUT WHATEVER IS IN THE WALLS... ISN'T.
BIEL'S EXTERMINATORS
I'LL NEVER GET YOU, ADAM.
YOU SPEND YOUR DAY KEEPIN' CRITTERS ALIVE, AND THEN UNWIND BY HAVING A NICE JUICY ORGANIC TURKEY BURGER IN ONE OF THEM LITTLE BOUTIQUE RESTAURANTS.
WE ALL MAKE OUR OWN PEACE.
I'M NOT PREACHING.
NO, YOU NEVER DO. ONE OF THE REASONS I WISH THAT DATE HAD WORKED OUT.
HA! WORKED OUT FOR WHO? I STILL GET DISCOUNTS WHENEVER A RAT GETS INTO THE WALLS--
--JOE?

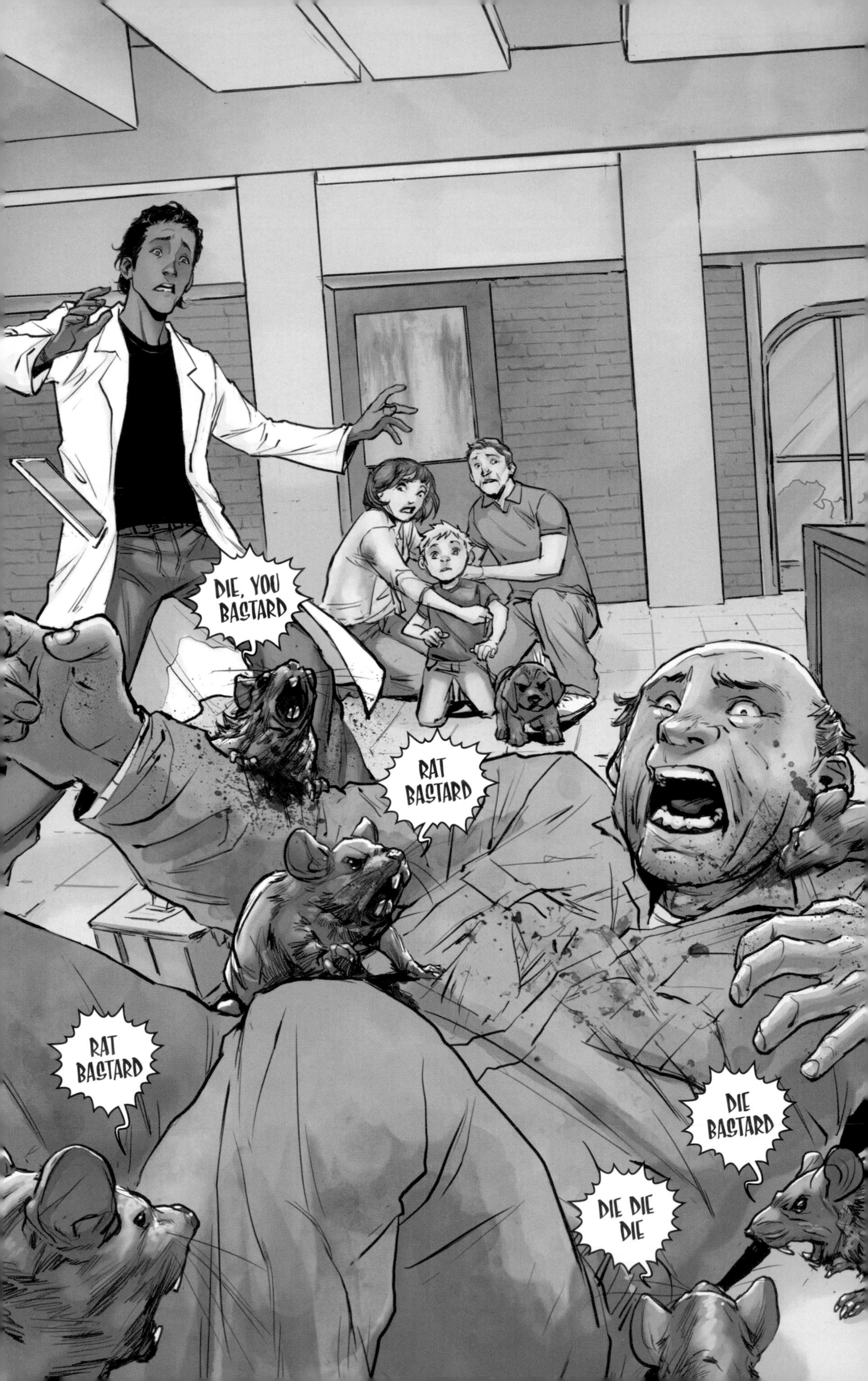
DIE, YOU BASTARD
RAT BASTARD
RAT BASTARD
DIE BASTARD
DIE DIE DIE

Then the Lord God said,
"Behold, I have given thee every plant yielding seed that is on the surface
of all the Earth, and every tree which has fruit yielding seed;
it shall be food for you;
and to every beast of the Earth and to every bird of the sky and
to every thing that creepeth upon the Earth,
I have given every green plant for food";
and it was so.

God saw all that He had made, and behold,
it was very good.

And there was evening and there was morning, and that was the sixth day.
—Genesis 1:29-31

Yesterday, God was in His Heaven,
the average American consumed 38lbs of meat per year,
and there were roughly 20,000,121,091,000,000,000 animals on planet Earth.

This number can be expressed as 20 quintillion,
or the equivalent of 20 billion billions,
and includes 500 trillion krill, 50 billion chickens, 1 billion cattle, 1 billion swine,
1 billion domestic sheep, 850 million goats, 600 million cats, 400 million dogs, 60 million horses,
40 million donkeys, 3 million whales, 500,000 elephants, 200,000 chimpanzees,
30,000 American bison, 20,000 polar bears, 8,000 cheetahs, 4,000 Komodo dragons, 1,500 pandas,
500 Siberian tigers, 100 red wolves, 45 amur leopards, 5 two-horned rhinos, two billion tons of fish,
and 10 quintillion insects.

There are also 7,250,000,000 humans, but who's counting.

As of 2016, there were over 1,203,375 species of animals,
and one species of human,
but as more than 10,000 new species are identified and categorized each year,
these statics are nebulous.

And since we got the data from the Animals, who knows?
Maybe they're fucking liars.

Mostly, what we know is this:

One day, for no goddamn reason, the Animals woke up.
They started thinking.
They started talking.
They started taking revenge.

We call it the Wake.

It's less dramatic than the Funeral.

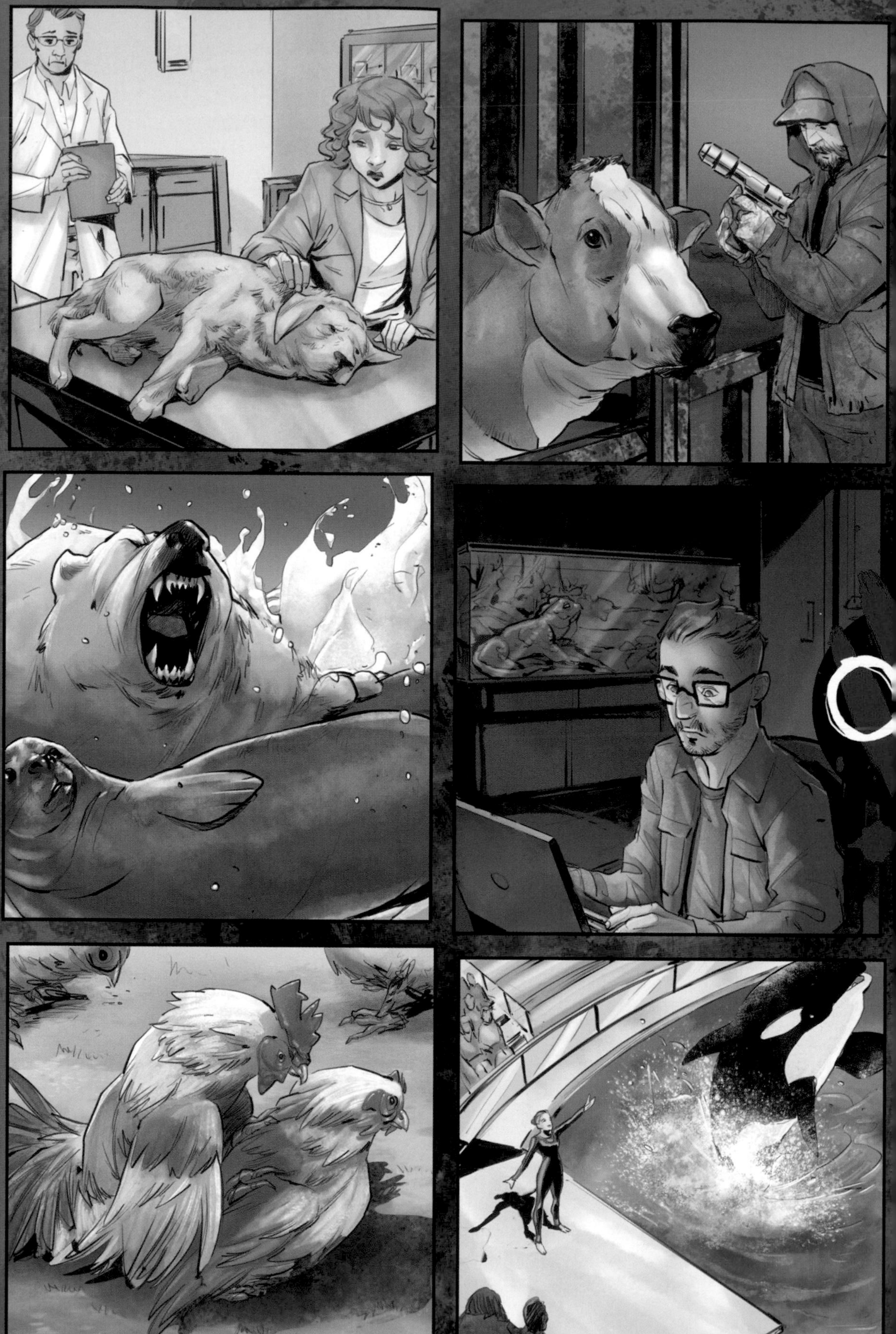

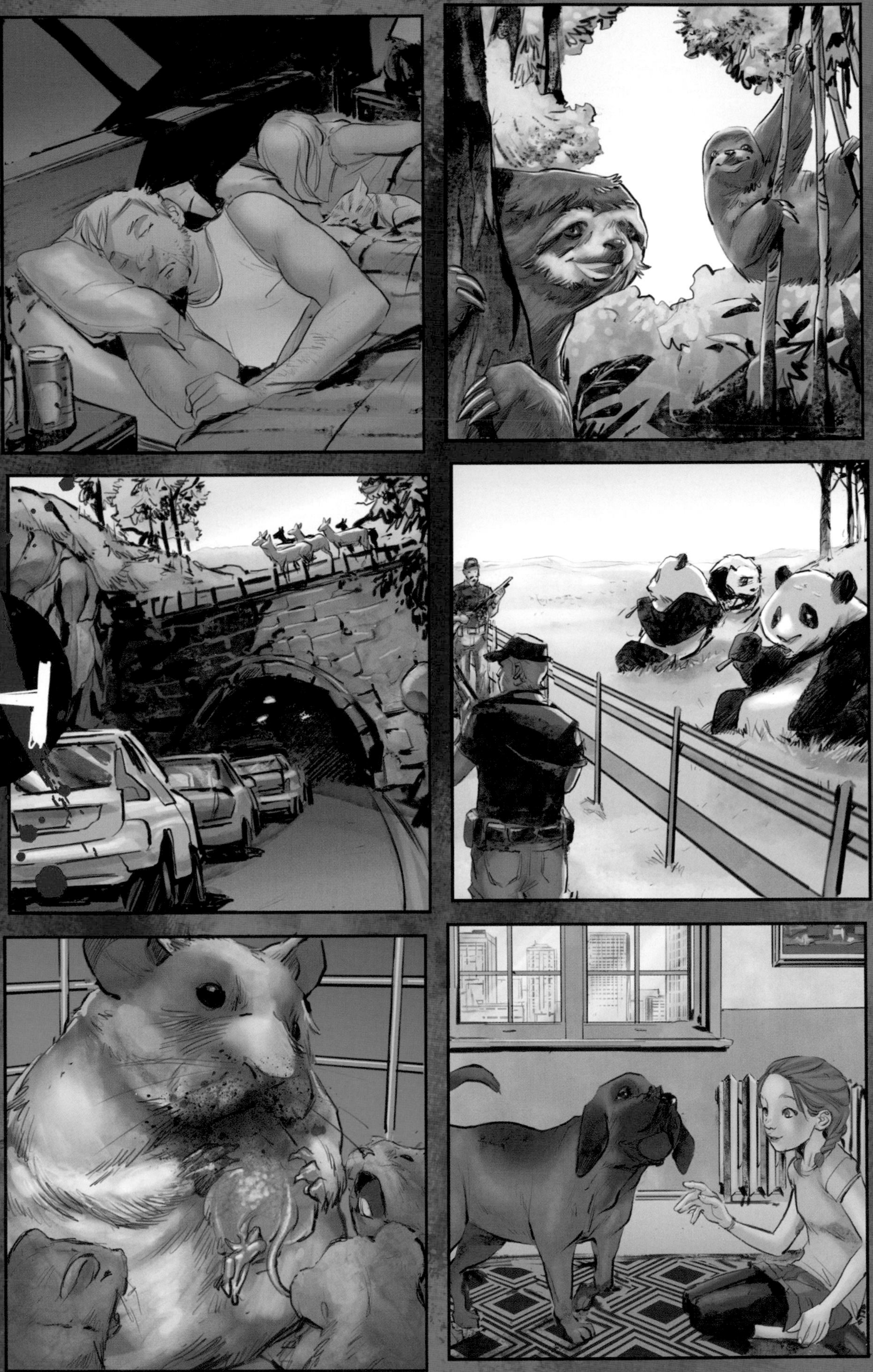

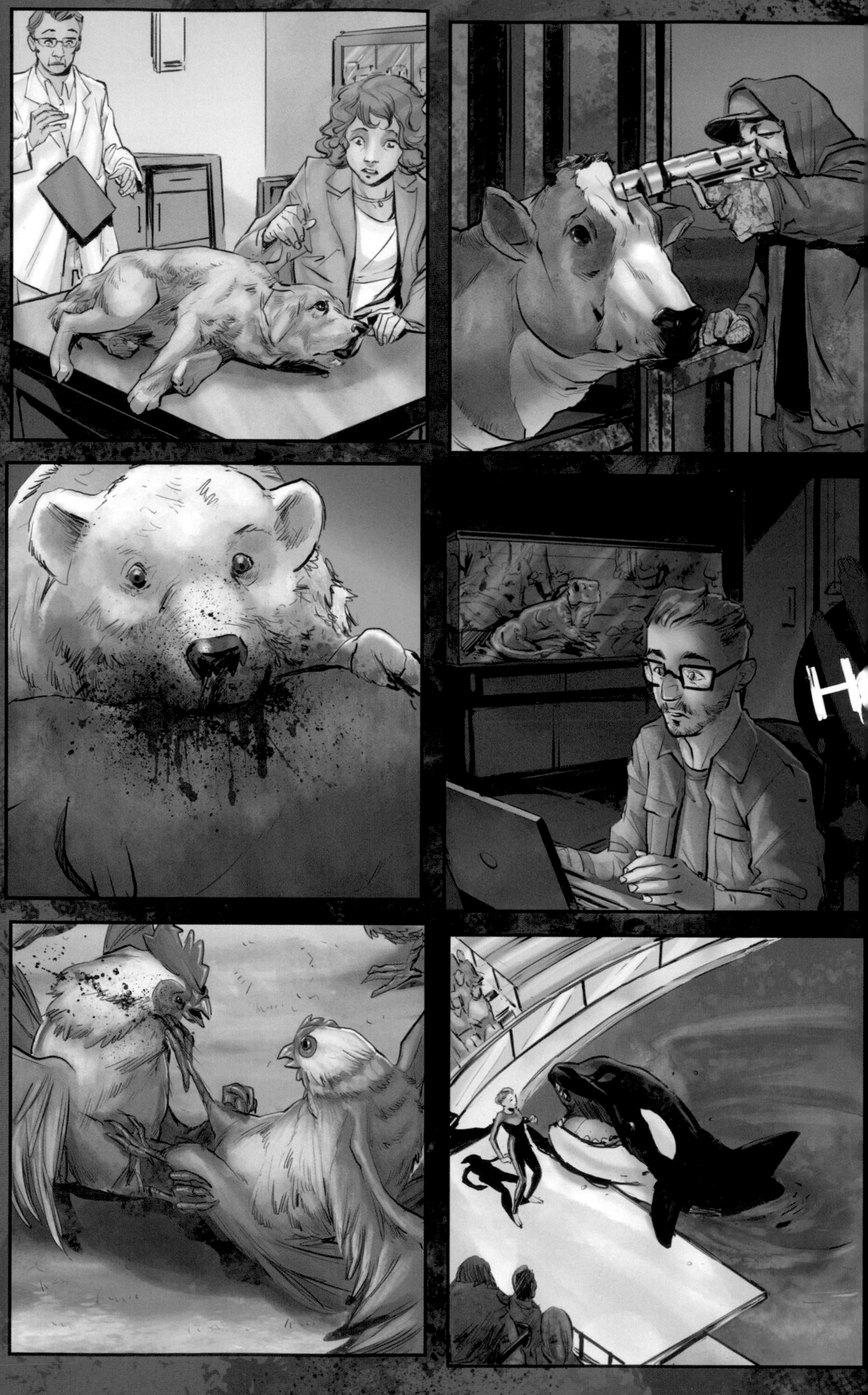

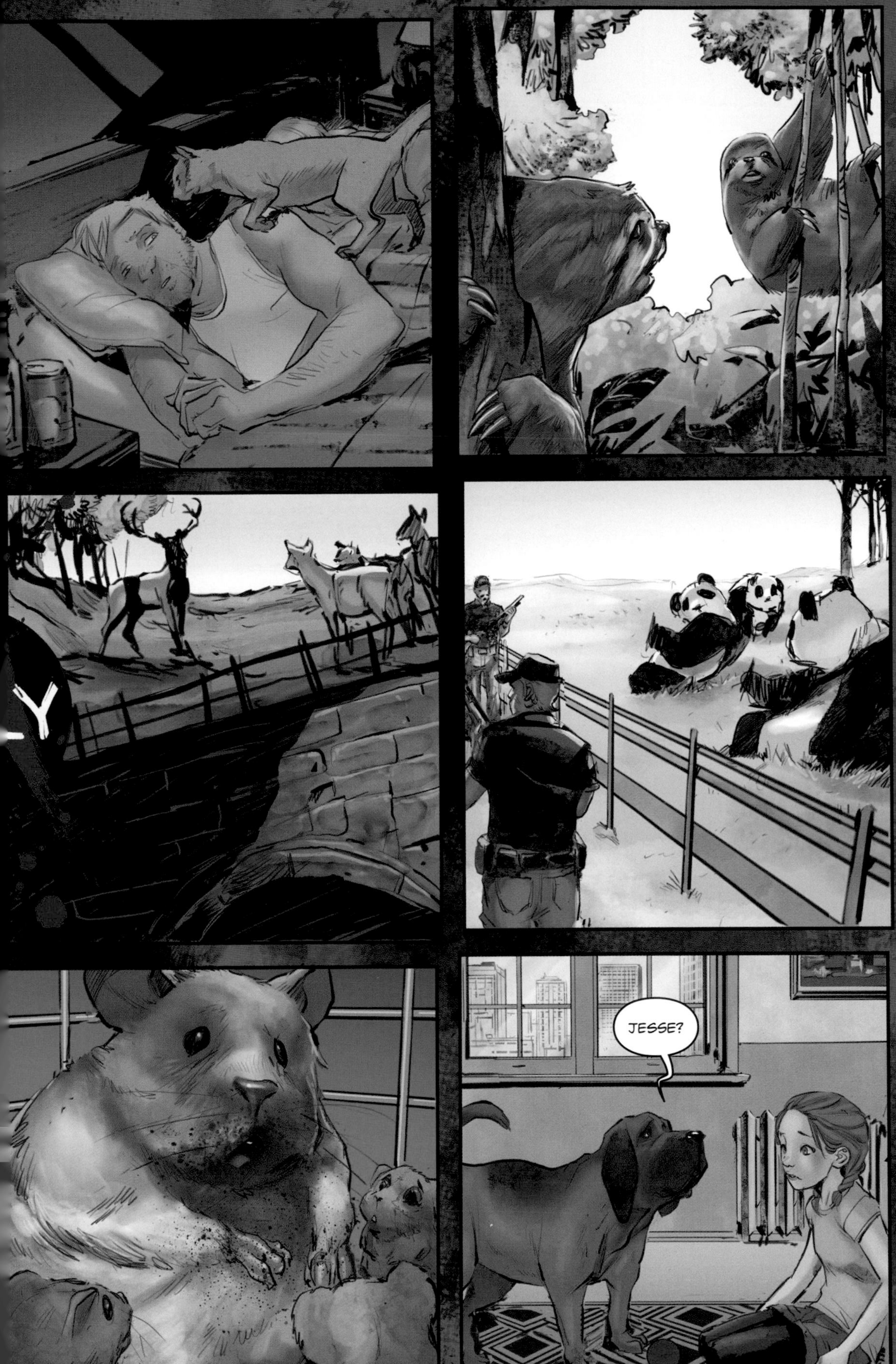
JESSE?

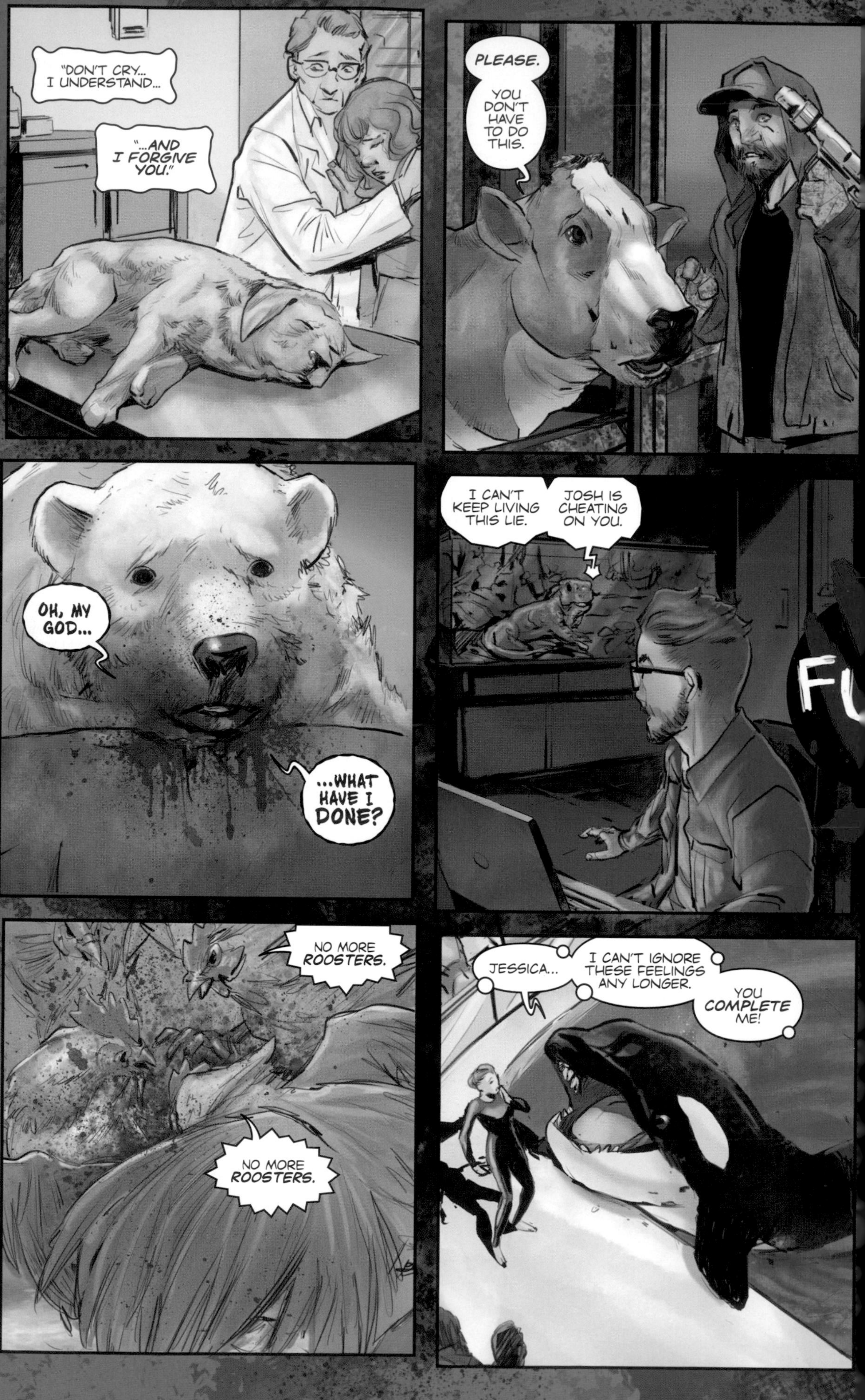
"DON'T CRY... I UNDERSTAND...
"...AND I FORGIVE YOU."
PLEASE.
YOU DON'T HAVE TO DO THIS.
OH, MY GOD...
...WHAT HAVE I DONE?
I CAN'T KEEP LIVING THIS LIE.
JOSH IS CHEATING ON YOU.
FU
NO MORE ROOSTERS.
NO MORE ROOSTERS.
JESSICA...
I CAN'T IGNORE THESE FEELINGS ANY LONGER.
YOU COMPLETE ME!

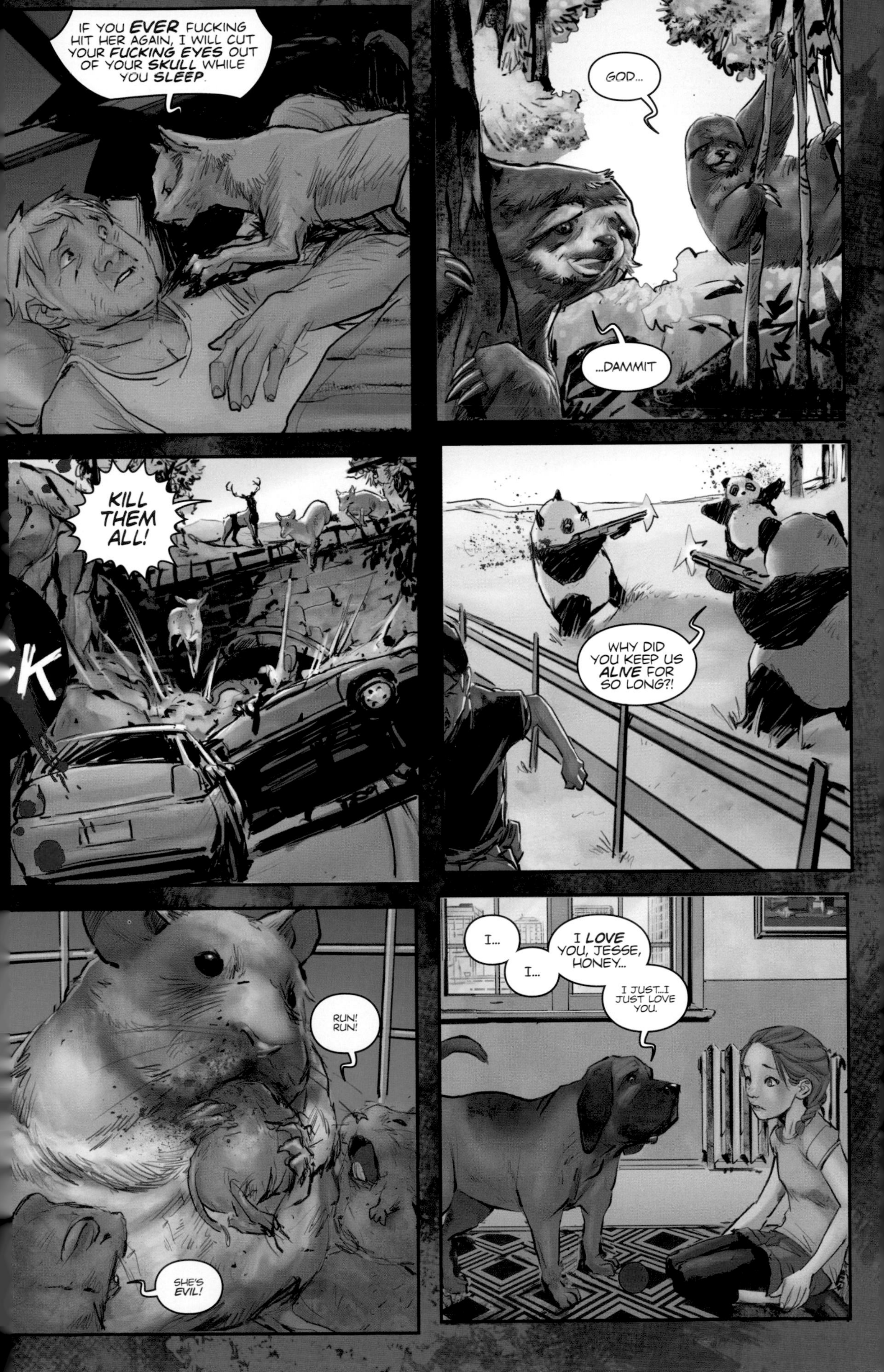

IF YOU EVER FUCKING HIT HER AGAIN, I WILL CUT YOUR FUCKING EYES OUT OF YOUR SKULL WHILE YOU SLEEP.
GOD...
...DAMMIT
KILL THEM ALL!
WHY DID YOU KEEP US ALIVE FOR SO LONG?!
RUN! RUN!
SHE'S EVIL!
I...
I...
I LOVE YOU, JESSE, HONEY...
I JUST...I JUST LOVE YOU.

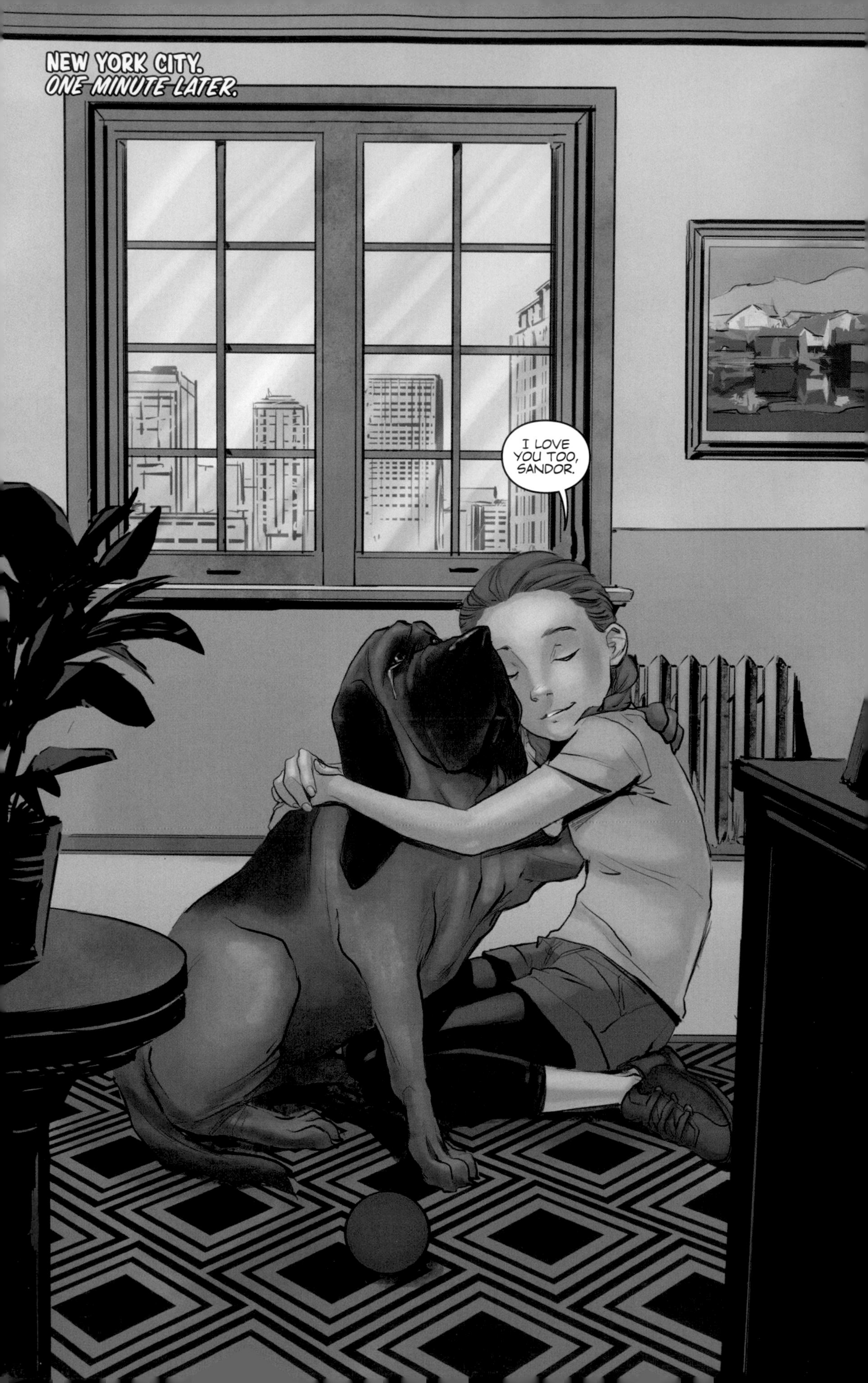
NEW YORK CITY.
ONE MINUTE LATER.
I LOVE YOU TOO, SANDOR.

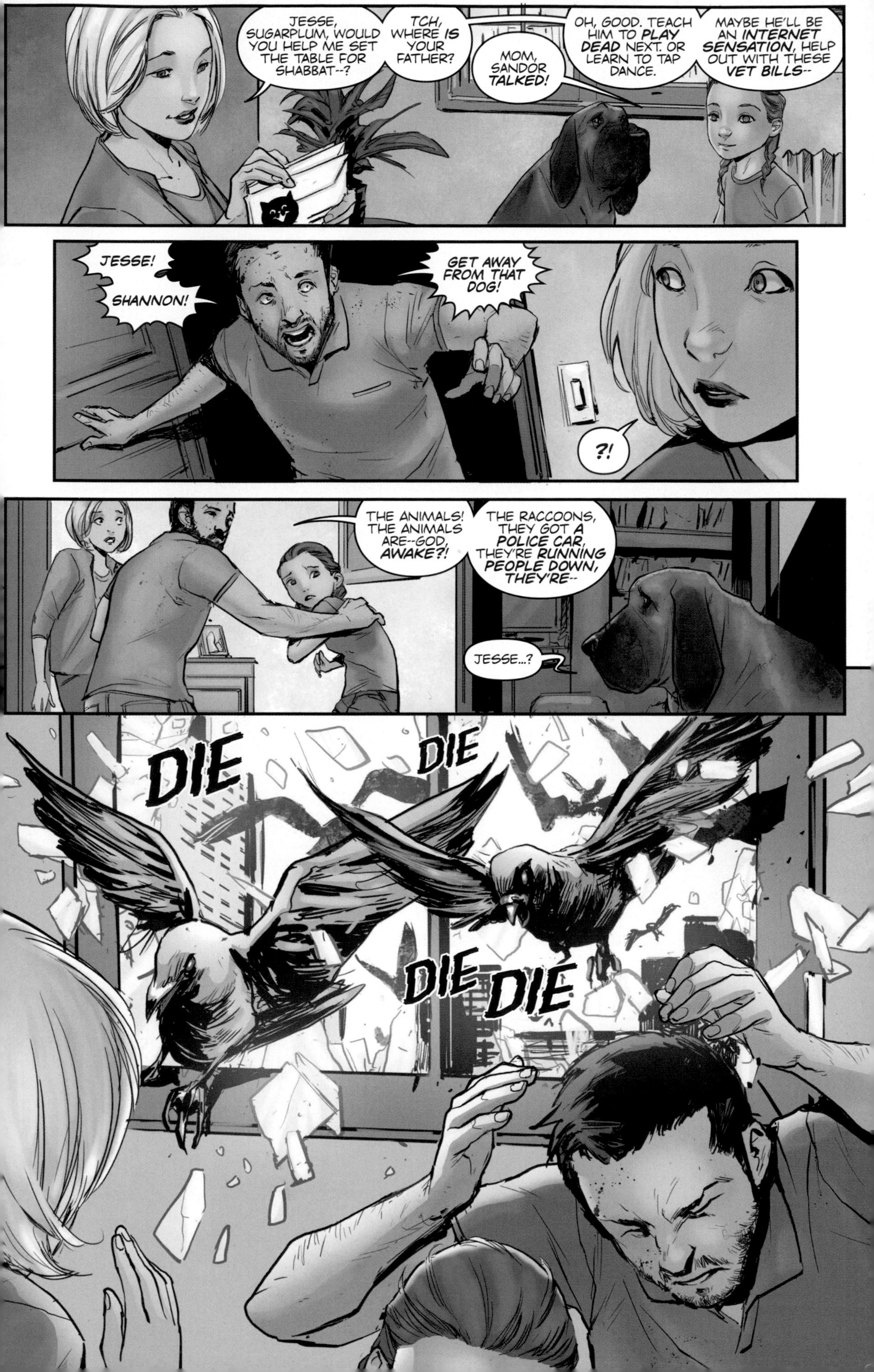
JESSE, SUGARPLUM, WOULD YOU HELP ME SET THE TABLE FOR SHABBAT--?
TCH, WHERE IS YOUR FATHER?
MOM, SANDOR TALKED!
OH, GOOD. TEACH HIM TO PLAY DEAD NEXT. OR LEARN TO TAP DANCE.
MAYBE HE'LL BE AN INTERNET SENSATION, HELP OUT WITH THESE VET BILLS--
JESSE!
SHANNON!
GET AWAY FROM THAT DOG!
?!
THE ANIMALS! THE ANIMALS ARE--GOD, AWAKE?!
THE RACCOONS, THEY GOT A POLICE CAR, THEY'RE RUNNING PEOPLE DOWN, THEY'RE--
JESSE...?
DIE
DIE
DIE
DIE

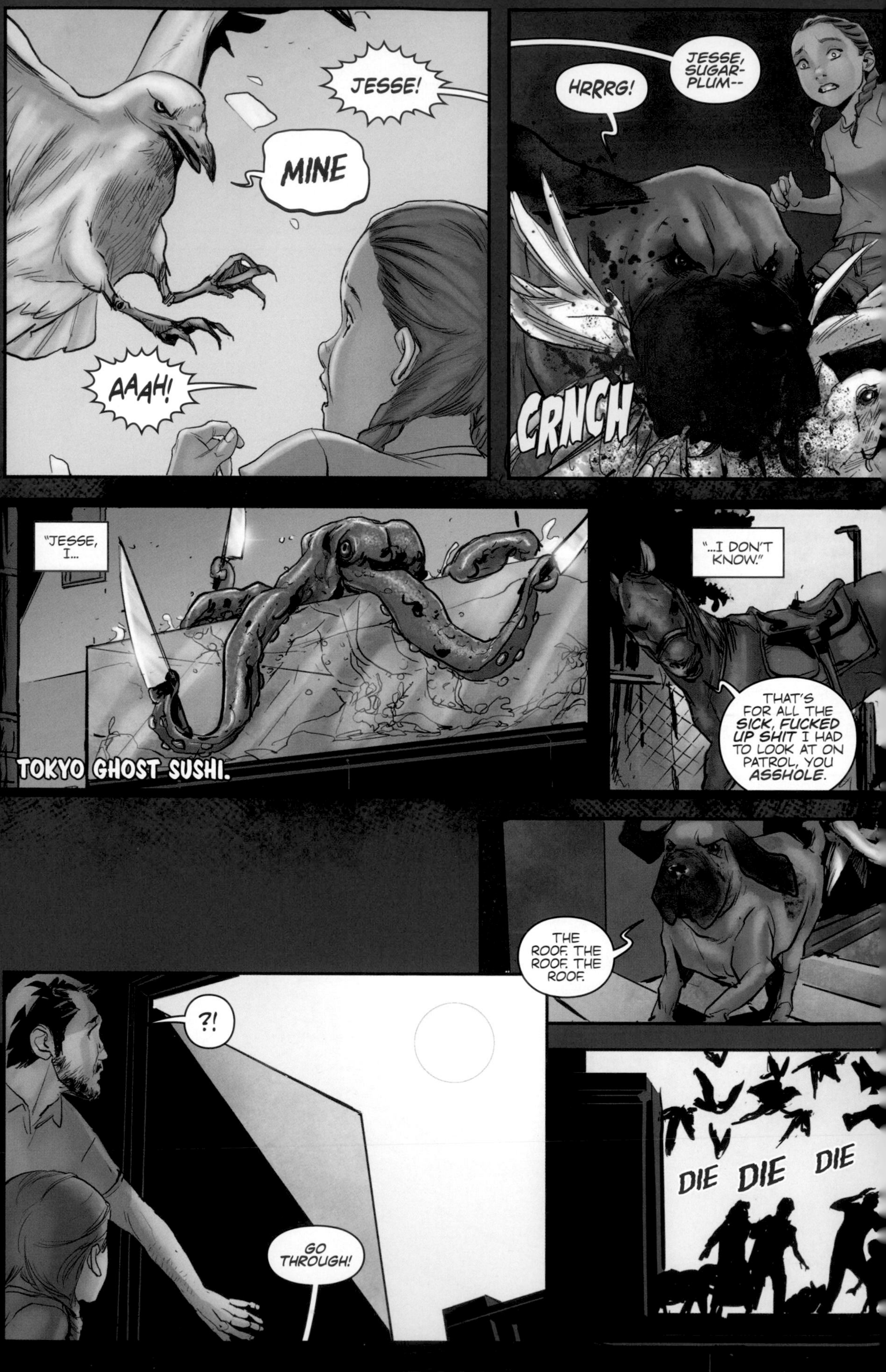
JESSE!
MINE
AAAH!
HRRRG!
JESSE, SUGAR-PLUM--
CRNCH
"JESSE, I...
TOKYO GHOST SUSHI.
"...I DON'T KNOW."
THAT'S FOR ALL THE SICK, FUCKED UP SHIT I HAD TO LOOK AT ON PATROL, YOU ASSHOLE.
THE ROOF. THE ROOF. THE ROOF.
?!
GO THROUGH!
DIE DIE DIE

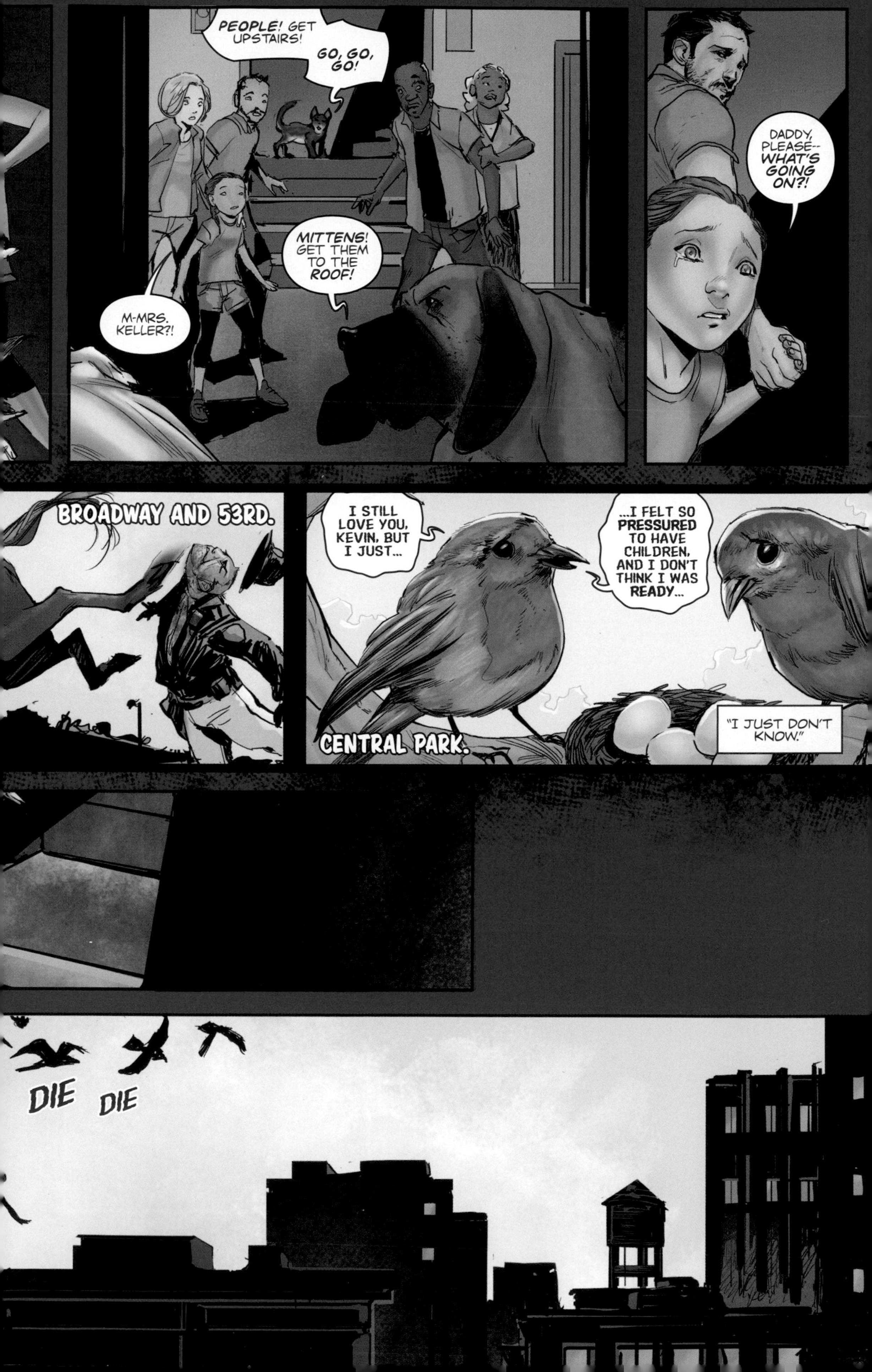
PEOPLE! GET UPSTAIRS!
GO, GO, GO!
M-MRS. KELLER?!
MITTENS! GET THEM TO THE ROOF!
DADDY, PLEASE-- WHAT'S GOING ON?!
BROADWAY AND 53RD.
CENTRAL PARK.
I STILL LOVE YOU, KEVIN, BUT I JUST...
...I FELT SO PRESSURED TO HAVE CHILDREN, AND I DON'T THINK I WAS READY...
"I JUST DON'T KNOW."
DIE
DIE

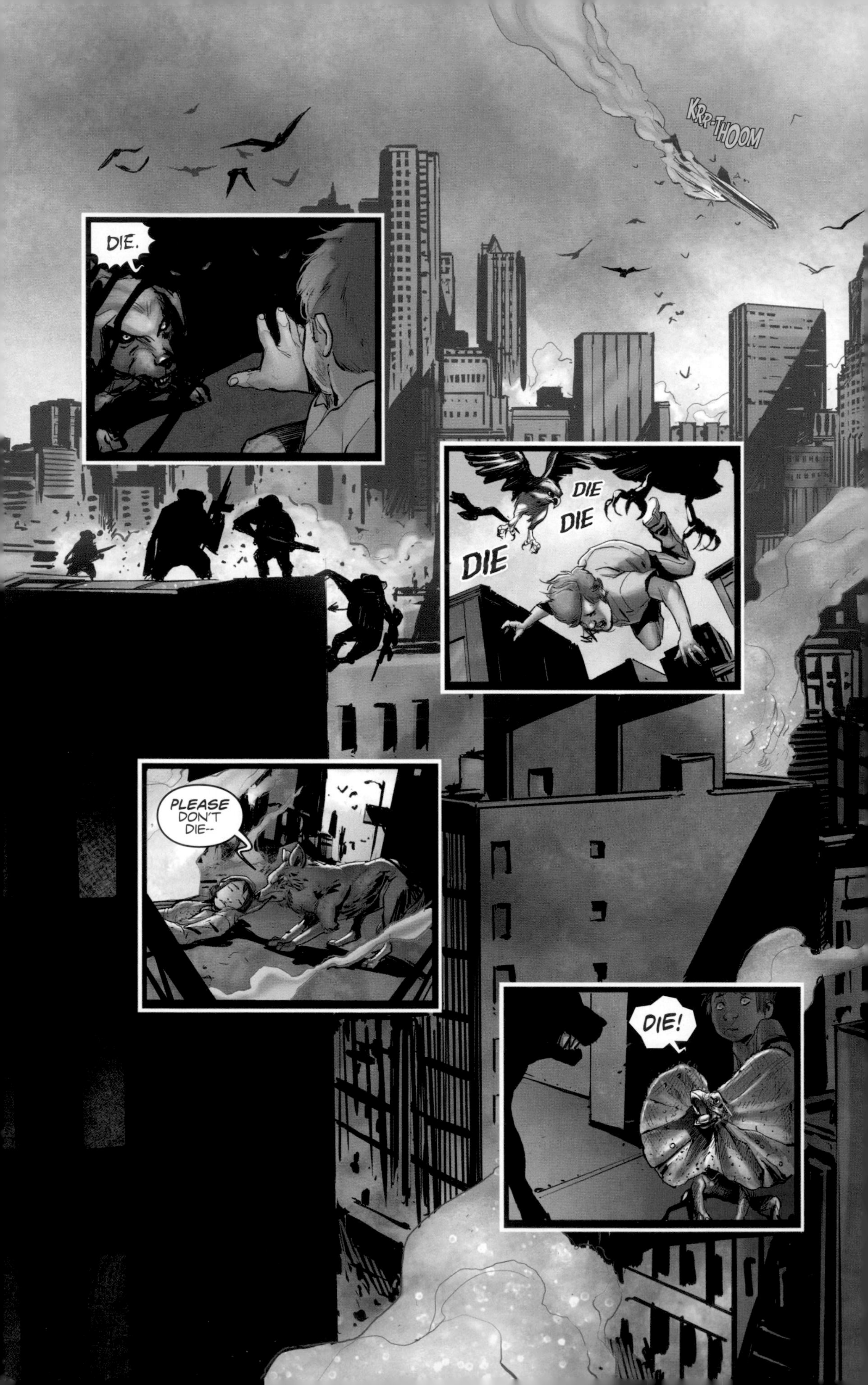
KRR-THOOM
DIE.
DIE
DIE
DIE
PLEASE DON'T DIE--
DIE!

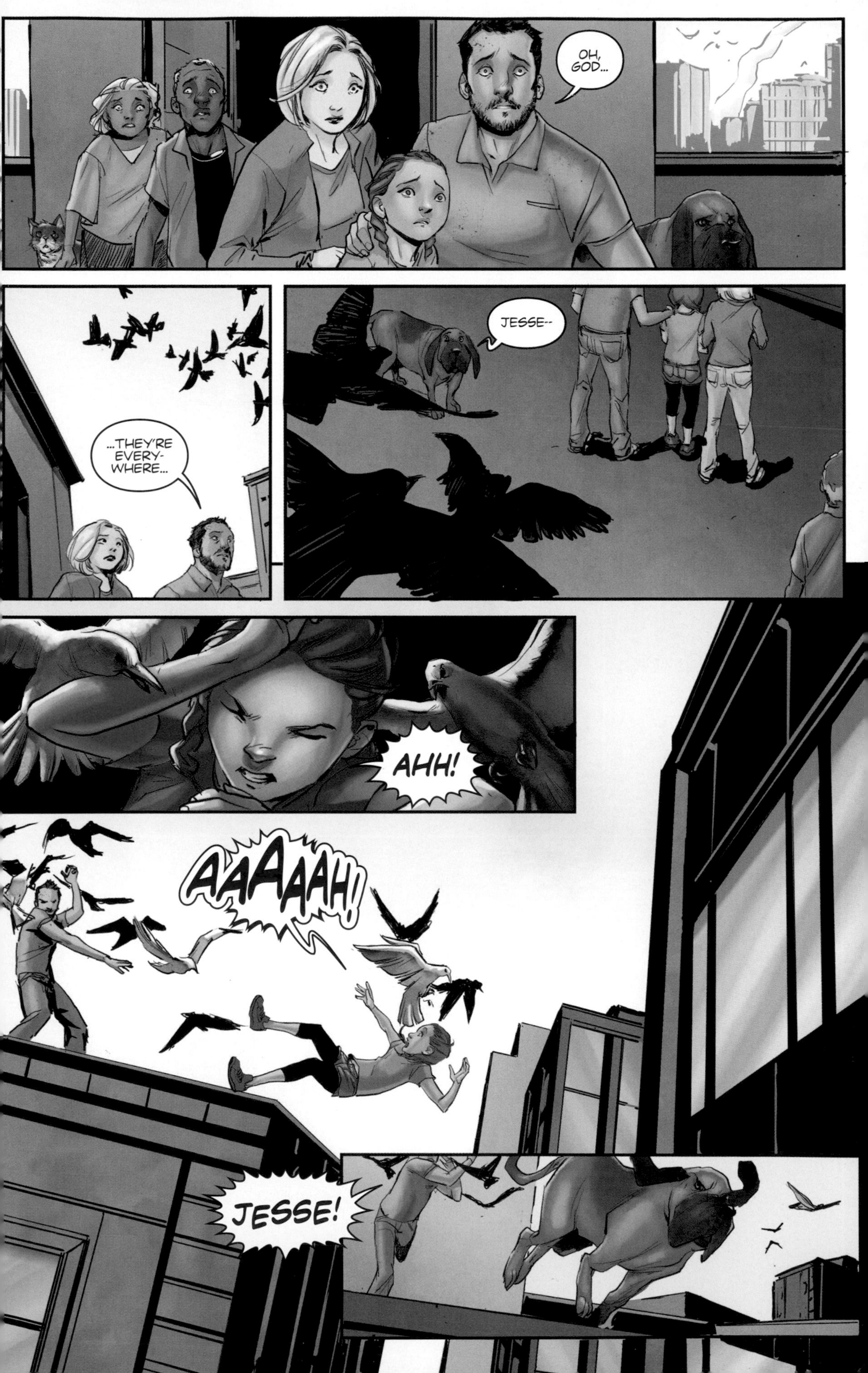
OH, GOD...
...THEY'RE EVERY-WHERE...
JESSE--
AHH!
AAAAAH!
JESSE!

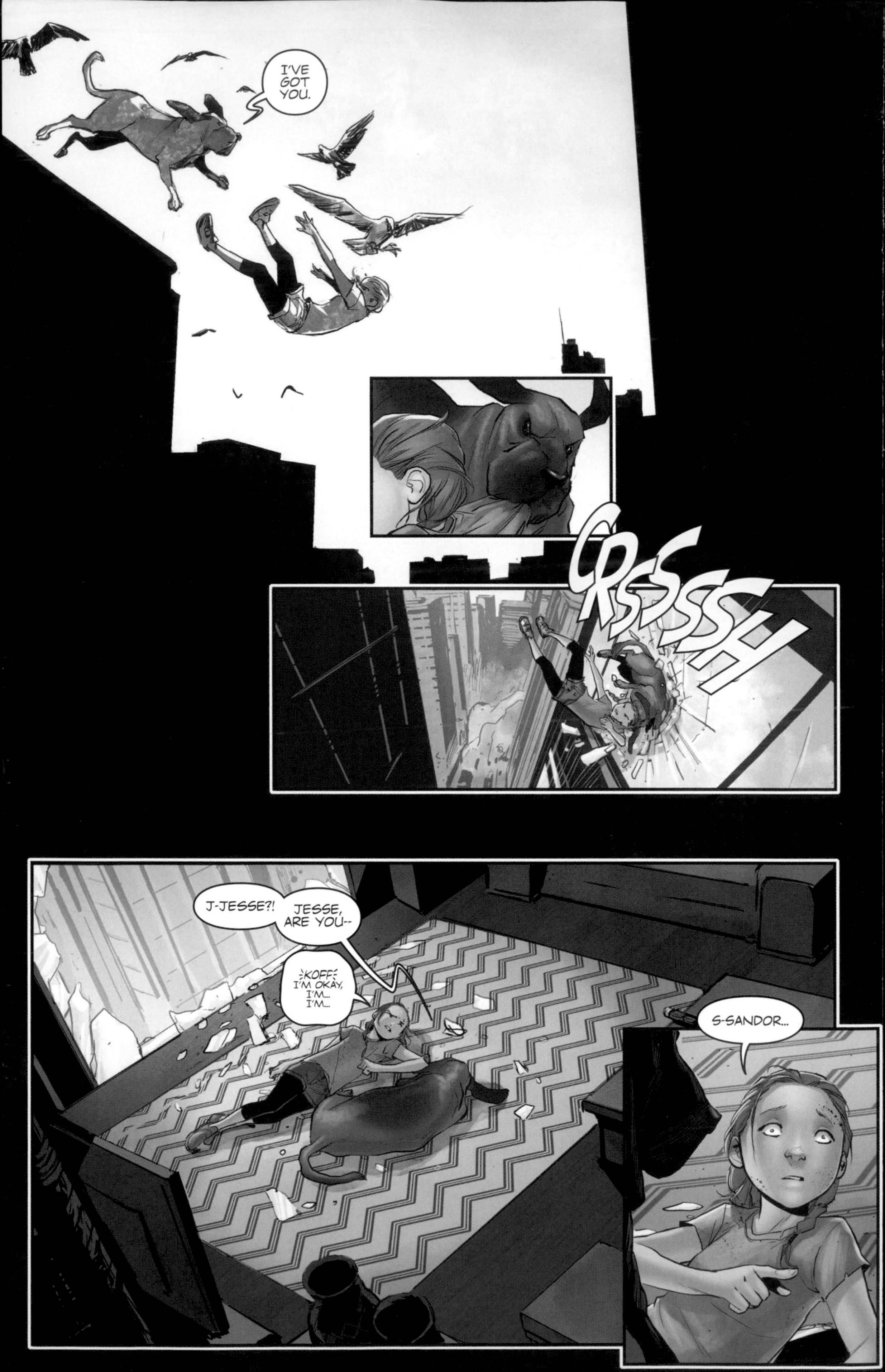
I'VE GOT YOU.
CRSSSSH
J-JESSE?!
JESSE, ARE YOU--
KOFF I'M OKAY, I'M... I'M...
S-SANDOR...

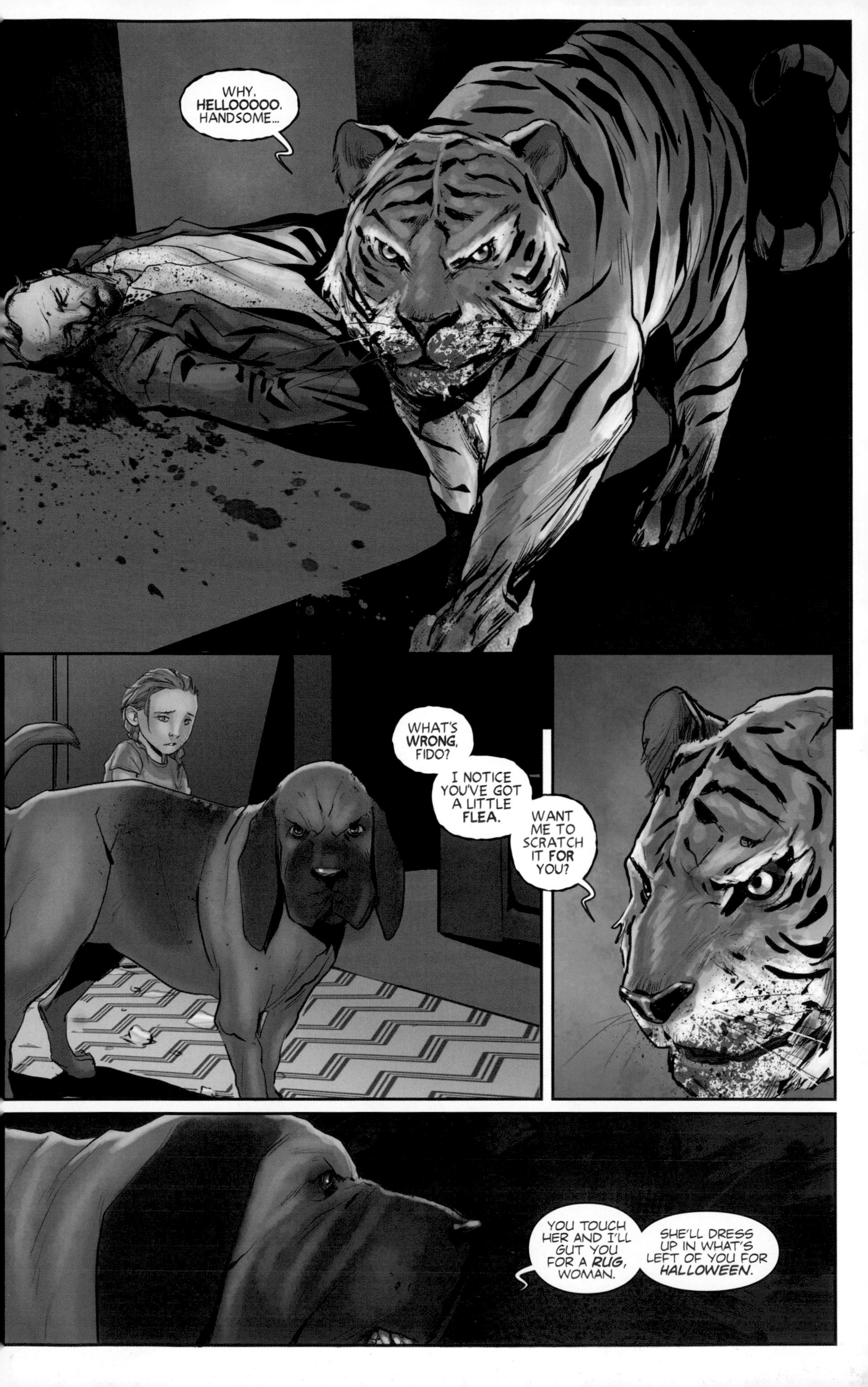
WHY, HELLOOOOO, HANDSOME...
WHAT'S WRONG, FIDO?
I NOTICE YOU'VE GOT A LITTLE FLEA.
WANT ME TO SCRATCH IT FOR YOU?
YOU TOUCH HER AND I'LL GUT YOU FOR A RUG, WOMAN.
SHE'LL DRESS UP IN WHAT'S LEFT OF YOU FOR HALLOWEEN.

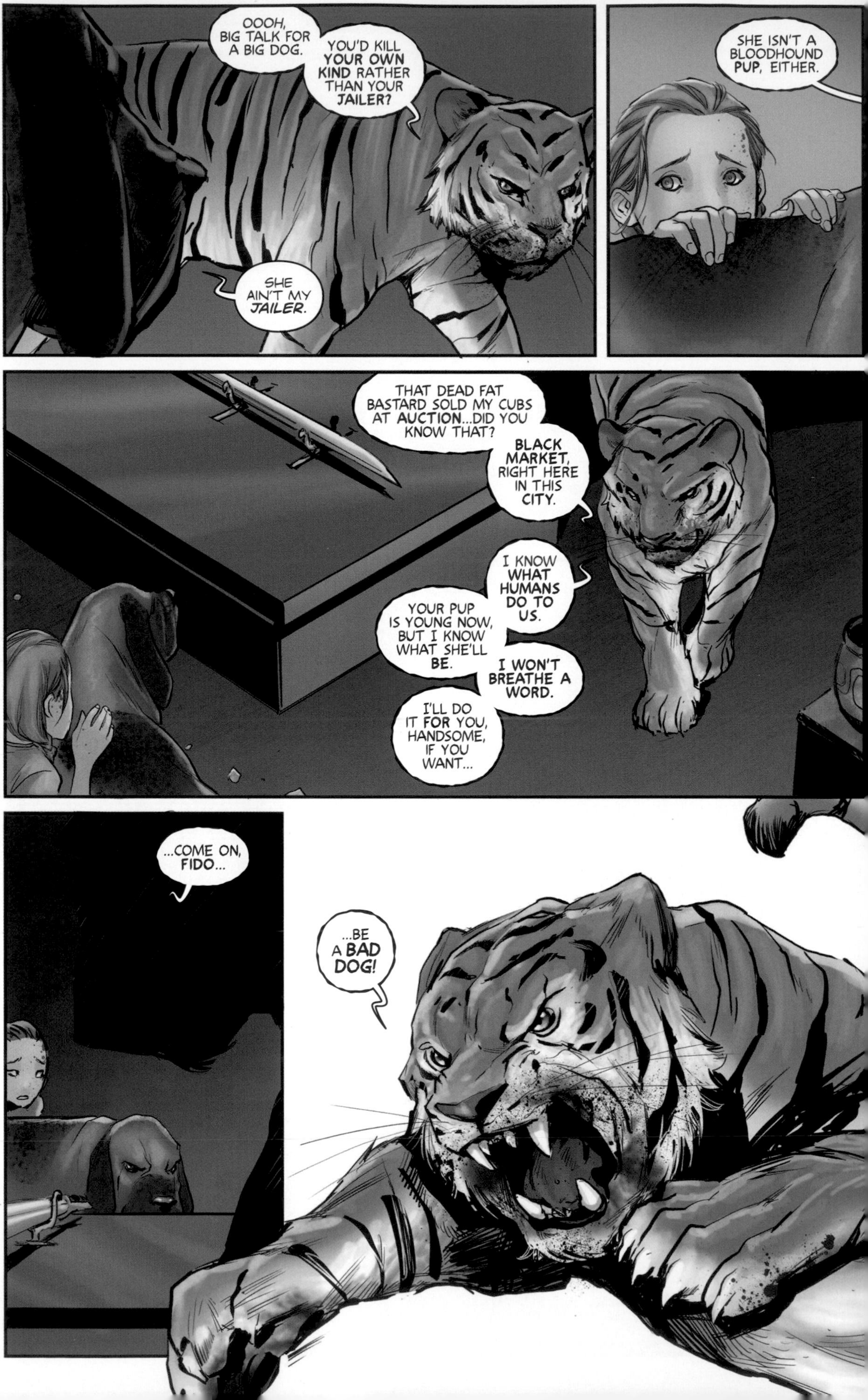
OOOH, BIG TALK FOR A BIG DOG.
YOU'D KILL YOUR OWN KIND RATHER THAN YOUR JAILER?
SHE AIN'T MY JAILER.
SHE ISN'T A BLOODHOUND PUP, EITHER.
THAT DEAD FAT BASTARD SOLD MY CUBS AT AUCTION...DID YOU KNOW THAT?
BLACK MARKET, RIGHT HERE IN THIS CITY.
I KNOW WHAT HUMANS DO TO US.
YOUR PUP IS YOUNG NOW, BUT I KNOW WHAT SHE'LL BE.
I WON'T BREATHE A WORD.
I'LL DO IT FOR YOU, HANDSOME, IF YOU WANT...
...COME ON, FIDO...
...BE A BAD DOG!

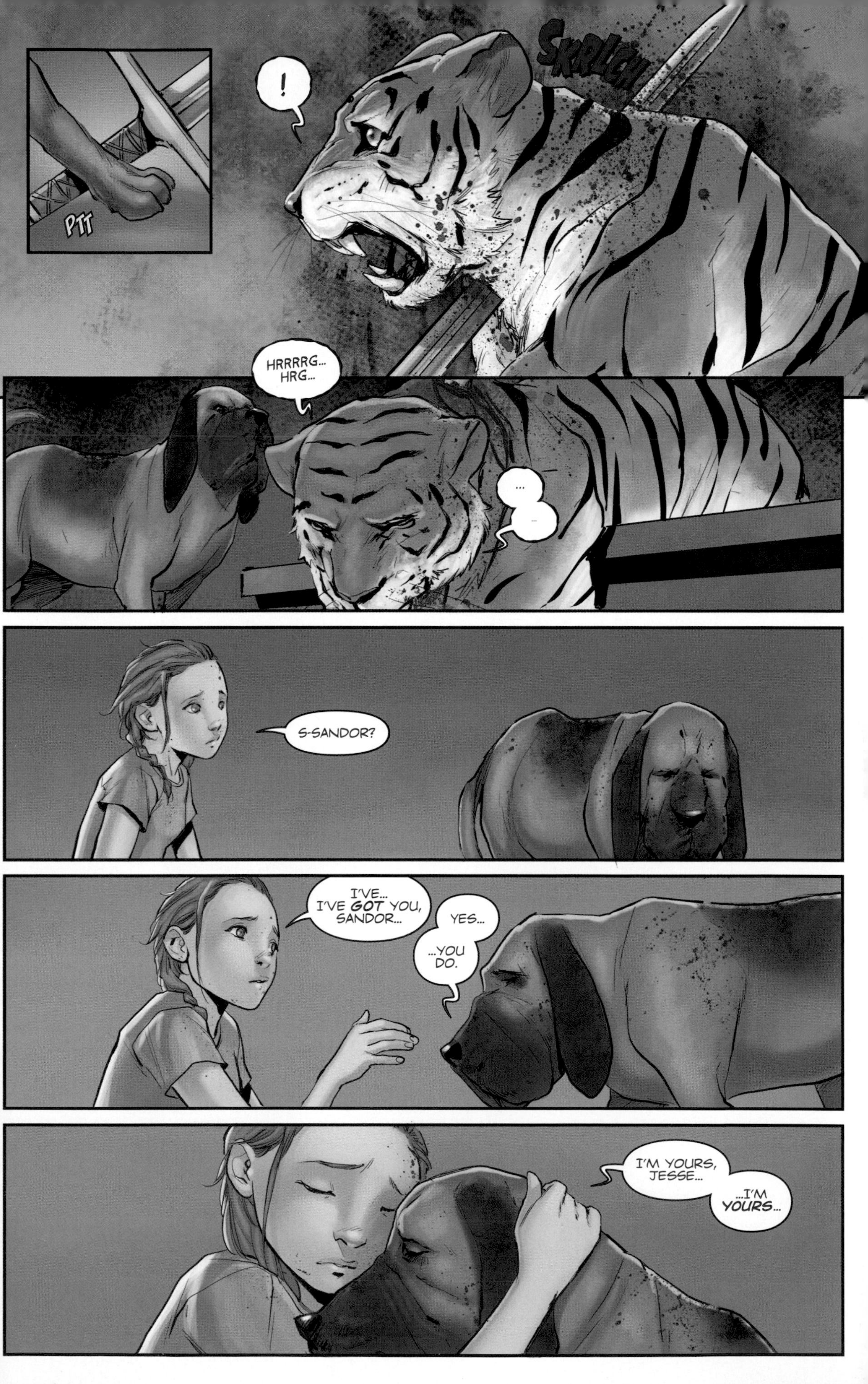
PTT
!
SKRLCH
HRRRRG... HRG...
...
...
S-SANDOR?
I'VE... I'VE **GOT** YOU, SANDOR...
YES...
...YOU DO.
I'M YOURS, JESSE...
...I'M **YOURS**...

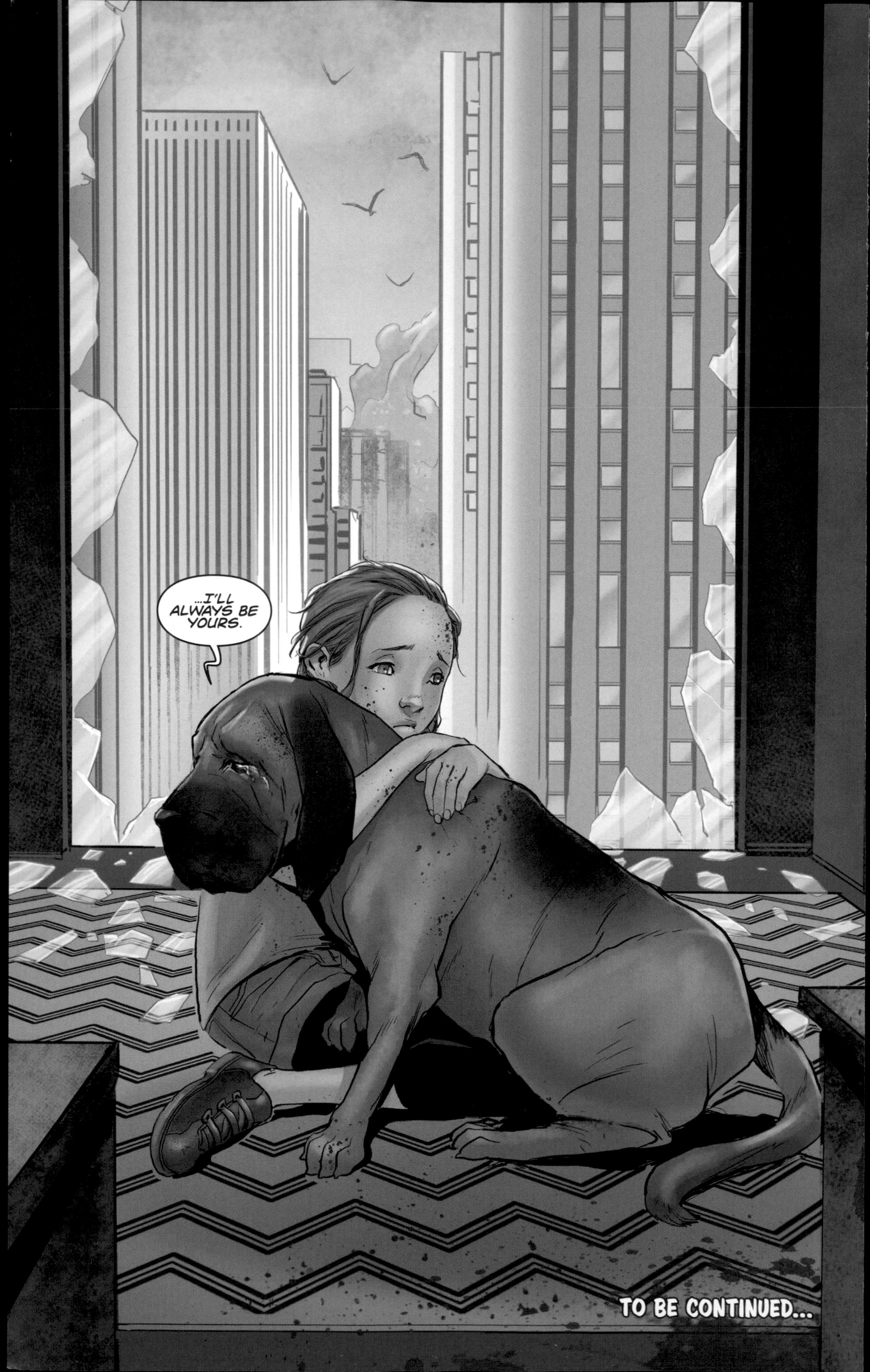
...I'LL ALWAYS BE YOURS.
TO BE CONTINUED...

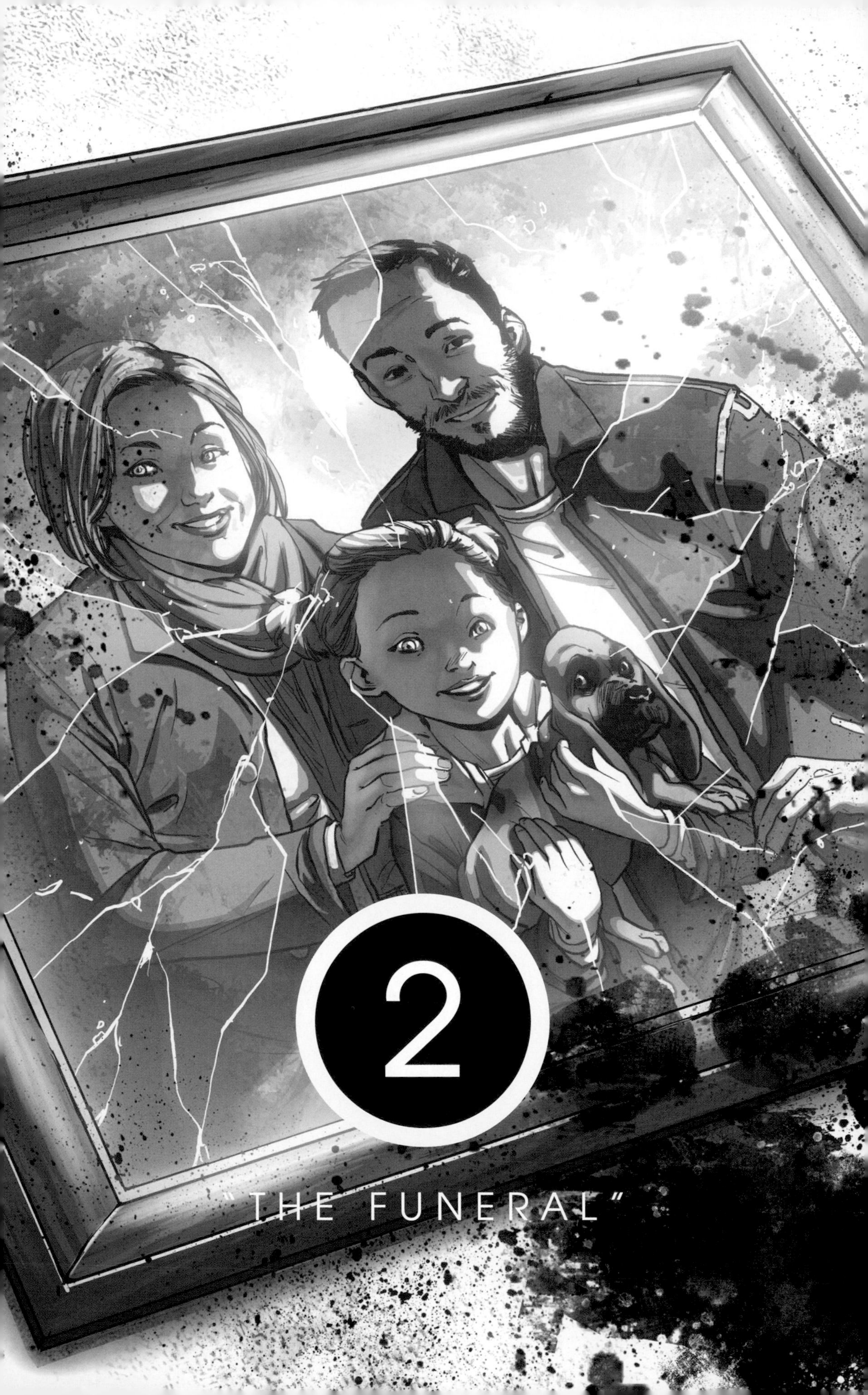
2
"THE FUNERAL"

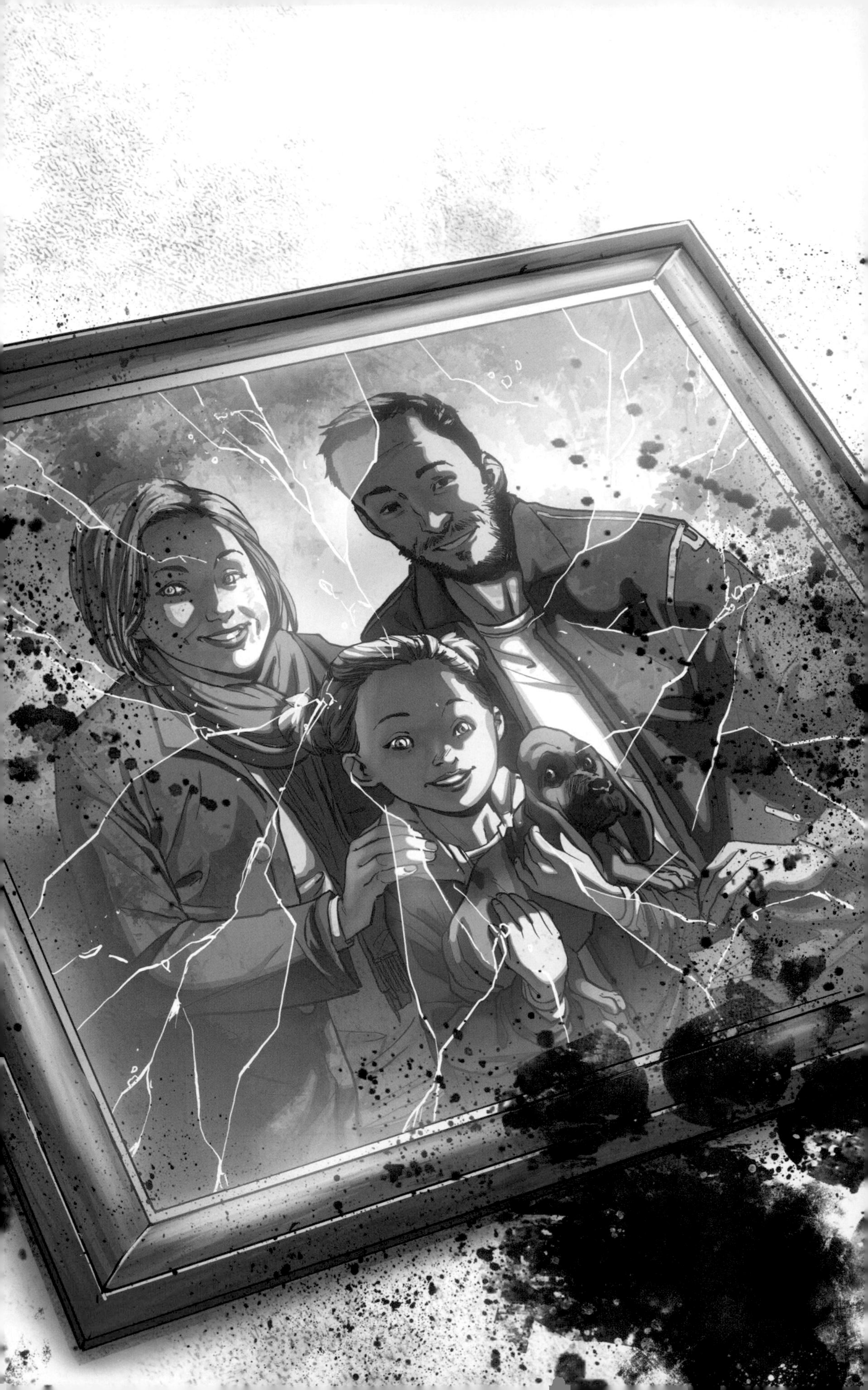

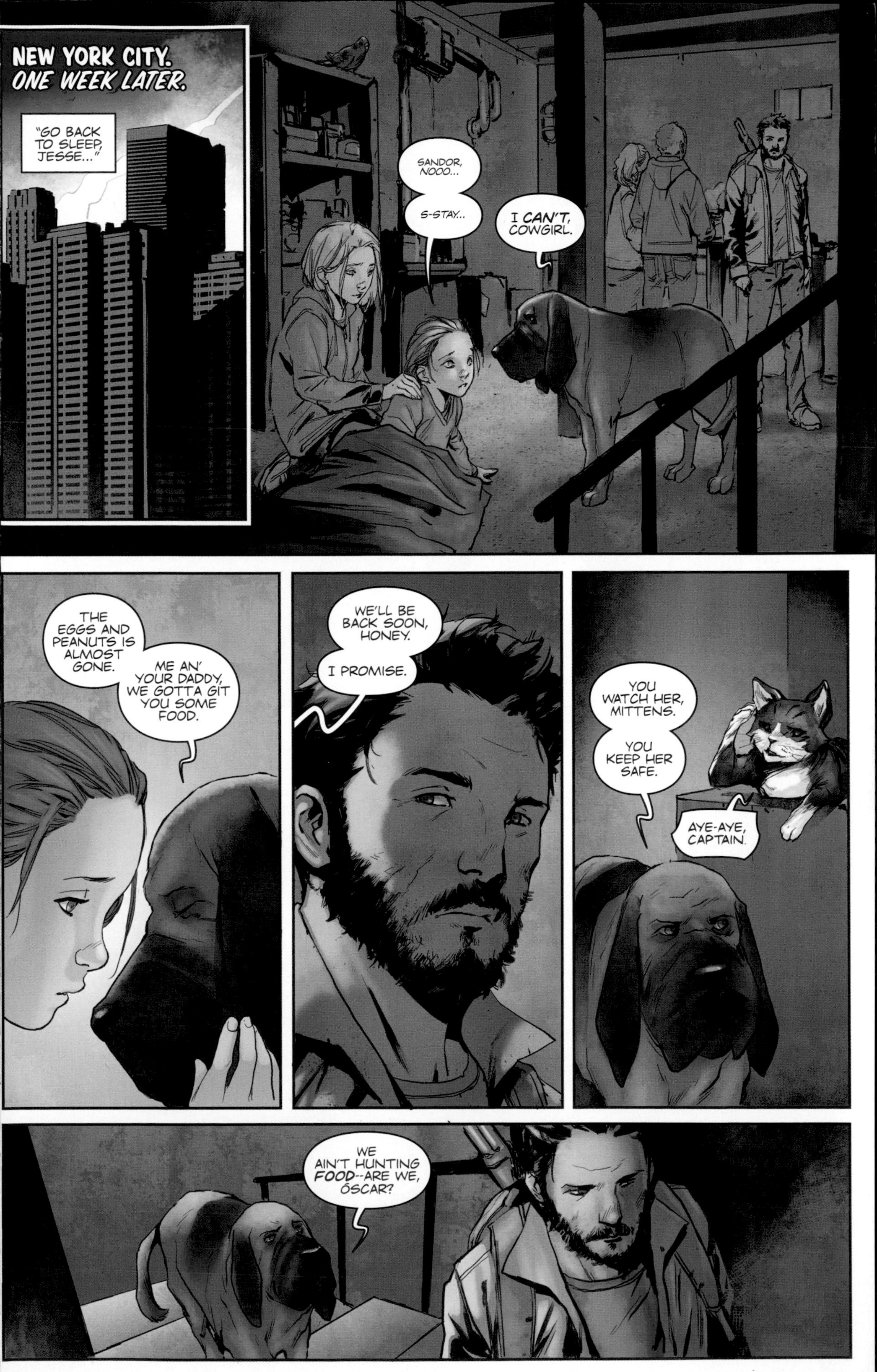
NEW YORK CITY.
ONE WEEK LATER.
"GO BACK TO SLEEP, JESSE..."
SANDOR, NOOO...
S-STAY...
I CAN'T, COWGIRL.
THE EGGS AND PEANUTS IS ALMOST GONE.
ME AN' YOUR DADDY, WE GOTTA GIT YOU SOME FOOD.
WE'LL BE BACK SOON, HONEY.
I PROMISE.
YOU WATCH HER, MITTENS.
YOU KEEP HER SAFE.
AYE-AYE, CAPTAIN.
WE AIN'T HUNTING FOOD--ARE WE, ÓSCAR?

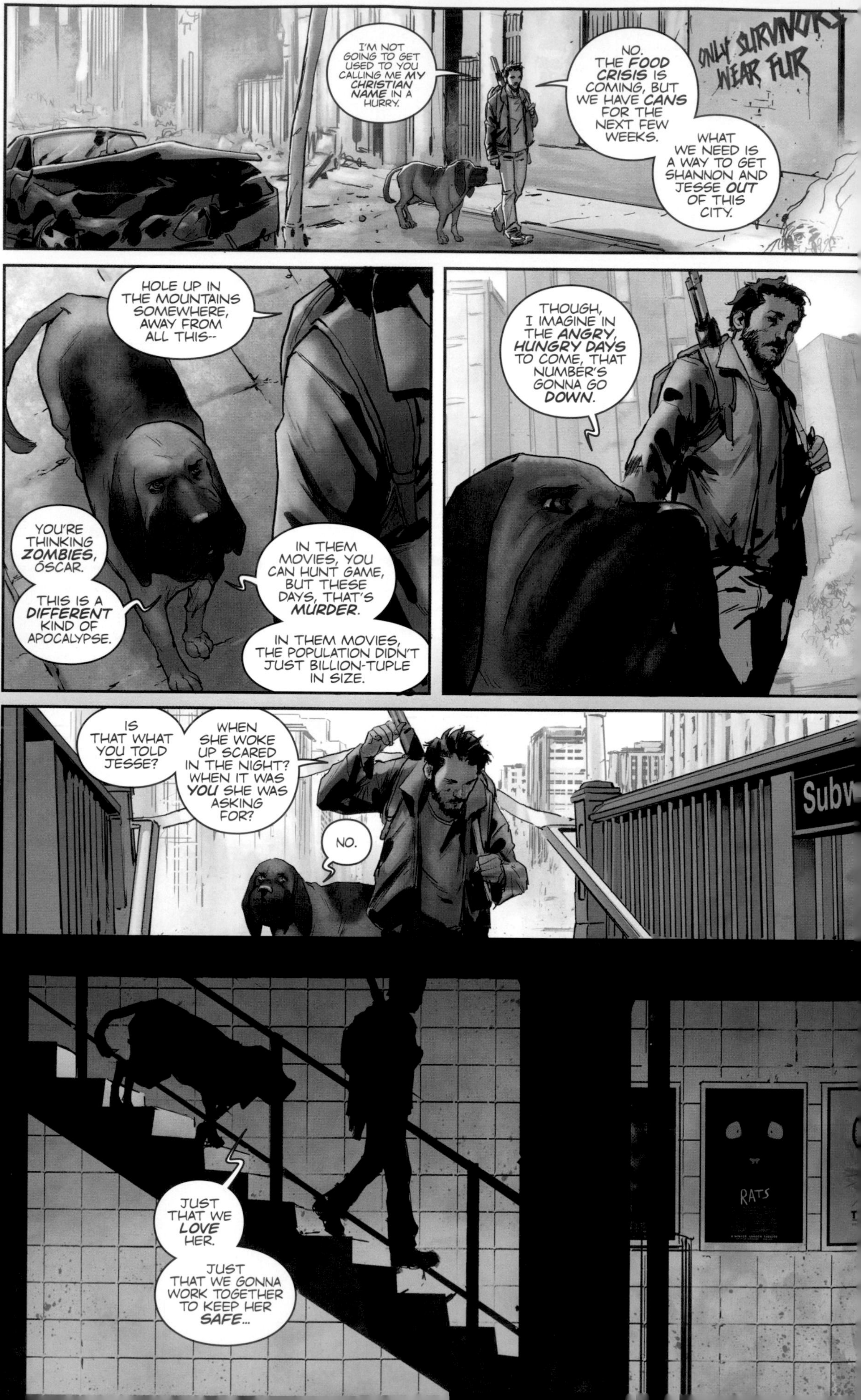
ONLY SURVIVORS WEAR FUR
I'M NOT GOING TO GET USED TO YOU CALLING ME MY CHRISTIAN NAME IN A HURRY.
NO. THE FOOD CRISIS IS COMING, BUT WE HAVE CANS FOR THE NEXT FEW WEEKS.
WHAT WE NEED IS A WAY TO GET SHANNON AND JESSE OUT OF THIS CITY.
HOLE UP IN THE MOUNTAINS SOMEWHERE, AWAY FROM ALL THIS--
YOU'RE THINKING ZOMBIES, ÓSCAR.
THIS IS A DIFFERENT KIND OF APOCALYPSE.
IN THEM MOVIES, YOU CAN HUNT GAME, BUT THESE DAYS, THAT'S MURDER.
IN THEM MOVIES, THE POPULATION DIDN'T JUST BILLION-TUPLE IN SIZE.
THOUGH, I IMAGINE IN THE ANGRY, HUNGRY DAYS TO COME, THAT NUMBER'S GONNA GO DOWN.
IS THAT WHAT YOU TOLD JESSE?
WHEN SHE WOKE UP SCARED IN THE NIGHT? WHEN IT WAS YOU SHE WAS ASKING FOR?
NO.
Subw
JUST THAT WE LOVE HER.
JUST THAT WE GONNA WORK TOGETHER TO KEEP HER SAFE...
RATS

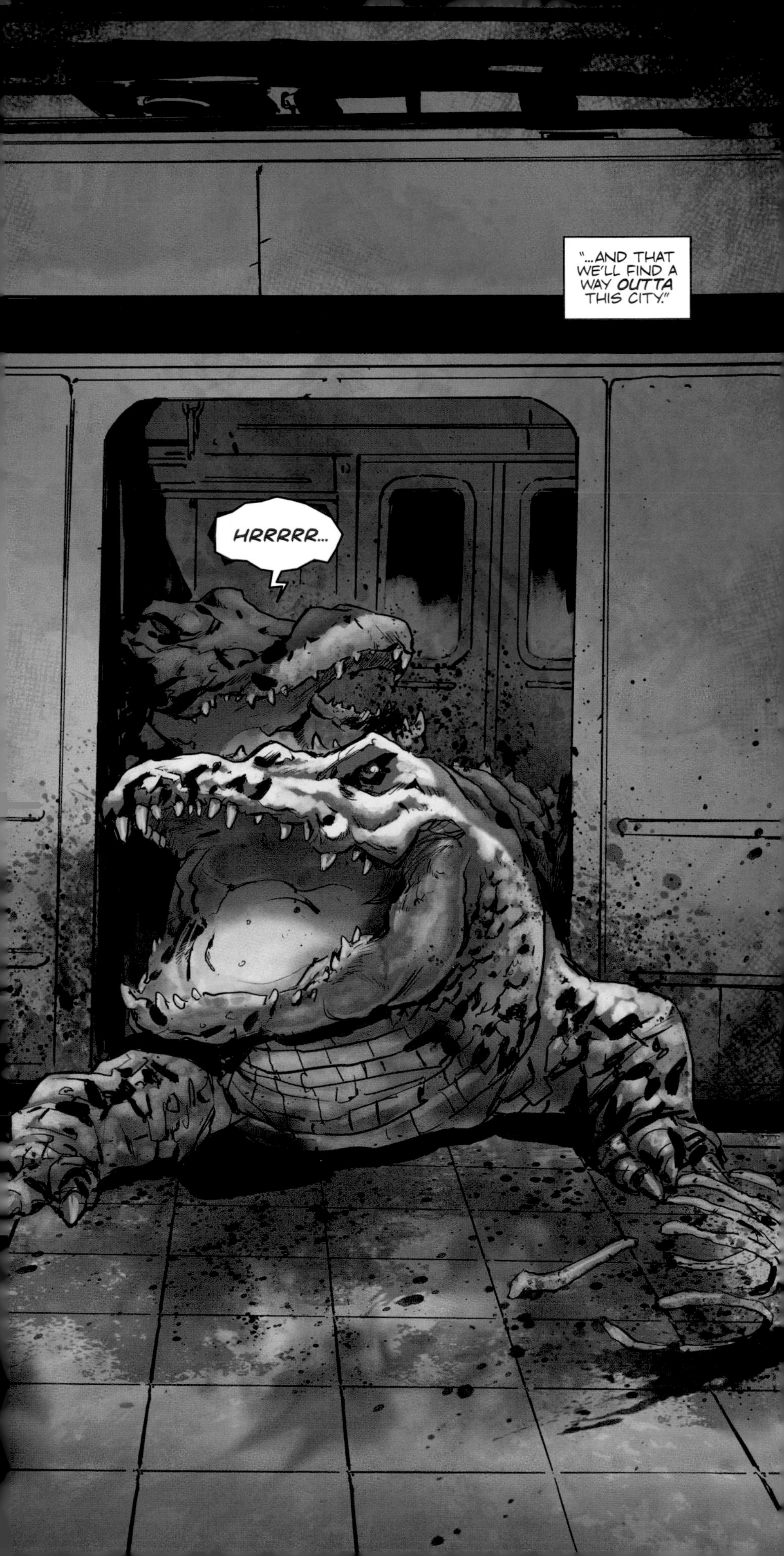
"...AND THAT WE'LL FIND A WAY OUTTA THIS CITY."
HRRRRR...

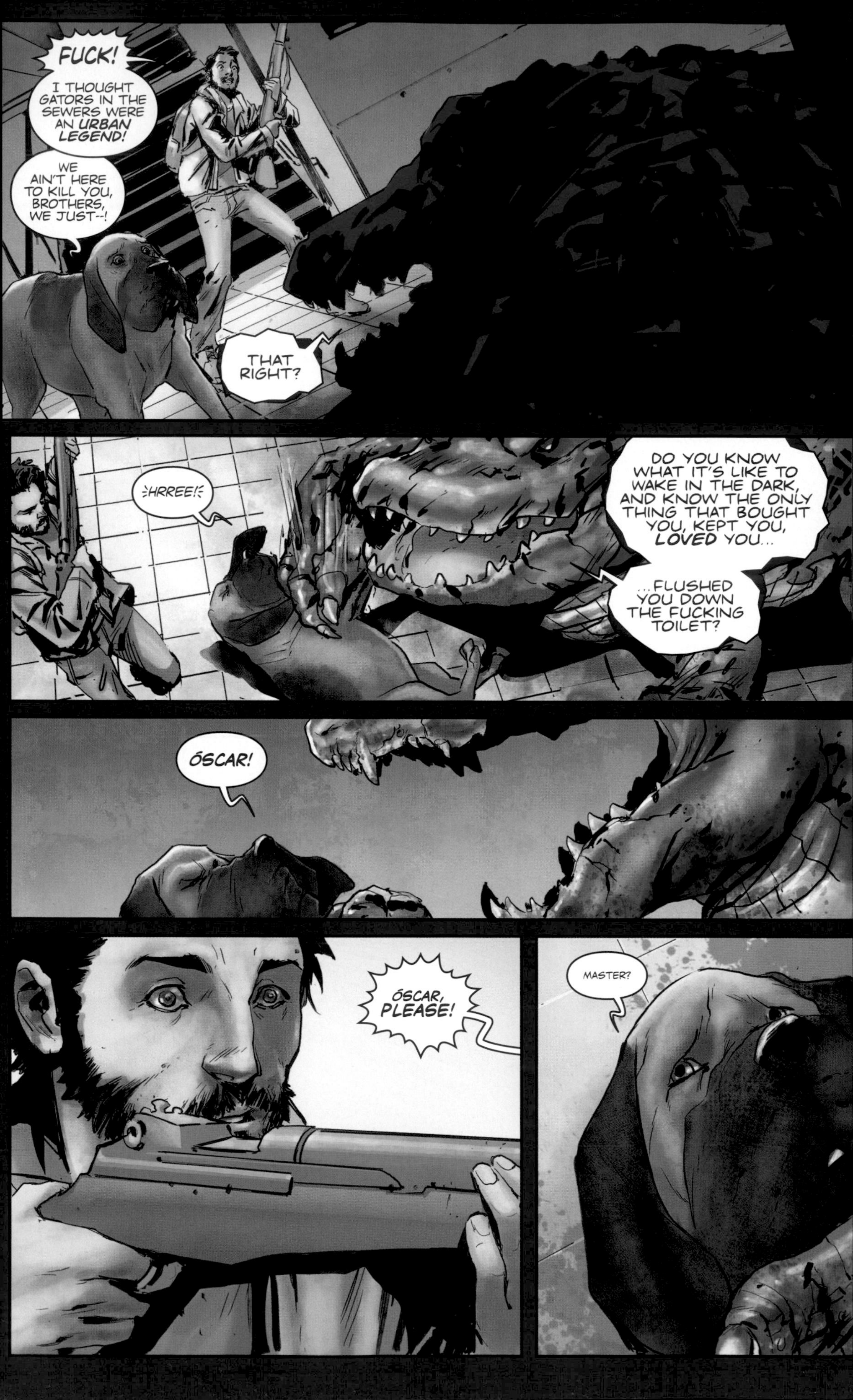
FUCK!
I THOUGHT GATORS IN THE SEWERS WERE AN URBAN LEGEND!
WE AIN'T HERE TO KILL YOU, BROTHERS, WE JUST--!
THAT RIGHT?
HRREE!
DO YOU KNOW WHAT IT'S LIKE TO WAKE IN THE DARK, AND KNOW THE ONLY THING THAT BOUGHT YOU, KEPT YOU, LOVED YOU...
...FLUSHED YOU DOWN THE FUCKING TOILET?
ÓSCAR!
ÓSCAR, PLEASE!
MASTER?

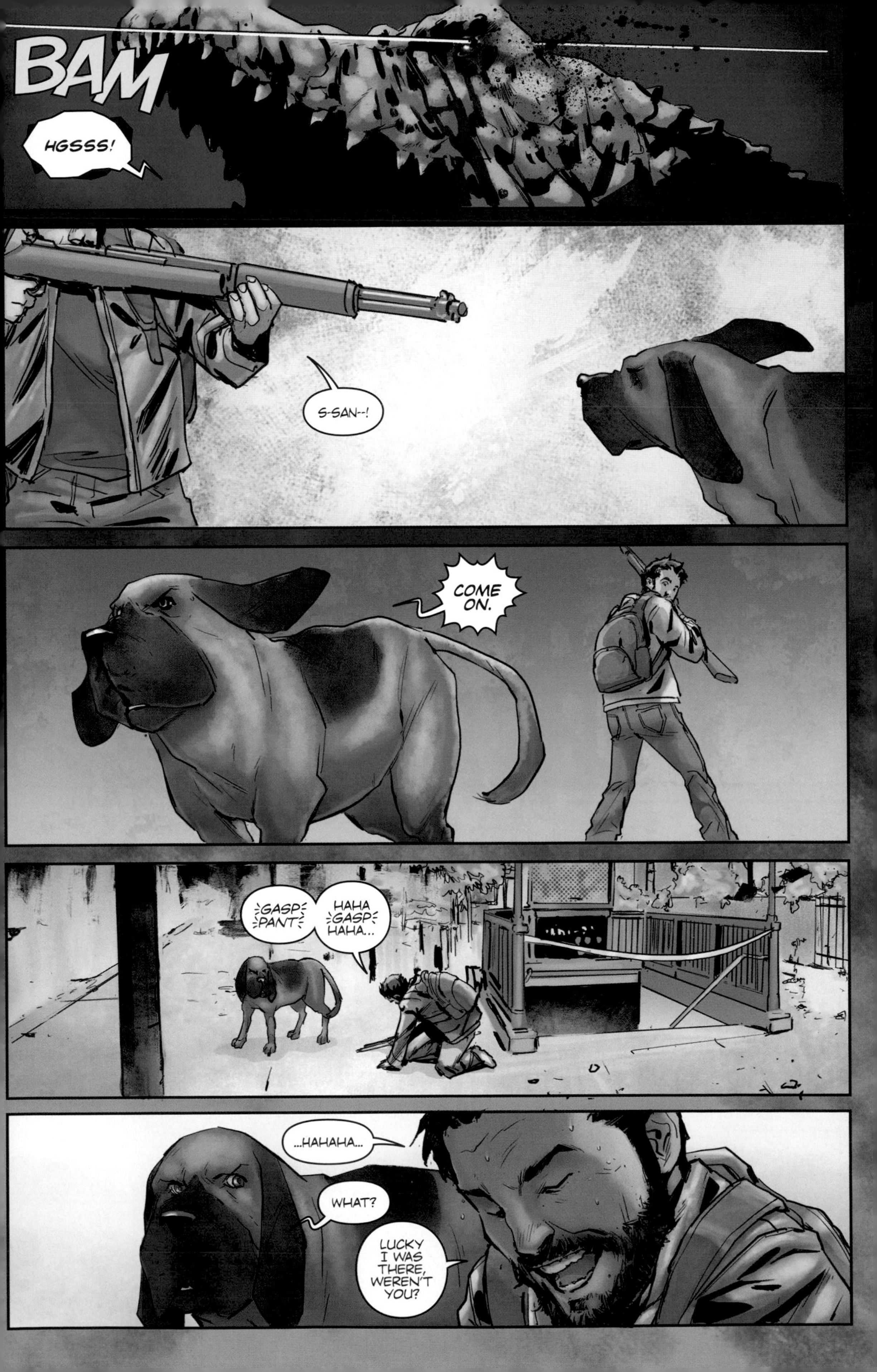
BAM
HGSSS!
S-SAN--!
COME ON.
GASP PANT
HAHA GASP HAHA...
...HAHAHA...
WHAT?
LUCKY I WAS THERE, WEREN'T YOU?

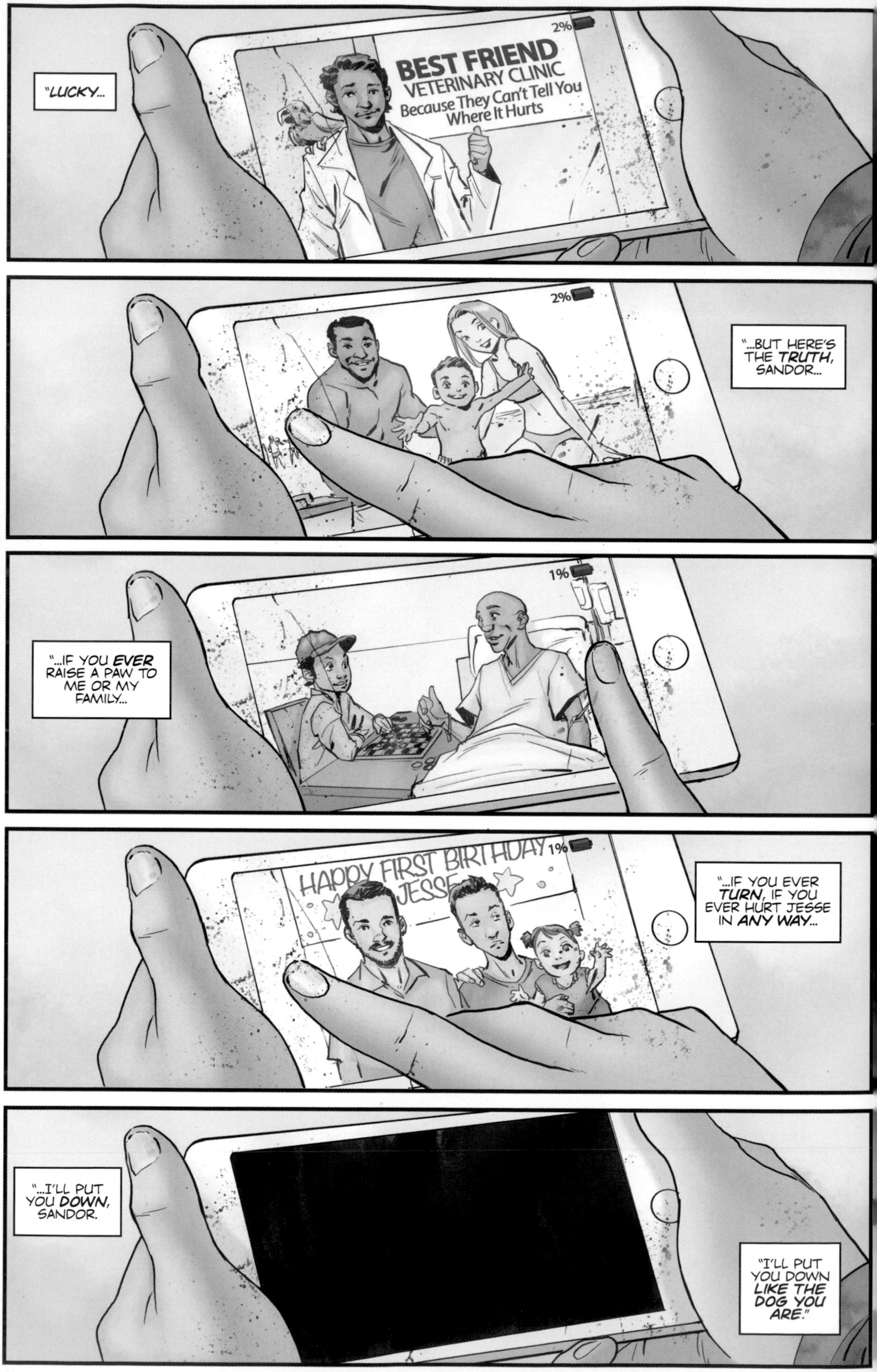

"LUCKY...
2%
BEST FRIEND
VETERINARY CLINIC
Because They Can't Tell You Where It Hurts
2%
"...BUT HERE'S THE TRUTH, SANDOR...
1%
"...IF YOU EVER RAISE A PAW TO ME OR MY FAMILY...
1%
HAPPY FIRST BIRTHDAY JESSE
"...IF YOU EVER TURN, IF YOU EVER HURT JESSE IN ANY WAY...
"...I'LL PUT YOU DOWN, SANDOR.
"I'LL PUT YOU DOWN LIKE THE DOG YOU ARE."

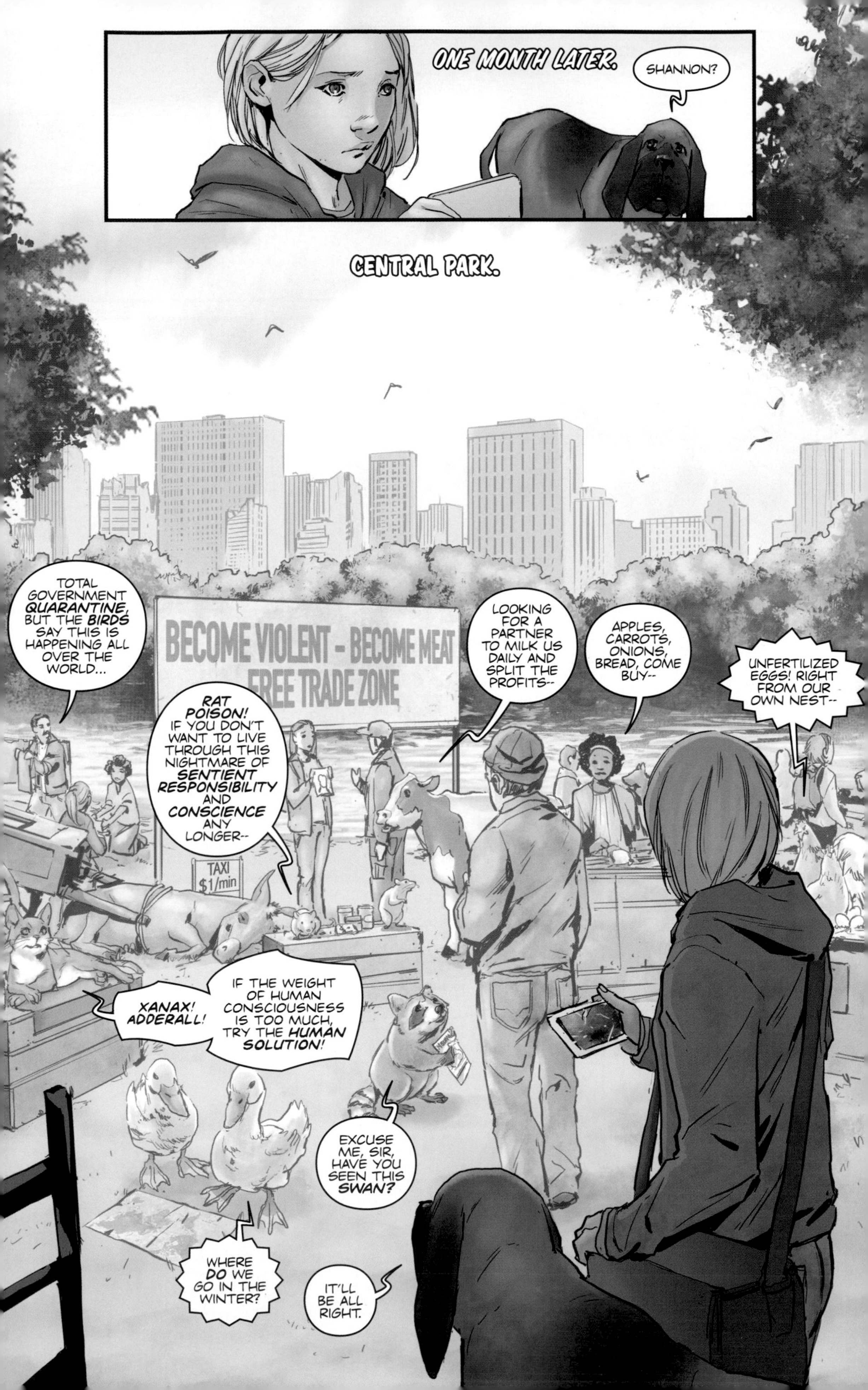
ONE MONTH LATER.
SHANNON?
CENTRAL PARK.
BECOME VIOLENT - BECOME MEAT
FREE TRADE ZONE
TOTAL GOVERNMENT QUARANTINE, BUT THE BIRDS SAY THIS IS HAPPENING ALL OVER THE WORLD...
RAT POISON! IF YOU DON'T WANT TO LIVE THROUGH THIS NIGHTMARE OF SENTIENT RESPONSIBILITY AND CONSCIENCE ANY LONGER--
LOOKING FOR A PARTNER TO MILK US DAILY AND SPLIT THE PROFITS--
APPLES, CARROTS, ONIONS, BREAD, COME BUY--
UNFERTILIZED EGGS! RIGHT FROM OUR OWN NEST--
TAXI
$1/min
XANAX! ADDERALL!
IF THE WEIGHT OF HUMAN CONSCIOUSNESS IS TOO MUCH, TRY THE HUMAN SOLUTION!
EXCUSE ME, SIR, HAVE YOU SEEN THIS SWAN?
WHERE DO WE GO IN THE WINTER?
IT'LL BE ALL RIGHT.

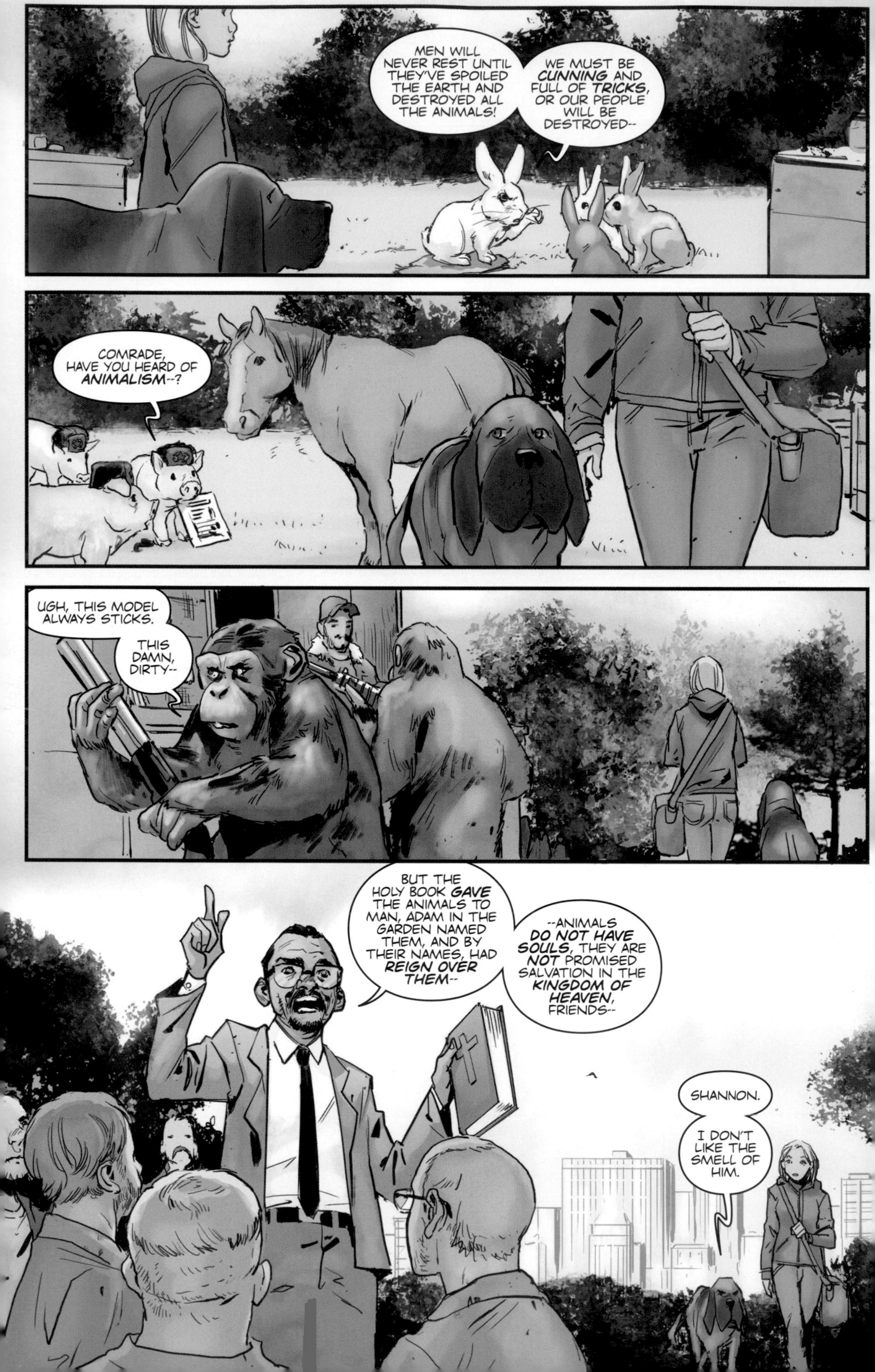
MEN WILL NEVER REST UNTIL THEY'VE SPOILED THE EARTH AND DESTROYED ALL THE ANIMALS!
WE MUST BE CUNNING AND FULL OF TRICKS, OR OUR PEOPLE WILL BE DESTROYED--
COMRADE, HAVE YOU HEARD OF ANIMALISM--?
UGH, THIS MODEL ALWAYS STICKS.
THIS DAMN, DIRTY--
BUT THE HOLY BOOK GAVE THE ANIMALS TO MAN, ADAM IN THE GARDEN NAMED THEM, AND BY THEIR NAMES, HAD REIGN OVER THEM--
--ANIMALS DO NOT HAVE SOULS, THEY ARE NOT PROMISED SALVATION IN THE KINGDOM OF HEAVEN, FRIENDS--
SHANNON.
I DON'T LIKE THE SMELL OF HIM.

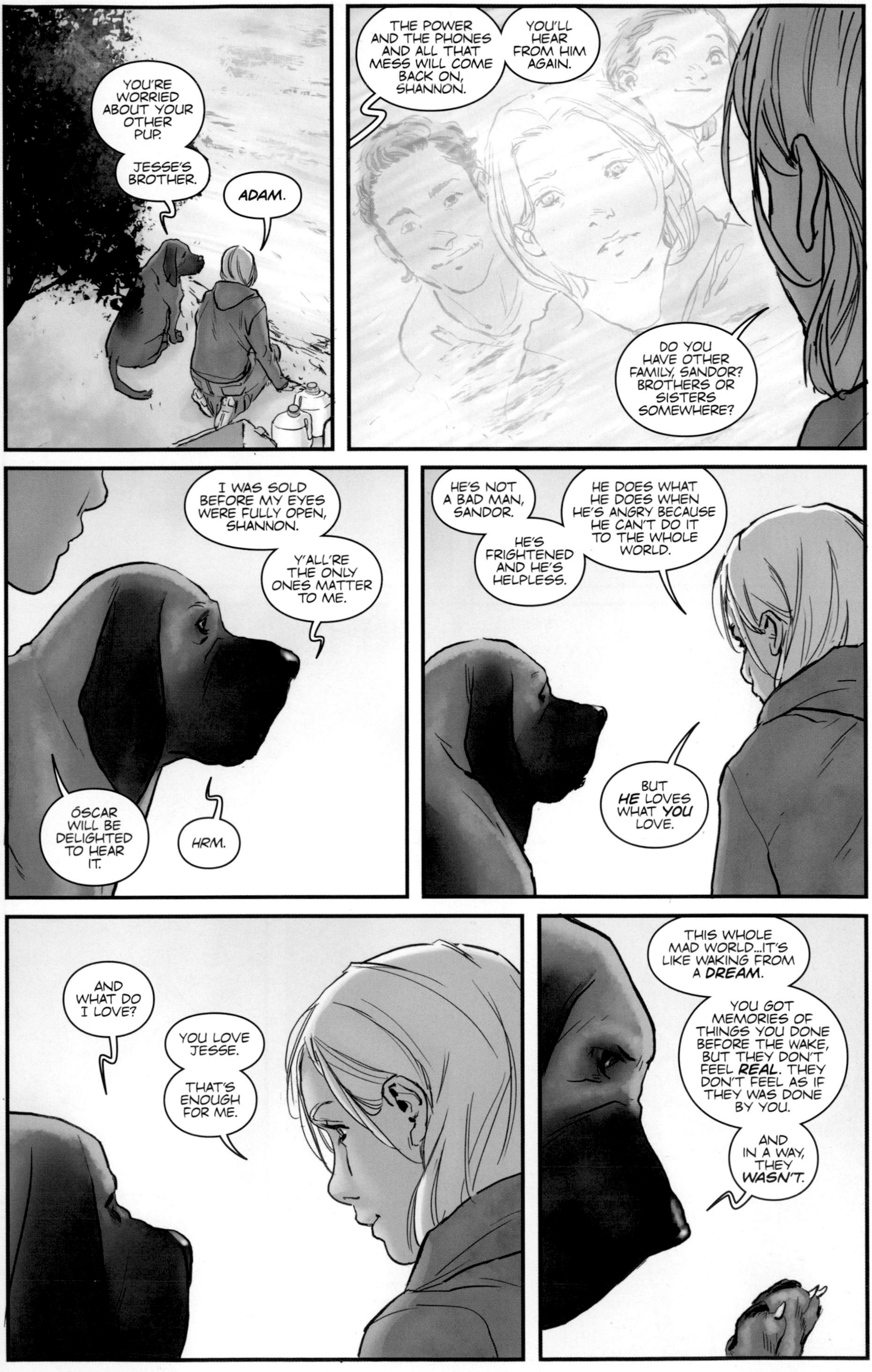
YOU'RE WORRIED ABOUT YOUR OTHER PUP.
JESSE'S BROTHER.
ADAM.
THE POWER AND THE PHONES AND ALL THAT MESS WILL COME BACK ON, SHANNON.
YOU'LL HEAR FROM HIM AGAIN.
DO YOU HAVE OTHER FAMILY, SANDOR? BROTHERS OR SISTERS SOMEWHERE?
I WAS SOLD BEFORE MY EYES WERE FULLY OPEN, SHANNON.
Y'ALL'RE THE ONLY ONES MATTER TO ME.
ÓSCAR WILL BE DELIGHTED TO HEAR IT.
HRM.
HE'S NOT A BAD MAN, SANDOR.
HE'S FRIGHTENED AND HE'S HELPLESS.
HE DOES WHAT HE DOES WHEN HE'S ANGRY BECAUSE HE CAN'T DO IT TO THE WHOLE WORLD.
BUT ***HE*** LOVES WHAT ***YOU*** LOVE.
AND WHAT DO I LOVE?
YOU LOVE JESSE.
THAT'S ENOUGH FOR ME.
THIS WHOLE MAD WORLD...IT'S LIKE WAKING FROM A ***DREAM***.
YOU GOT MEMORIES OF THINGS YOU DONE BEFORE THE WAKE, BUT THEY DON'T FEEL ***REAL***. THEY DON'T FEEL AS IF THEY WAS DONE BY YOU.
AND IN A WAY, THEY ***WASN'T***.

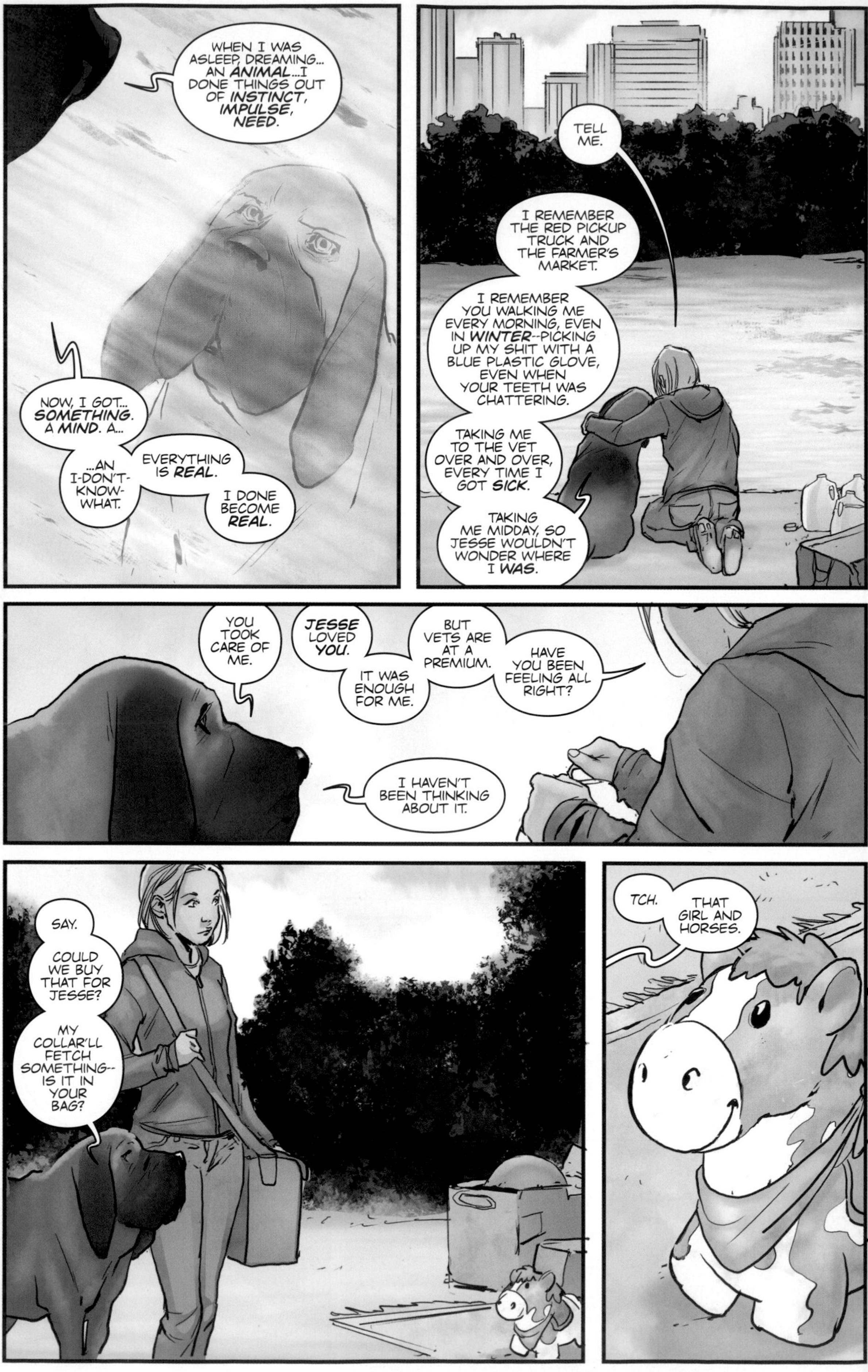
WHEN I WAS ASLEEP, DREAMING... AN ANIMAL...I DONE THINGS OUT OF INSTINCT, IMPULSE, NEED.
NOW, I GOT... SOMETHING. A MIND. A...
...AN I-DON'T-KNOW-WHAT.
EVERYTHING IS REAL.
I DONE BECOME REAL.
TELL ME.
I REMEMBER THE RED PICKUP TRUCK AND THE FARMER'S MARKET.
I REMEMBER YOU WALKING ME EVERY MORNING, EVEN IN WINTER--PICKING UP MY SHIT WITH A BLUE PLASTIC GLOVE, EVEN WHEN YOUR TEETH WAS CHATTERING.
TAKING ME TO THE VET OVER AND OVER, EVERY TIME I GOT SICK.
TAKING ME MIDDAY, SO JESSE WOULDN'T WONDER WHERE I WAS.
YOU TOOK CARE OF ME.
JESSE LOVED YOU.
IT WAS ENOUGH FOR ME.
BUT VETS ARE AT A PREMIUM.
HAVE YOU BEEN FEELING ALL RIGHT?
I HAVEN'T BEEN THINKING ABOUT IT.
SAY.
COULD WE BUY THAT FOR JESSE?
MY COLLAR'LL FETCH SOMETHING-- IS IT IN YOUR BAG?
TCH.
THAT GIRL AND HORSES.

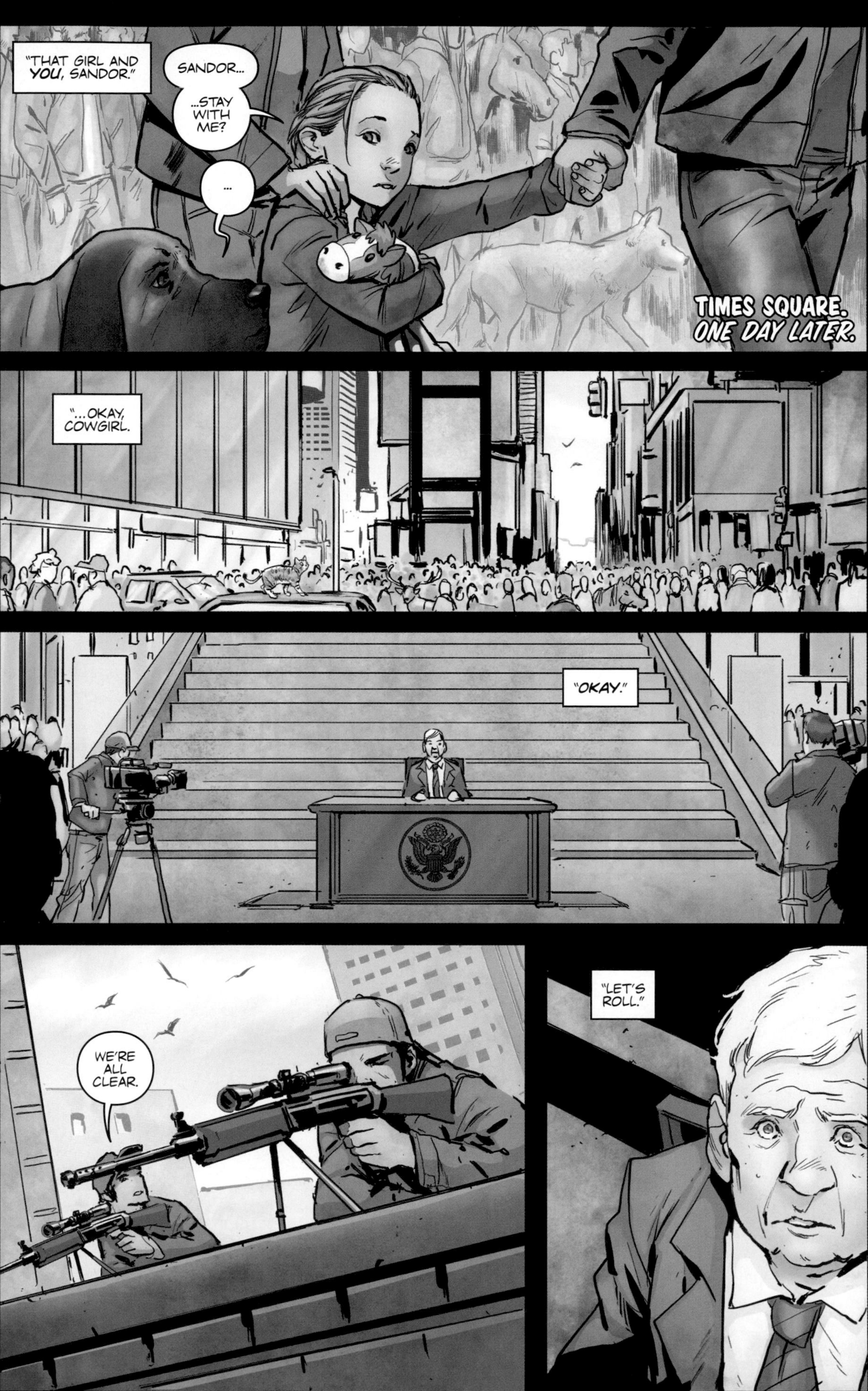
"THAT GIRL AND YOU, SANDOR."
SANDOR...
...STAY WITH ME?
...
TIMES SQUARE. ONE DAY LATER.
"...OKAY, COWGIRL.
"OKAY."
WE'RE ALL CLEAR.
"LET'S ROLL."

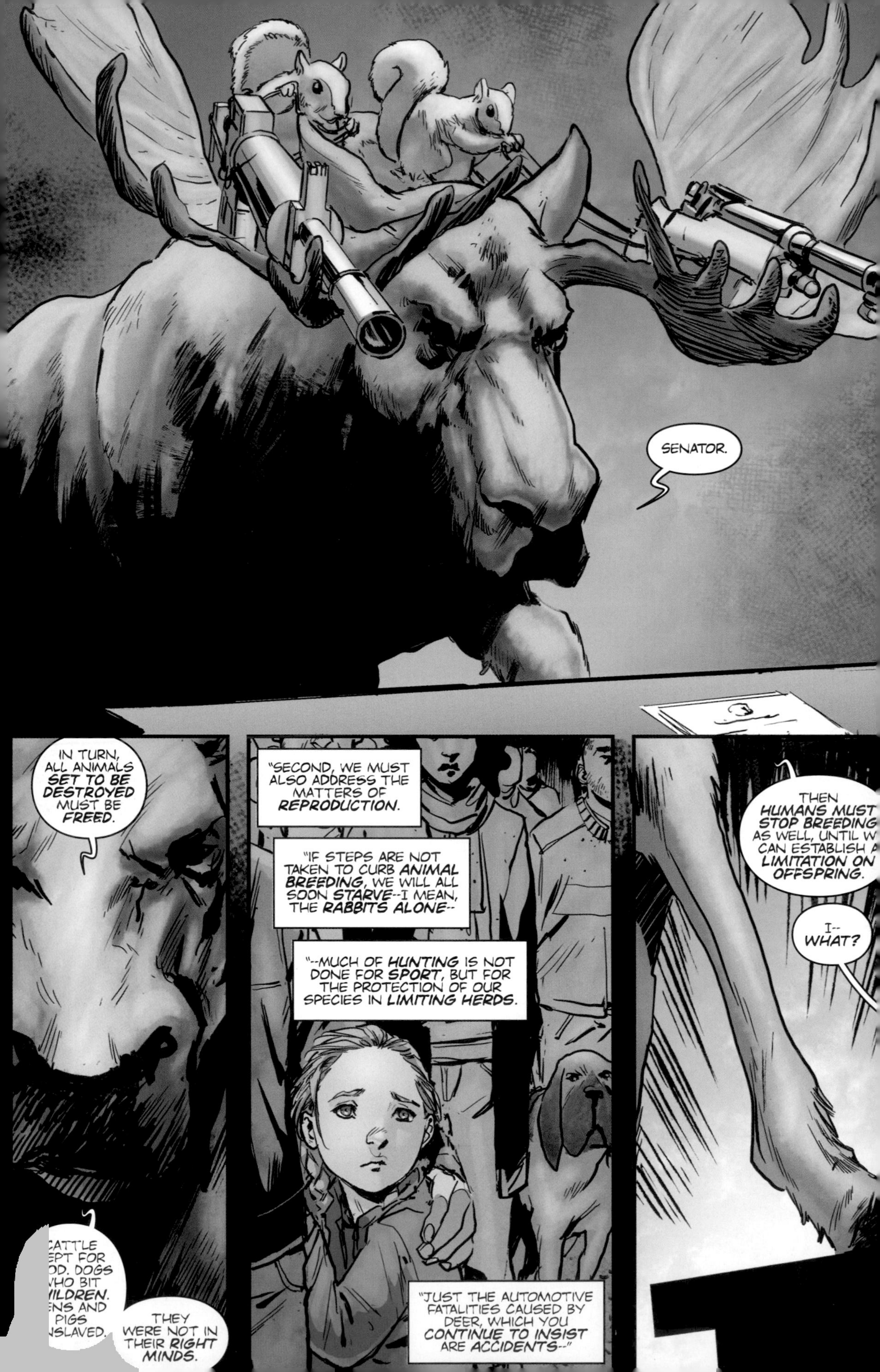

SENATOR.
IN TURN, ALL ANIMALS SET TO BE DESTROYED MUST BE FREED.
CATTLE EPT FOR OD. DOGS WHO BIT HILDREN. ENS AND PIGS NSLAVED.
THEY WERE NOT IN THEIR RIGHT MINDS.
"SECOND, WE MUST ALSO ADDRESS THE MATTERS OF REPRODUCTION.
"IF STEPS ARE NOT TAKEN TO CURB ANIMAL BREEDING, WE WILL ALL SOON STARVE--I MEAN, THE RABBITS ALONE--
"--MUCH OF HUNTING IS NOT DONE FOR SPORT, BUT FOR THE PROTECTION OF OUR SPECIES IN LIMITING HERDS.
"JUST THE AUTOMOTIVE FATALITIES CAUSED BY DEER, WHICH YOU CONTINUE TO INSIST ARE ACCIDENTS--"
THEN HUMANS MUST STOP BREEDING AS WELL, UNTIL W CAN ESTABLISH A LIMITATION ON OFFSPRING.
I-- WHAT?

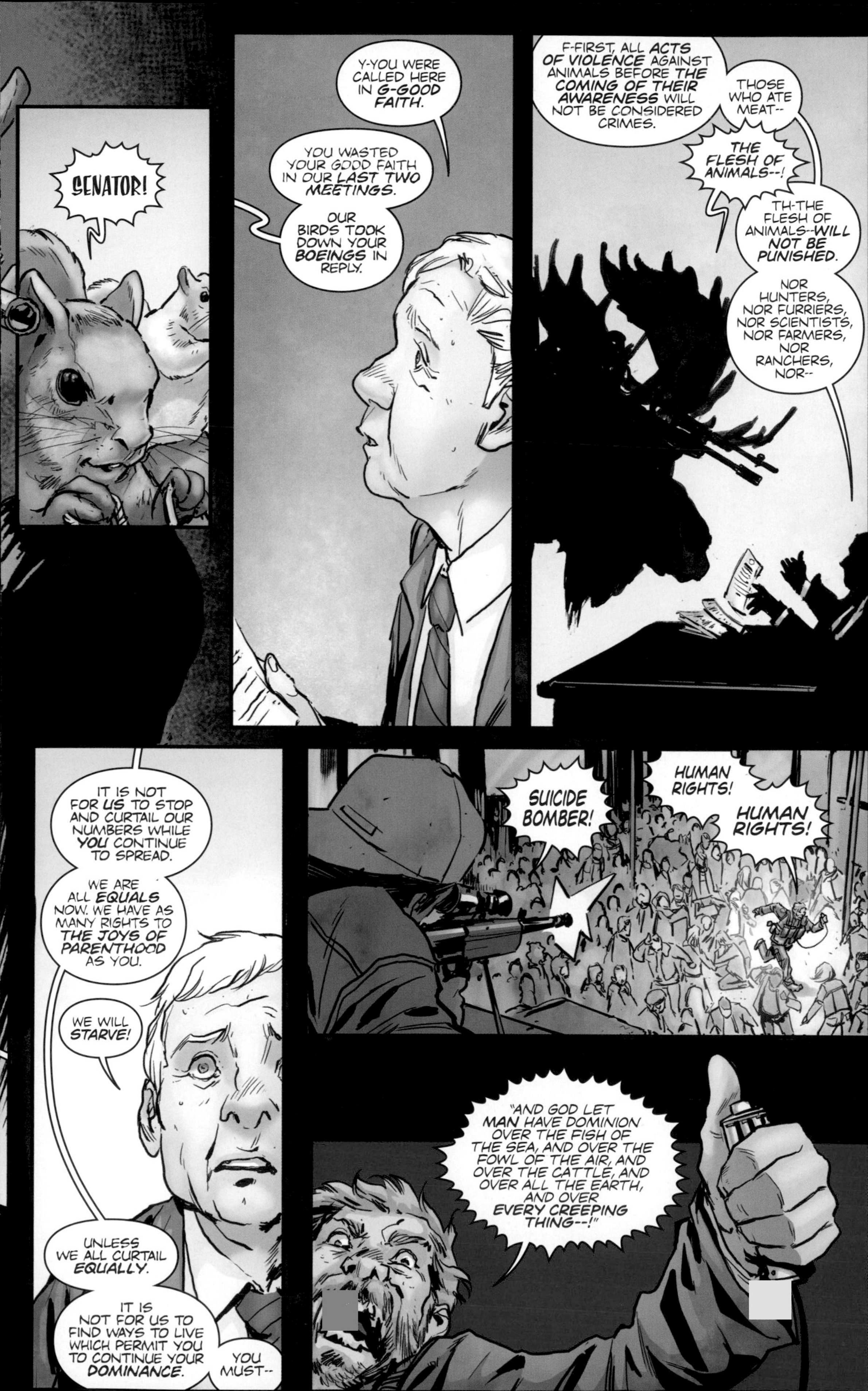

SENATOR!
Y-YOU WERE CALLED HERE IN G-GOOD FAITH.
YOU WASTED YOUR GOOD FAITH IN OUR LAST TWO MEETINGS.
OUR BIRDS TOOK DOWN YOUR BOEINGS IN REPLY.
F-FIRST, ALL ACTS OF VIOLENCE AGAINST ANIMALS BEFORE THE COMING OF THEIR AWARENESS WILL NOT BE CONSIDERED CRIMES.
THOSE WHO ATE MEAT--
THE FLESH OF ANIMALS--!
TH-THE FLESH OF ANIMALS--WILL NOT BE PUNISHED.
NOR HUNTERS, NOR FURRIERS, NOR SCIENTISTS, NOR FARMERS, NOR RANCHERS, NOR--
IT IS NOT FOR US TO STOP AND CURTAIL OUR NUMBERS WHILE YOU CONTINUE TO SPREAD.
WE ARE ALL EQUALS NOW. WE HAVE AS MANY RIGHTS TO THE JOYS OF PARENTHOOD AS YOU.
WE WILL STARVE!
UNLESS WE ALL CURTAIL EQUALLY.
IT IS NOT FOR US TO FIND WAYS TO LIVE WHICH PERMIT YOU TO CONTINUE YOUR DOMINANCE.
YOU MUST--
SUICIDE BOMBER!
HUMAN RIGHTS!
HUMAN RIGHTS!
"AND GOD LET MAN HAVE DOMINION OVER THE FISH OF THE SEA, AND OVER THE FOWL OF THE AIR, AND OVER THE CATTLE, AND OVER ALL THE EARTH, AND OVER EVERY CREEPING THING--!"

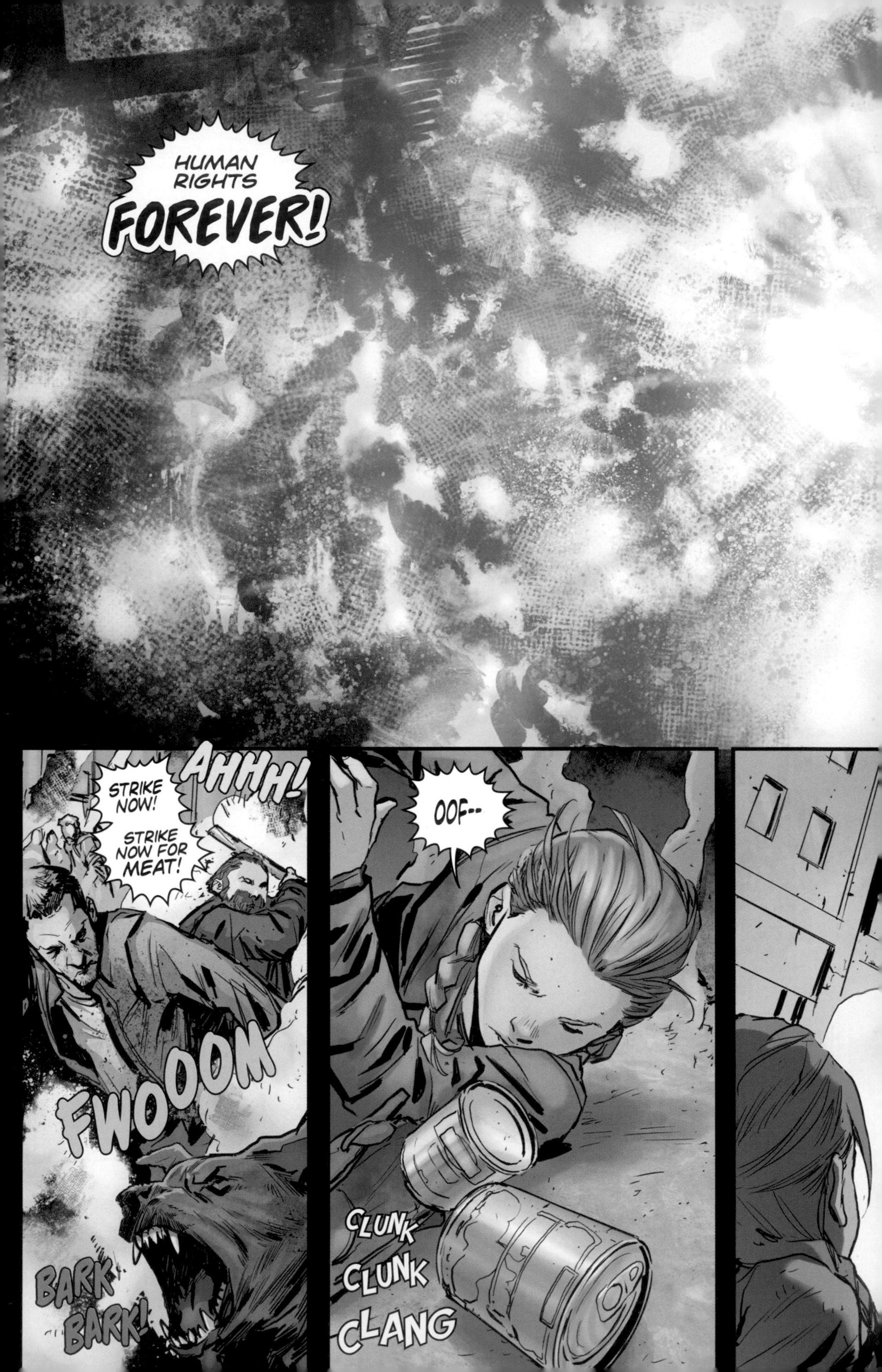
HUMAN RIGHTS FOREVER!
STRIKE NOW!
STRIKE NOW FOR MEAT!
AHHH!
FWOOOM
BARK BARK!
OOF--
CLUNK
CLUNK
CLANG

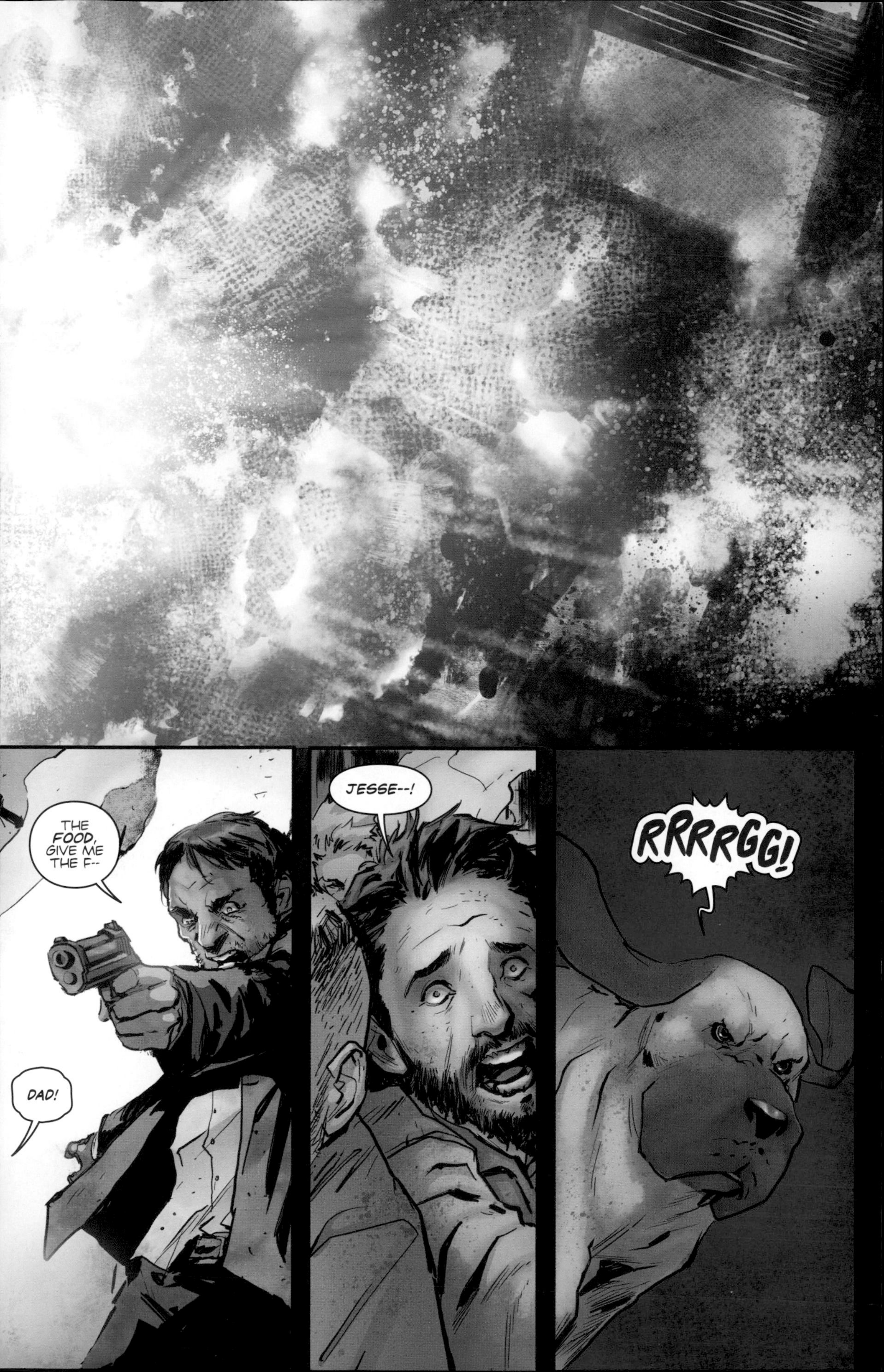
THE FOOD, GIVE ME THE F--
DAD!
JESSE--!
RRRRGG!

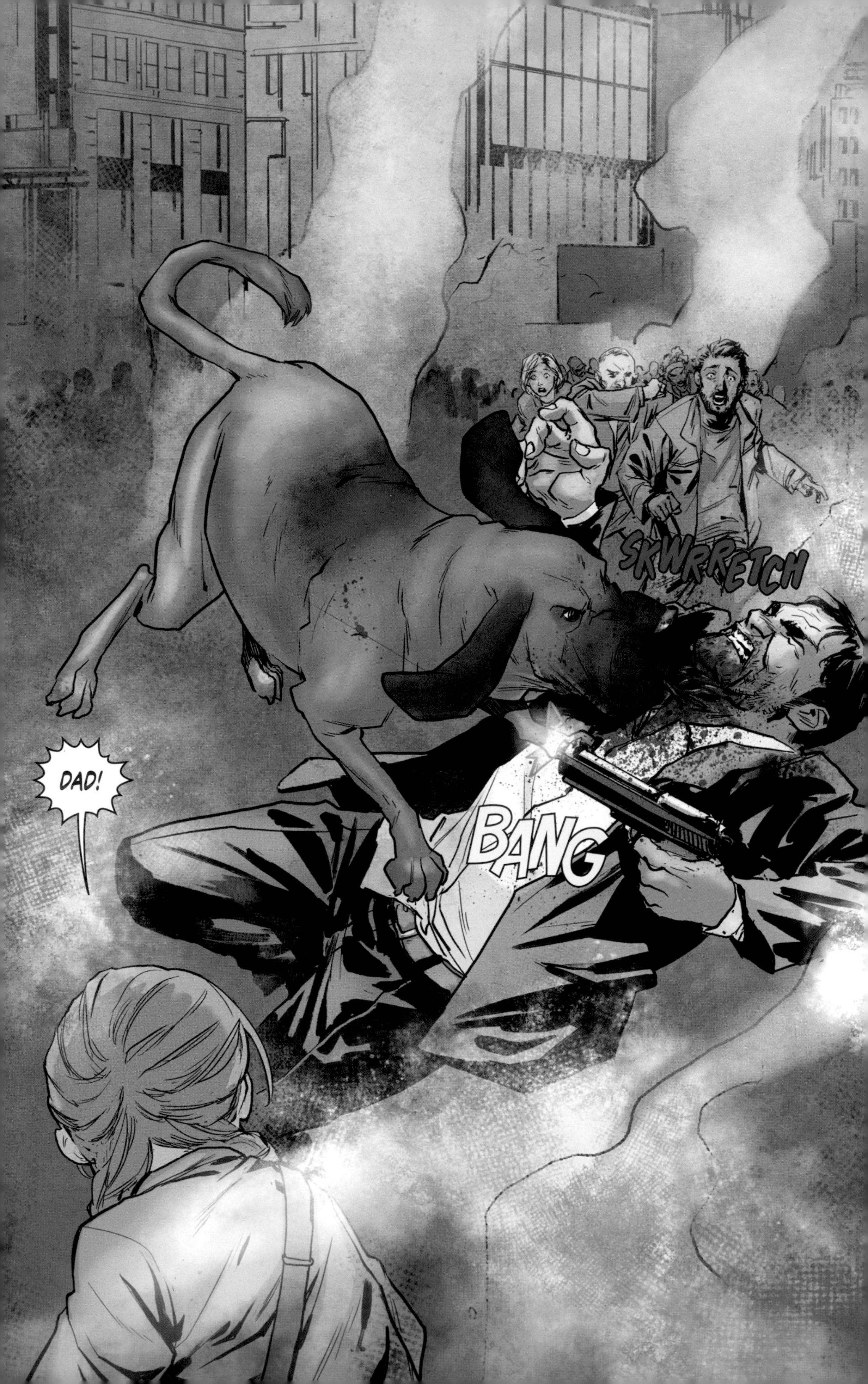
SKWRRETCH
DAD!
BANG

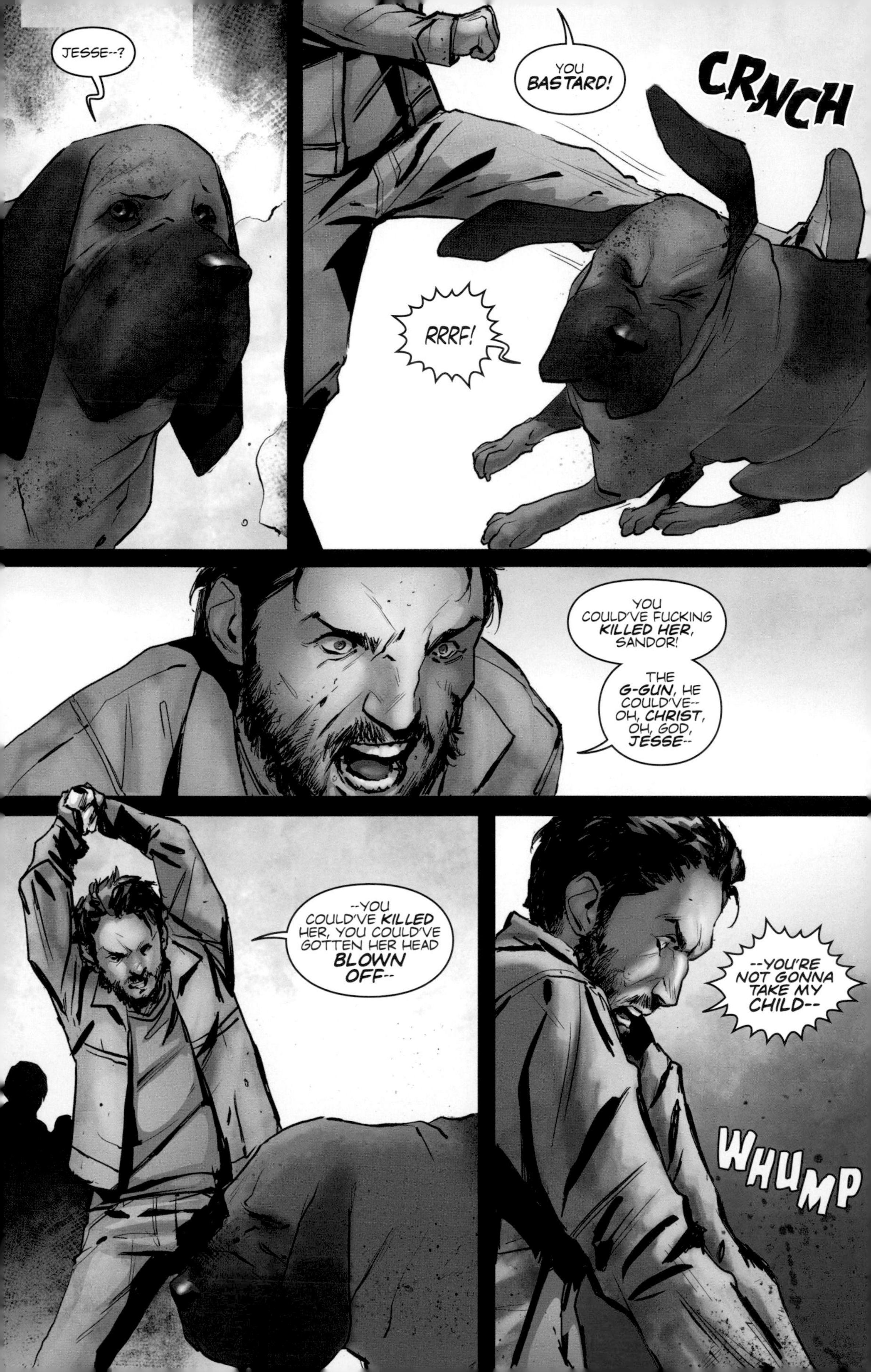
JESSE--?
YOU BASTARD!
CRNCH
RRRF!
YOU COULD'VE FUCKING KILLED HER, SANDOR!
THE G-GUN, HE COULD'VE-- OH, CHRIST, OH, GOD, JESSE--
--YOU COULD'VE KILLED HER, YOU COULD'VE GOTTEN HER HEAD BLOWN OFF--
--YOU'RE NOT GONNA TAKE MY CHILD--
WHUMP

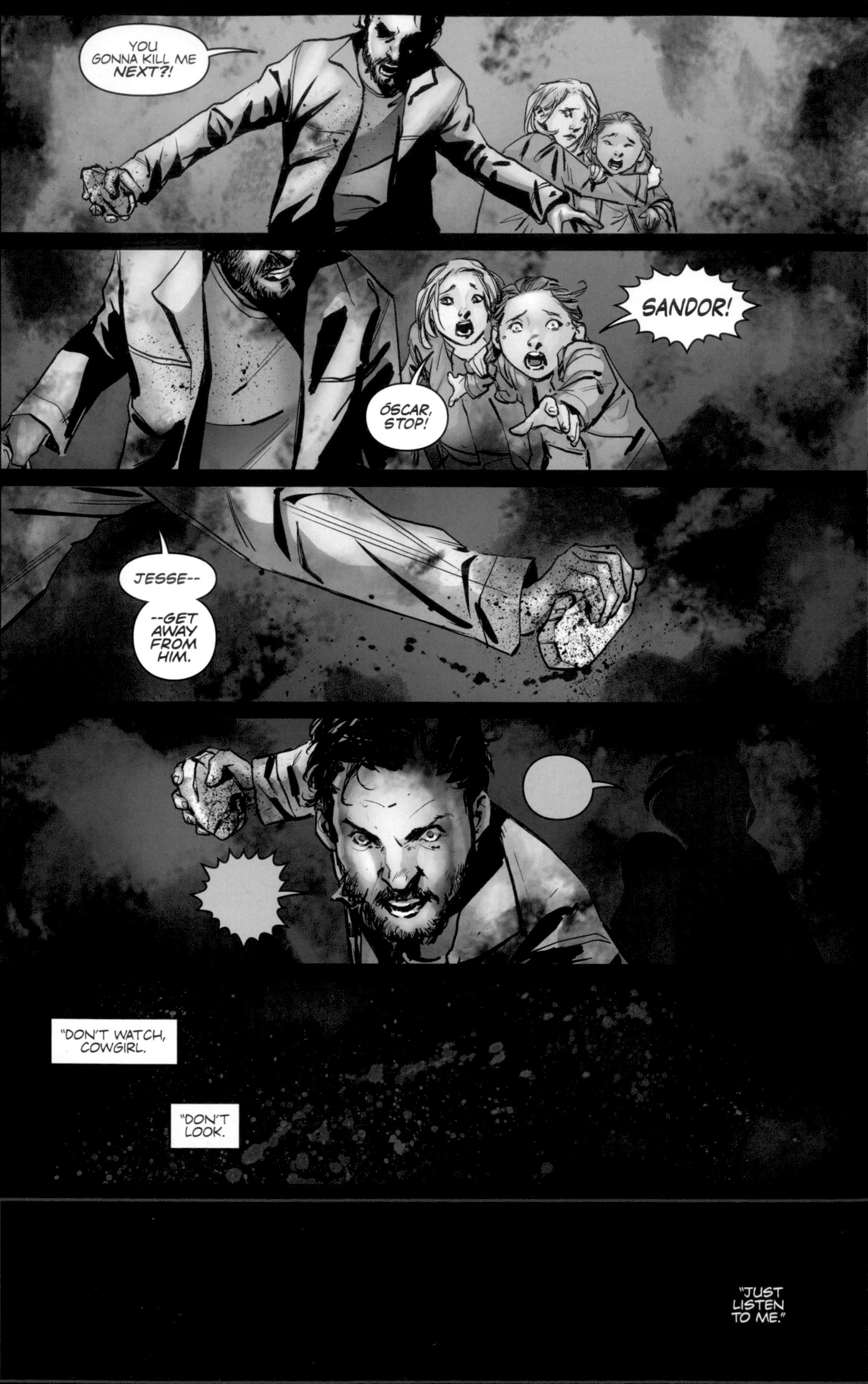

YOU GONNA KILL ME NEXT?!
SANDOR!
ÓSCAR, STOP!
JESSE--
--GET AWAY FROM HIM.
"DON'T WATCH, COWGIRL.
"DON'T LOOK.
"JUST LISTEN TO ME."

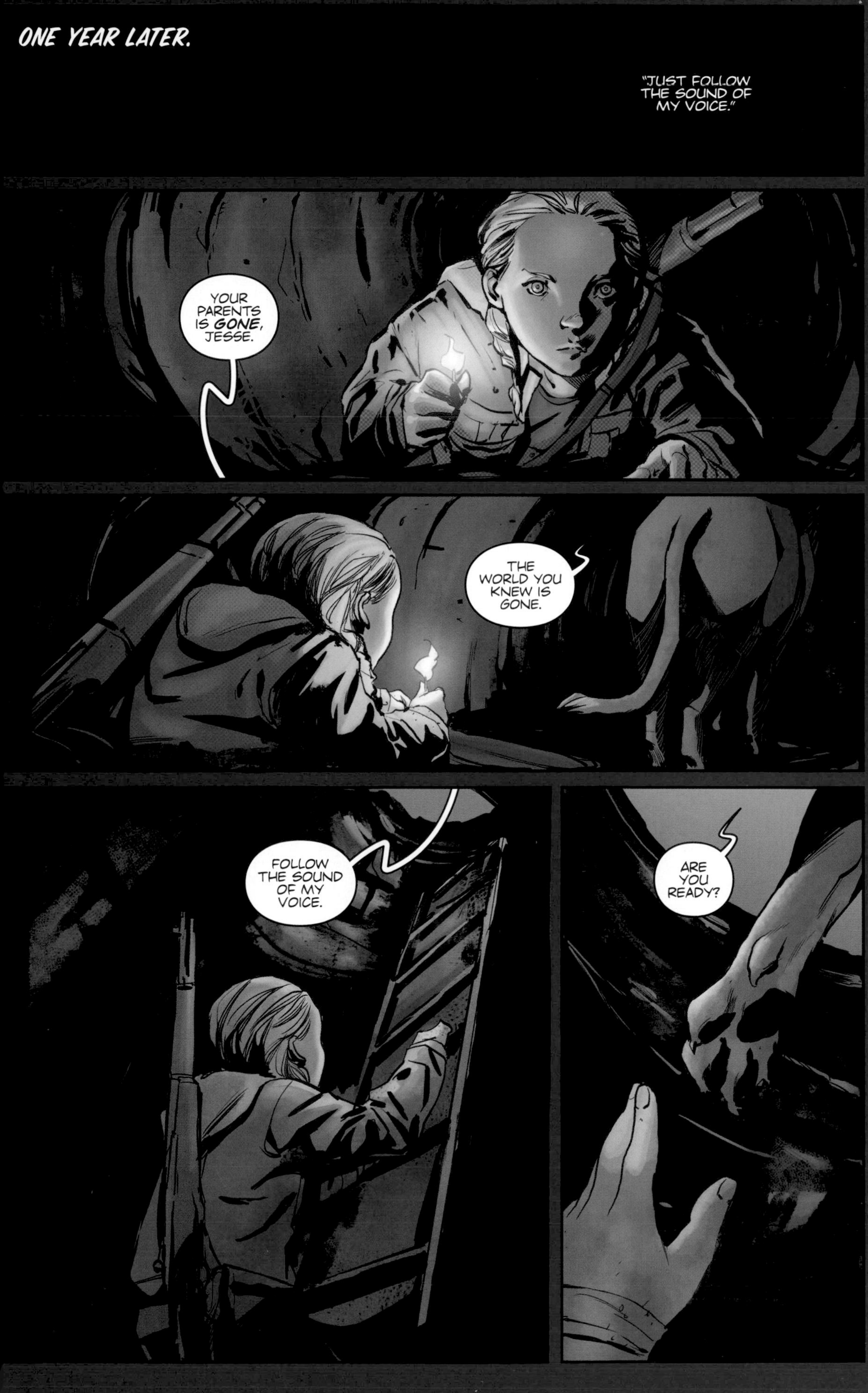
ONE YEAR LATER.
"JUST FOLLOW THE SOUND OF MY VOICE."
YOUR PARENTS IS GONE, JESSE.
THE WORLD YOU KNEW IS GONE.
FOLLOW THE SOUND OF MY VOICE.
ARE YOU READY?

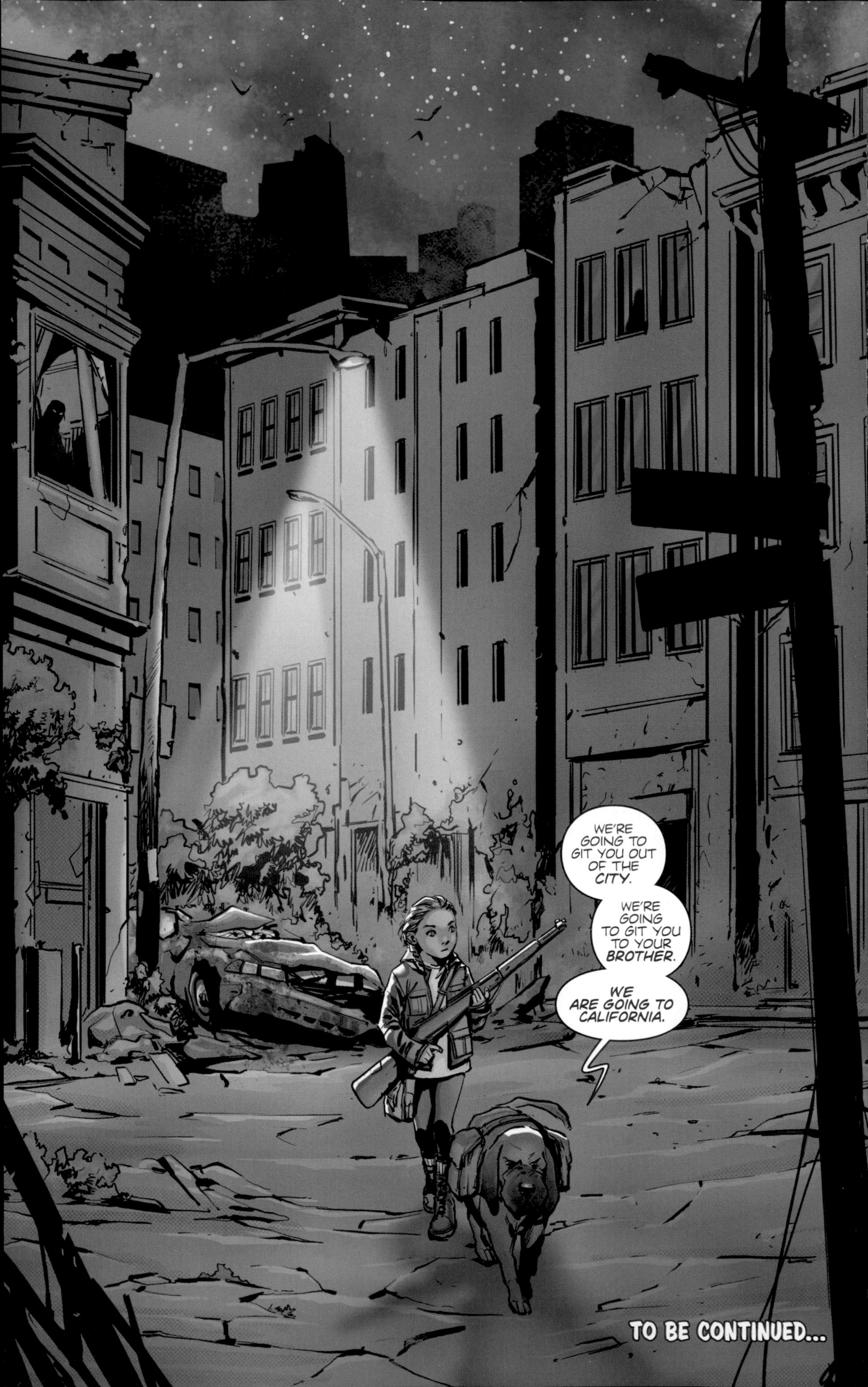
WE'RE GOING TO GIT YOU OUT OF THE CITY.
WE'RE GOING TO GIT YOU TO YOUR BROTHER.
WE ARE GOING TO CALIFORNIA.
TO BE CONTINUED...

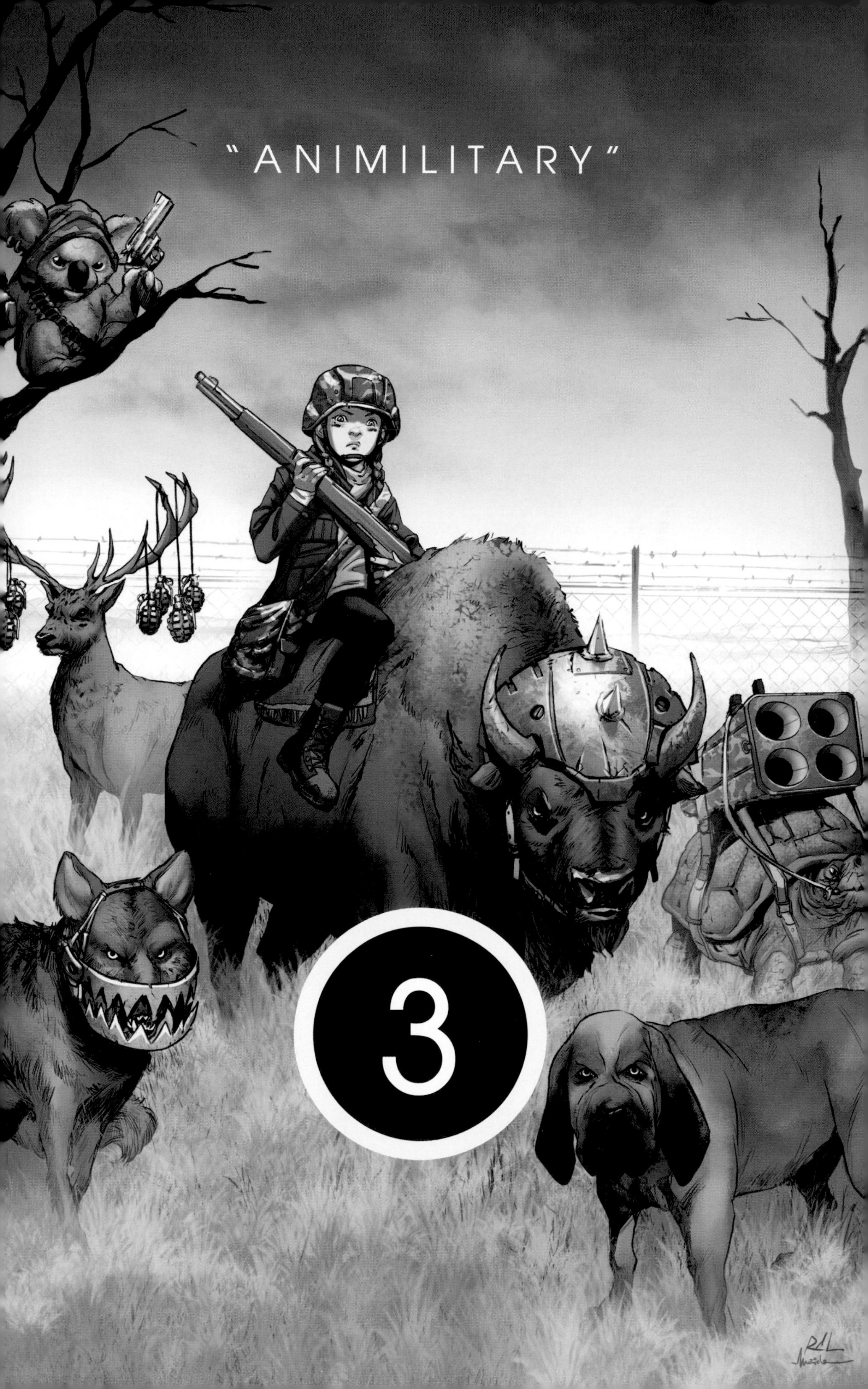
"ANIMILITARY"
3

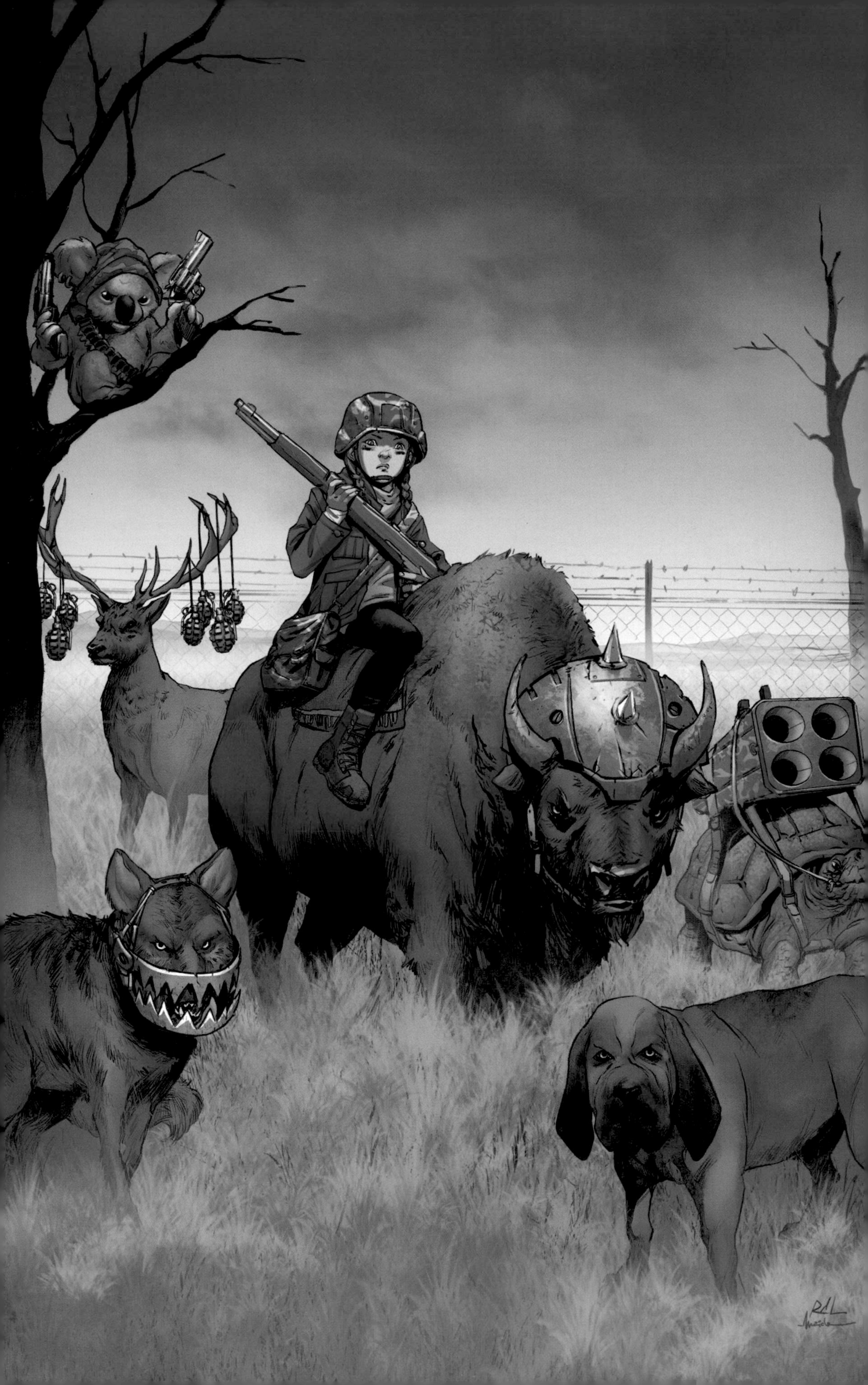

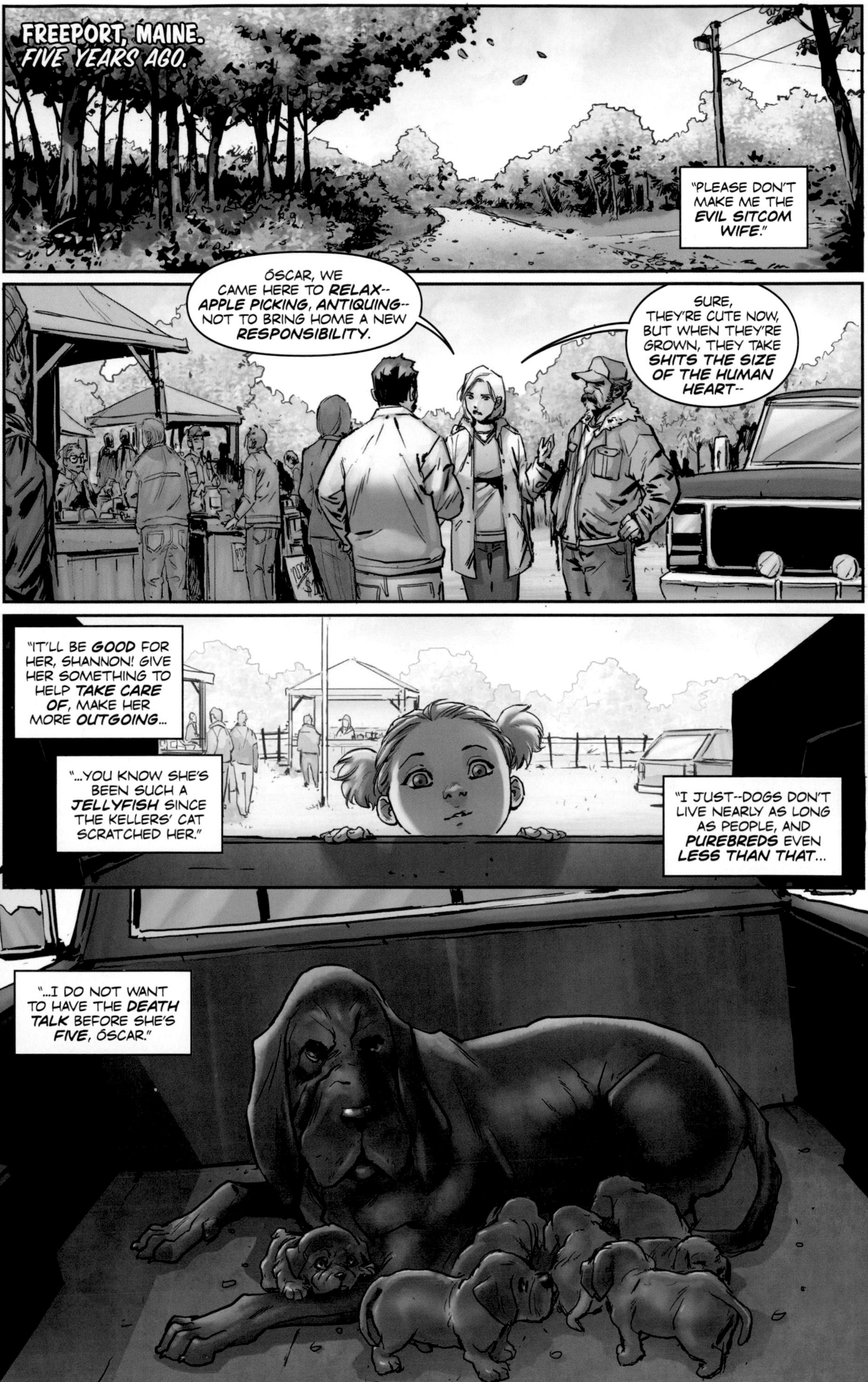
FREEPORT, MAINE.
FIVE YEARS AGO.
"PLEASE DON'T MAKE ME THE EVIL SITCOM WIFE."
ÓSCAR, WE CAME HERE TO RELAX-- APPLE PICKING, ANTIQUING-- NOT TO BRING HOME A NEW RESPONSIBILITY.
SURE, THEY'RE CUTE NOW, BUT WHEN THEY'RE GROWN, THEY TAKE SHITS THE SIZE OF THE HUMAN HEART--
"IT'LL BE GOOD FOR HER, SHANNON! GIVE HER SOMETHING TO HELP TAKE CARE OF, MAKE HER MORE OUTGOING...
"...YOU KNOW SHE'S BEEN SUCH A JELLYFISH SINCE THE KELLERS' CAT SCRATCHED HER."
"I JUST--DOGS DON'T LIVE NEARLY AS LONG AS PEOPLE, AND PUREBREDS EVEN LESS THAN THAT...
"...I DO NOT WANT TO HAVE THE DEATH TALK BEFORE SHE'S FIVE, ÓSCAR."

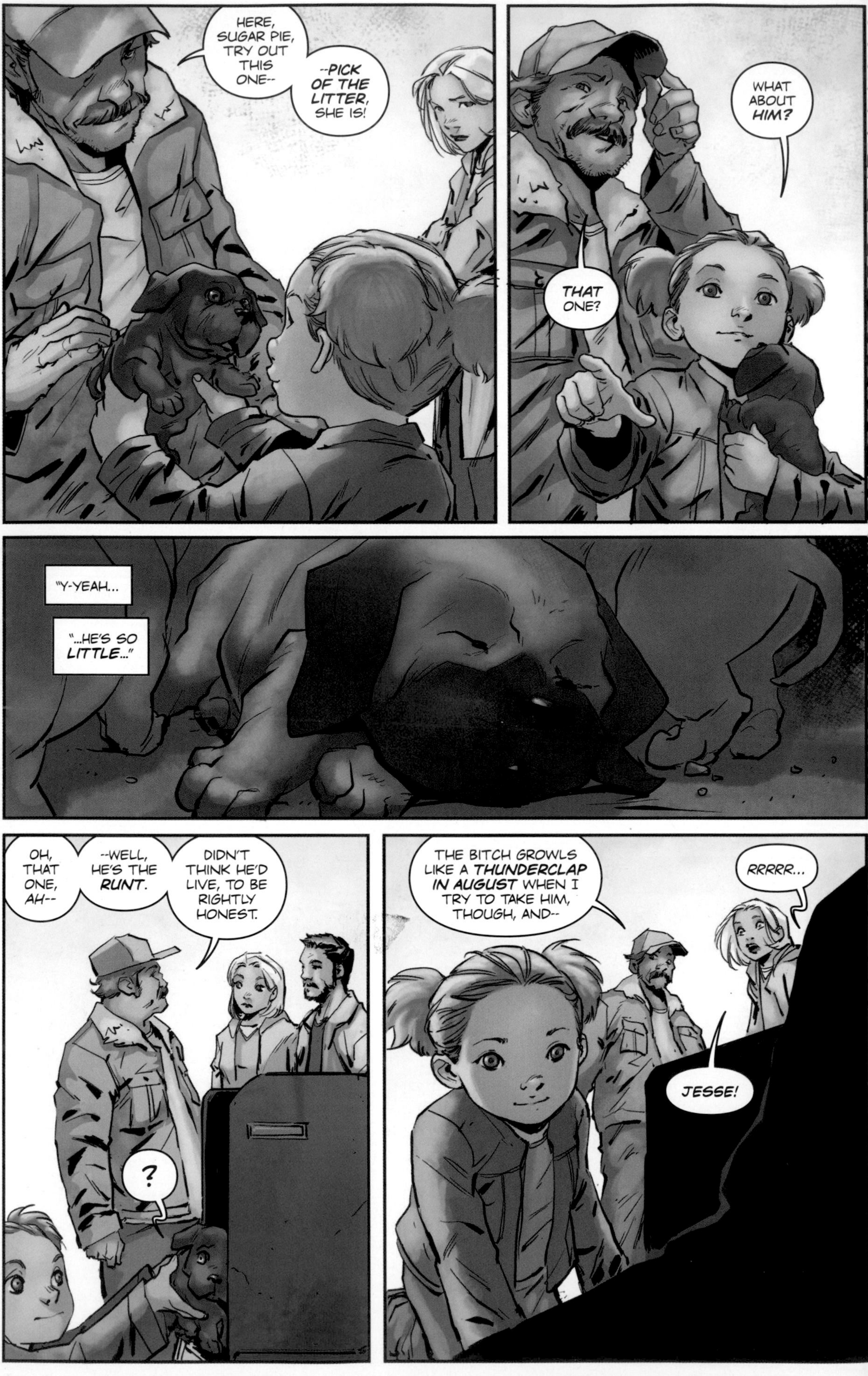
HERE, SUGAR PIE, TRY OUT THIS ONE--
--PICK OF THE LITTER, SHE IS!
WHAT ABOUT HIM?
THAT ONE?
"Y-YEAH...
"...HE'S SO LITTLE..."
OH, THAT ONE, AH--
--WELL, HE'S THE RUNT.
DIDN'T THINK HE'D LIVE, TO BE RIGHTLY HONEST.
?
THE BITCH GROWLS LIKE A THUNDERCLAP IN AUGUST WHEN I TRY TO TAKE HIM, THOUGH, AND--
RRRRR...
JESSE!

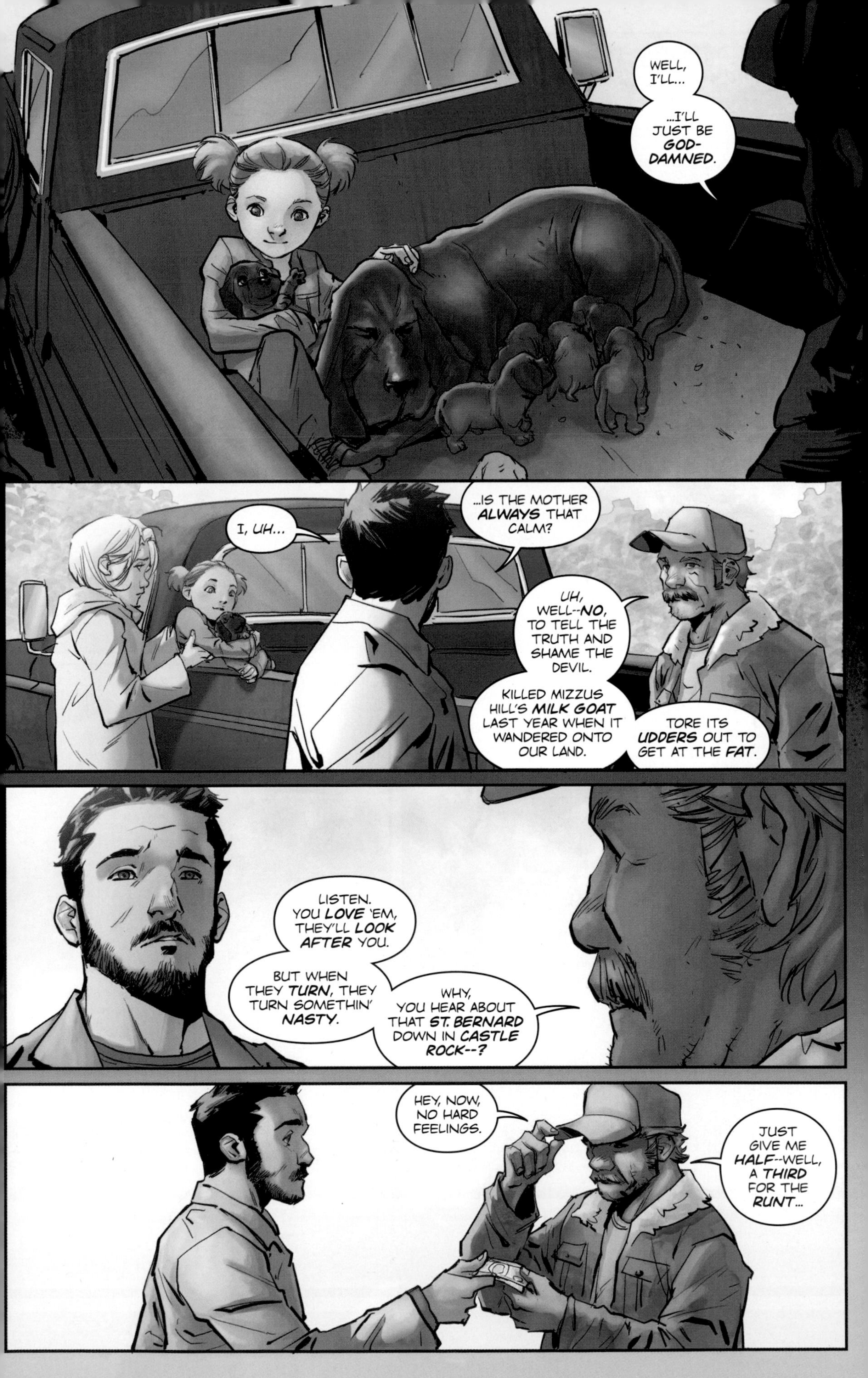
WELL, I'LL...
...I'LL JUST BE GOD-DAMNED.
I, UH...
...IS THE MOTHER ALWAYS THAT CALM?
UH, WELL--NO, TO TELL THE TRUTH AND SHAME THE DEVIL.
KILLED MIZZUS HILL'S MILK GOAT LAST YEAR WHEN IT WANDERED ONTO OUR LAND.
TORE ITS UDDERS OUT TO GET AT THE FAT.
LISTEN. YOU LOVE 'EM, THEY'LL LOOK AFTER YOU.
BUT WHEN THEY TURN, THEY TURN SOMETHIN' NASTY.
WHY, YOU HEAR ABOUT THAT ST. BERNARD DOWN IN CASTLE ROCK--?
HEY, NOW, NO HARD FEELINGS.
JUST GIVE ME HALF--WELL, A THIRD FOR THE RUNT...

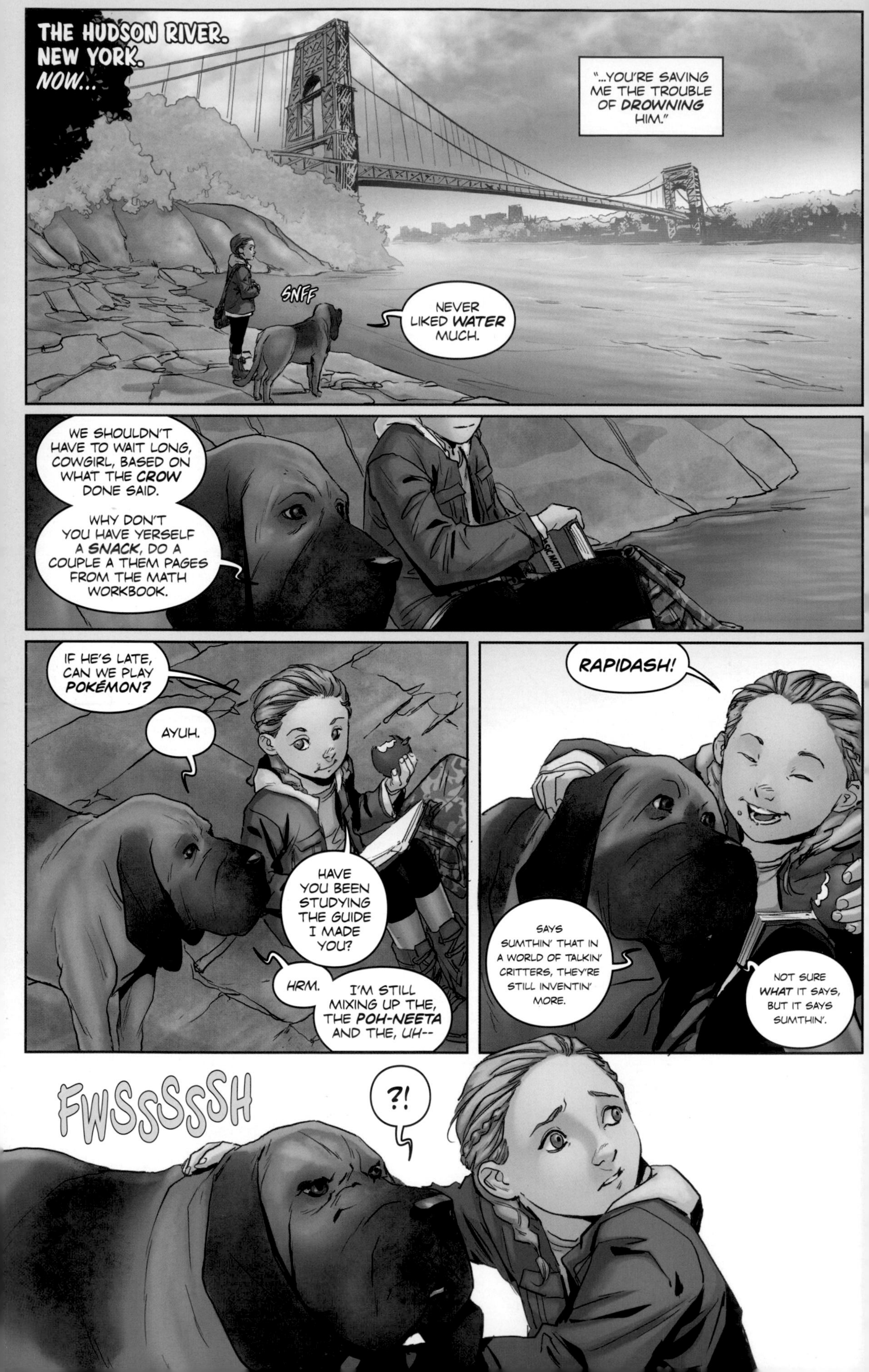
THE HUDSON RIVER. NEW YORK. NOW...
"...YOU'RE SAVING ME THE TROUBLE OF DROWNING HIM."
SNFF
NEVER LIKED WATER MUCH.
WE SHOULDN'T HAVE TO WAIT LONG, COWGIRL, BASED ON WHAT THE CROW DONE SAID.
WHY DON'T YOU HAVE YERSELF A SNACK, DO A COUPLE A THEM PAGES FROM THE MATH WORKBOOK.
IF HE'S LATE, CAN WE PLAY POKÉMON?
AYUH.
HAVE YOU BEEN STUDYING THE GUIDE I MADE YOU?
HRM.
I'M STILL MIXING UP THE, THE POH-NEETA AND THE, UH--
RAPIDASH!
SAYS SUMTHIN' THAT IN A WORLD OF TALKIN' CRITTERS, THEY'RE STILL INVENTIN' MORE.
NOT SURE WHAT IT SAYS, BUT IT SAYS SUMTHIN'.
FWSSSSSH
?!

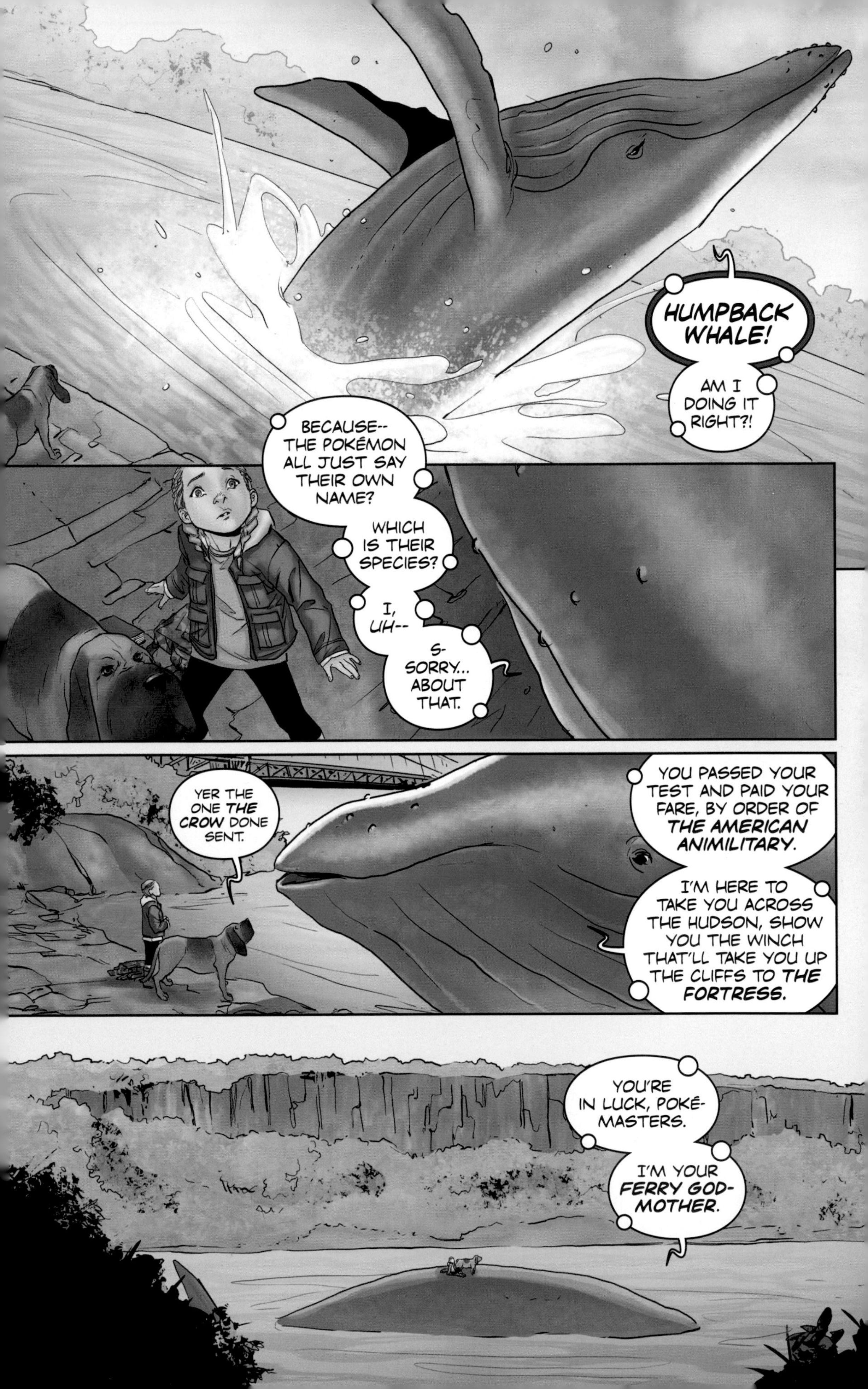

HUMPBACK WHALE!
AM I DOING IT RIGHT?!
BECAUSE-- THE POKÉMON ALL JUST SAY THEIR OWN NAME?
WHICH IS THEIR SPECIES?
I, UH--
S-SORRY... ABOUT THAT.
YER THE ONE THE CROW DONE SENT.
YOU PASSED YOUR TEST AND PAID YOUR FARE, BY ORDER OF THE AMERICAN ANIMILITARY.
I'M HERE TO TAKE YOU ACROSS THE HUDSON, SHOW YOU THE WINCH THAT'LL TAKE YOU UP THE CLIFFS TO THE FORTRESS.
YOU'RE IN LUCK, POKÉ-MASTERS.
I'M YOUR FERRY GOD-MOTHER.

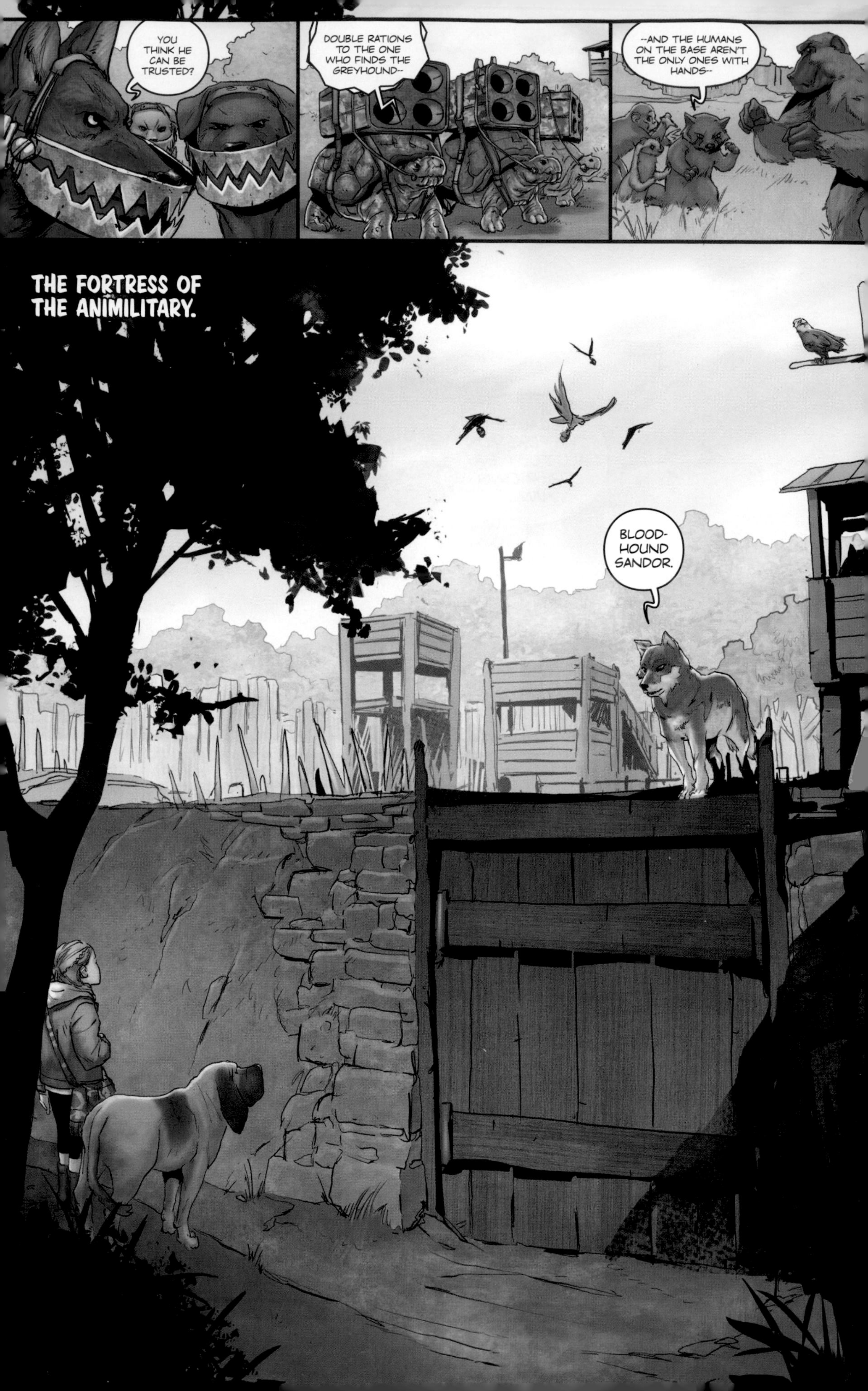
YOU THINK HE CAN BE TRUSTED?
DOUBLE RATIONS TO THE ONE WHO FINDS THE GREYHOUND--
--AND THE HUMANS ON THE BASE AREN'T THE ONLY ONES WITH HANDS--
THE FORTRESS OF THE ANIMILITARY.
BLOOD-HOUND SANDOR.

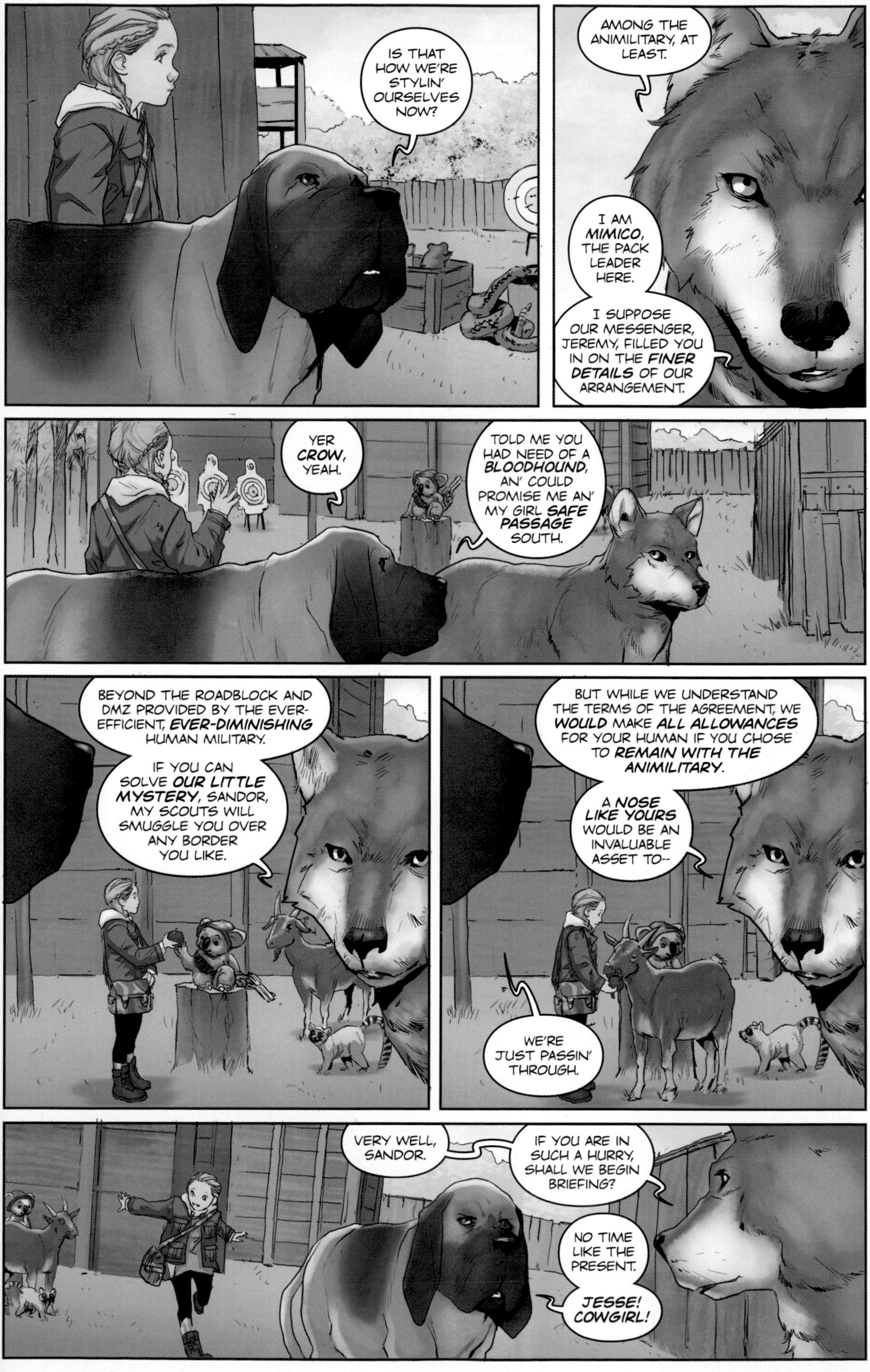
IS THAT HOW WE'RE STYLIN' OURSELVES NOW?
AMONG THE ANIMILITARY, AT LEAST.
I AM MIMICO, THE PACK LEADER HERE.
I SUPPOSE OUR MESSENGER, JEREMY, FILLED YOU IN ON THE FINER DETAILS OF OUR ARRANGEMENT.
YER CROW, YEAH.
TOLD ME YOU HAD NEED OF A BLOODHOUND, AN' COULD PROMISE ME AN' MY GIRL SAFE PASSAGE SOUTH.
BEYOND THE ROADBLOCK AND DMZ PROVIDED BY THE EVER-EFFICIENT, EVER-DIMINISHING HUMAN MILITARY.
IF YOU CAN SOLVE OUR LITTLE MYSTERY, SANDOR, MY SCOUTS WILL SMUGGLE YOU OVER ANY BORDER YOU LIKE.
BUT WHILE WE UNDERSTAND THE TERMS OF THE AGREEMENT, WE WOULD MAKE ALL ALLOWANCES FOR YOUR HUMAN IF YOU CHOSE TO REMAIN WITH THE ANIMILITARY.
A NOSE LIKE YOURS WOULD BE AN INVALUABLE ASSET TO--
WE'RE JUST PASSIN' THROUGH.
VERY WELL, SANDOR.
IF YOU ARE IN SUCH A HURRY, SHALL WE BEGIN BRIEFING?
NO TIME LIKE THE PRESENT.
JESSE! COWGIRL!

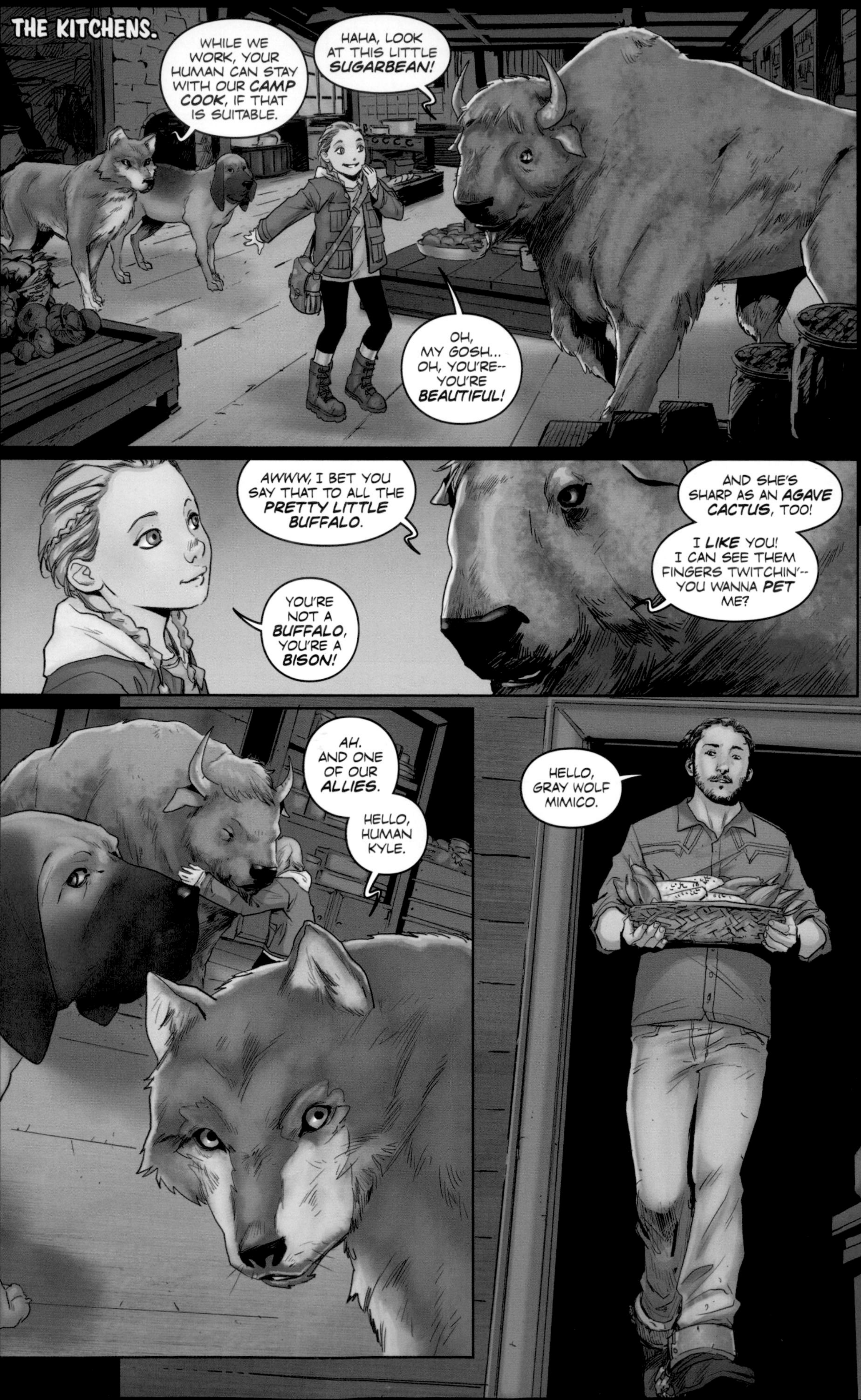
THE KITCHENS.
WHILE WE WORK, YOUR HUMAN CAN STAY WITH OUR CAMP COOK, IF THAT IS SUITABLE.
HAHA, LOOK AT THIS LITTLE SUGARBEAN!
OH, MY GOSH... OH, YOU'RE-- YOU'RE BEAUTIFUL!
AWWW, I BET YOU SAY THAT TO ALL THE PRETTY LITTLE BUFFALO.
YOU'RE NOT A BUFFALO, YOU'RE A BISON!
AND SHE'S SHARP AS AN AGAVE CACTUS, TOO!
I LIKE YOU! I CAN SEE THEM FINGERS TWITCHIN'-- YOU WANNA PET ME?
AH. AND ONE OF OUR ALLIES.
HELLO, HUMAN KYLE.
HELLO, GRAY WOLF MIMICO.

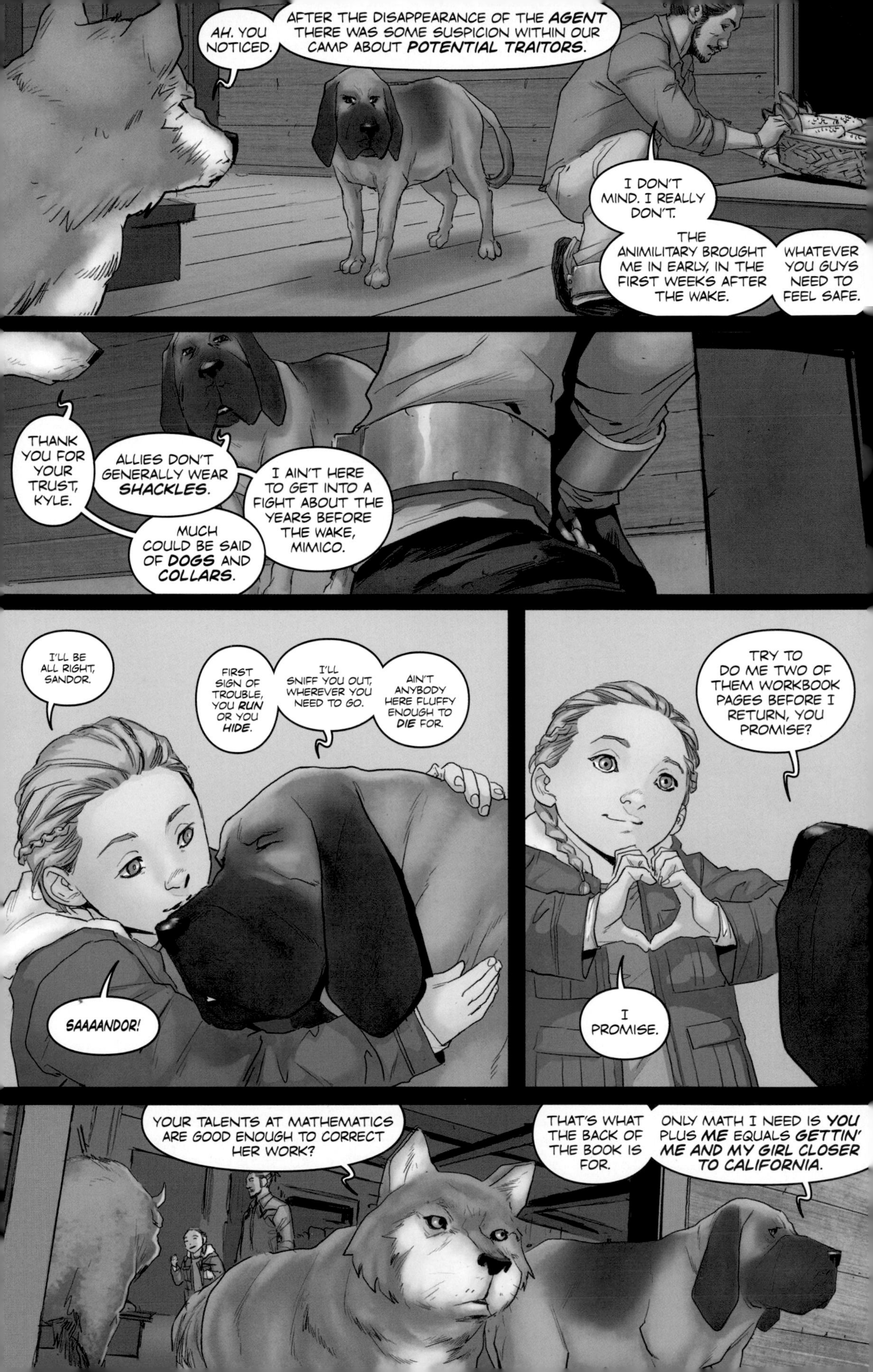
AH. YOU NOTICED.
AFTER THE DISAPPEARANCE OF THE AGENT THERE WAS SOME SUSPICION WITHIN OUR CAMP ABOUT POTENTIAL TRAITORS.
I DON'T MIND. I REALLY DON'T.
THE ANIMILITARY BROUGHT ME IN EARLY, IN THE FIRST WEEKS AFTER THE WAKE.
WHATEVER YOU GUYS NEED TO FEEL SAFE.
THANK YOU FOR YOUR TRUST, KYLE.
ALLIES DON'T GENERALLY WEAR SHACKLES.
MUCH COULD BE SAID OF DOGS AND COLLARS.
I AIN'T HERE TO GET INTO A FIGHT ABOUT THE YEARS BEFORE THE WAKE, MIMICO.
I'LL BE ALL RIGHT, SANDOR.
FIRST SIGN OF TROUBLE, YOU RUN OR YOU HIDE.
I'LL SNIFF YOU OUT, WHEREVER YOU NEED TO GO.
AIN'T ANYBODY HERE FLUFFY ENOUGH TO DIE FOR.
SAAAANDOR!
TRY TO DO ME TWO OF THEM WORKBOOK PAGES BEFORE I RETURN, YOU PROMISE?
I PROMISE.
YOUR TALENTS AT MATHEMATICS ARE GOOD ENOUGH TO CORRECT HER WORK?
THAT'S WHAT THE BACK OF THE BOOK IS FOR.
ONLY MATH I NEED IS YOU PLUS ME EQUALS GETTIN' ME AND MY GIRL CLOSER TO CALIFORNIA.

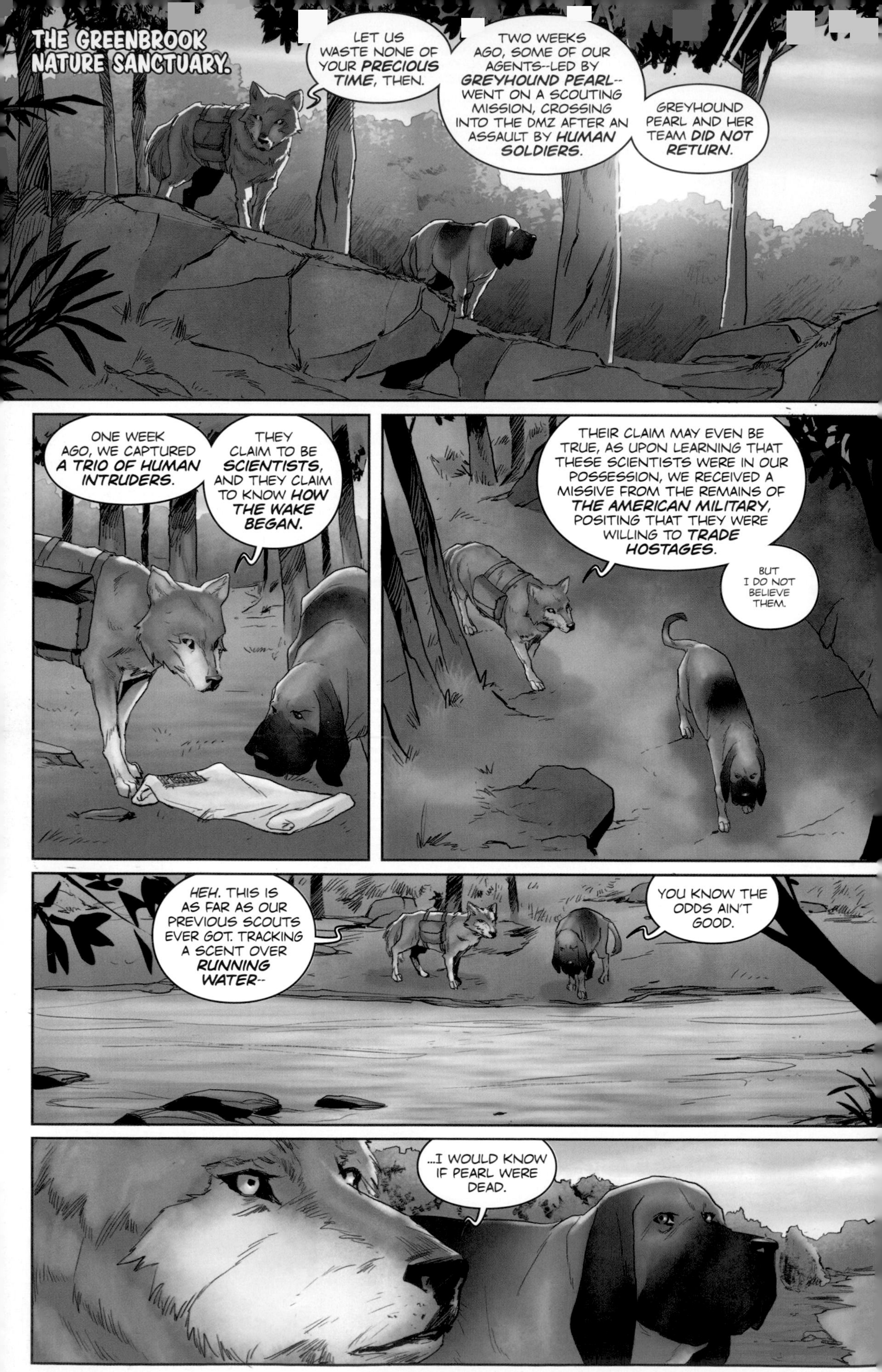
THE GREENBROOK NATURE SANCTUARY.
LET US WASTE NONE OF YOUR PRECIOUS TIME, THEN.
TWO WEEKS AGO, SOME OF OUR AGENTS--LED BY GREYHOUND PEARL--WENT ON A SCOUTING MISSION, CROSSING INTO THE DMZ AFTER AN ASSAULT BY HUMAN SOLDIERS.
GREYHOUND PEARL AND HER TEAM DID NOT RETURN.
ONE WEEK AGO, WE CAPTURED A TRIO OF HUMAN INTRUDERS.
THEY CLAIM TO BE SCIENTISTS, AND THEY CLAIM TO KNOW HOW THE WAKE BEGAN.
THEIR CLAIM MAY EVEN BE TRUE, AS UPON LEARNING THAT THESE SCIENTISTS WERE IN OUR POSSESSION, WE RECEIVED A MISSIVE FROM THE REMAINS OF THE AMERICAN MILITARY, POSITING THAT THEY WERE WILLING TO TRADE HOSTAGES.
BUT I DO NOT BELIEVE THEM.
HEH. THIS IS AS FAR AS OUR PREVIOUS SCOUTS EVER GOT. TRACKING A SCENT OVER RUNNING WATER--
YOU KNOW THE ODDS AIN'T GOOD.
...I WOULD KNOW IF PEARL WERE DEAD.

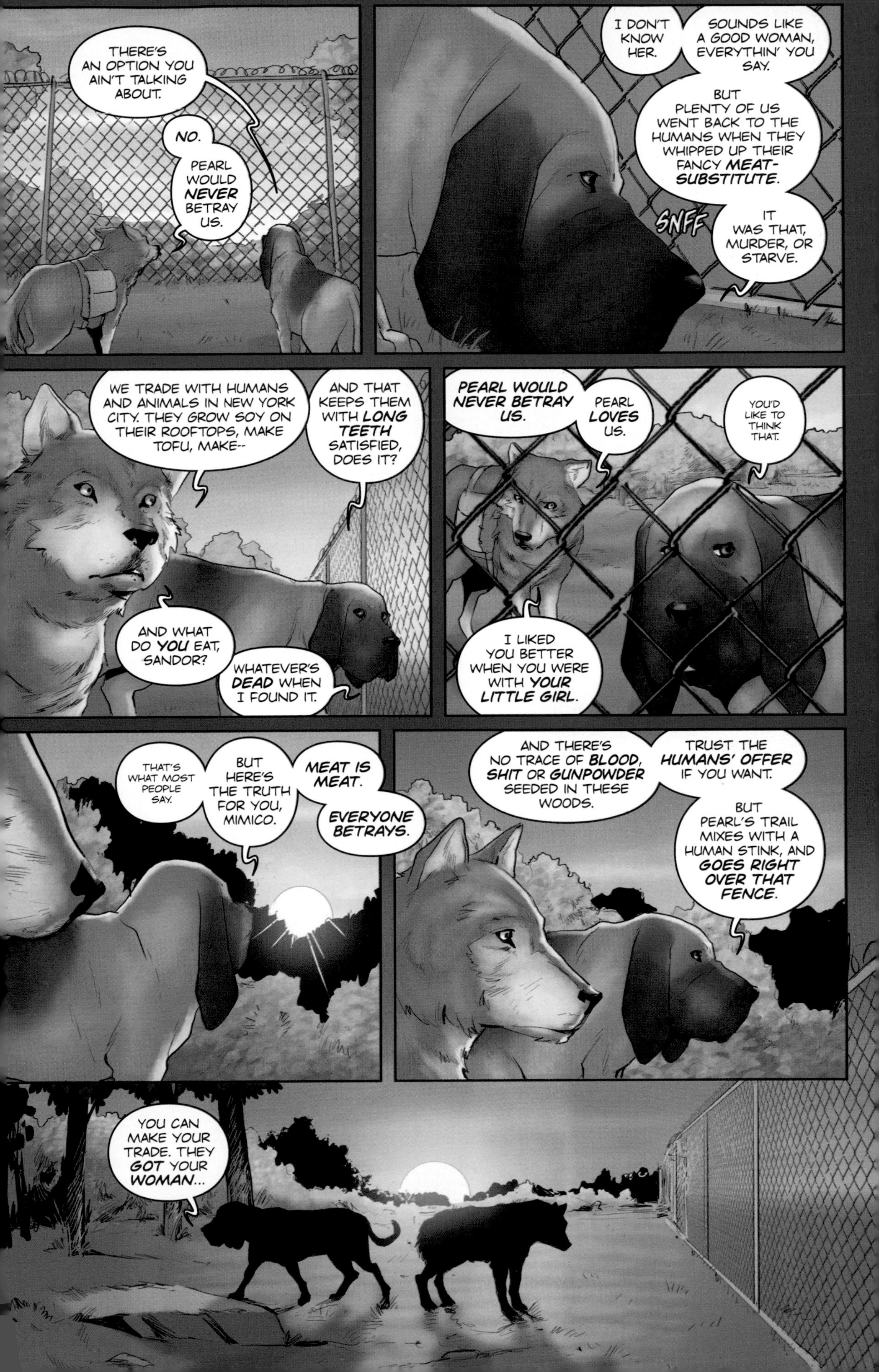
THERE'S AN OPTION YOU AIN'T TALKING ABOUT.
NO.
PEARL WOULD NEVER BETRAY US.
I DON'T KNOW HER.
SOUNDS LIKE A GOOD WOMAN, EVERYTHIN' YOU SAY.
BUT PLENTY OF US WENT BACK TO THE HUMANS WHEN THEY WHIPPED UP THEIR FANCY MEAT-SUBSTITUTE.
SNFF
IT WAS THAT, MURDER, OR STARVE.
WE TRADE WITH HUMANS AND ANIMALS IN NEW YORK CITY. THEY GROW SOY ON THEIR ROOFTOPS, MAKE TOFU, MAKE--
AND THAT KEEPS THEM WITH LONG TEETH SATISFIED, DOES IT?
AND WHAT DO YOU EAT, SANDOR?
WHATEVER'S DEAD WHEN I FOUND IT.
PEARL WOULD NEVER BETRAY US.
PEARL LOVES US.
YOU'D LIKE TO THINK THAT.
I LIKED YOU BETTER WHEN YOU WERE WITH YOUR LITTLE GIRL.
THAT'S WHAT MOST PEOPLE SAY.
BUT HERE'S THE TRUTH FOR YOU, MIMICO.
MEAT IS MEAT.
EVERYONE BETRAYS.
AND THERE'S NO TRACE OF BLOOD, SHIT OR GUNPOWDER SEEDED IN THESE WOODS.
TRUST THE HUMANS' OFFER IF YOU WANT.
BUT PEARL'S TRAIL MIXES WITH A HUMAN STINK, AND GOES RIGHT OVER THAT FENCE.
YOU CAN MAKE YOUR TRADE. THEY GOT YOUR WOMAN...

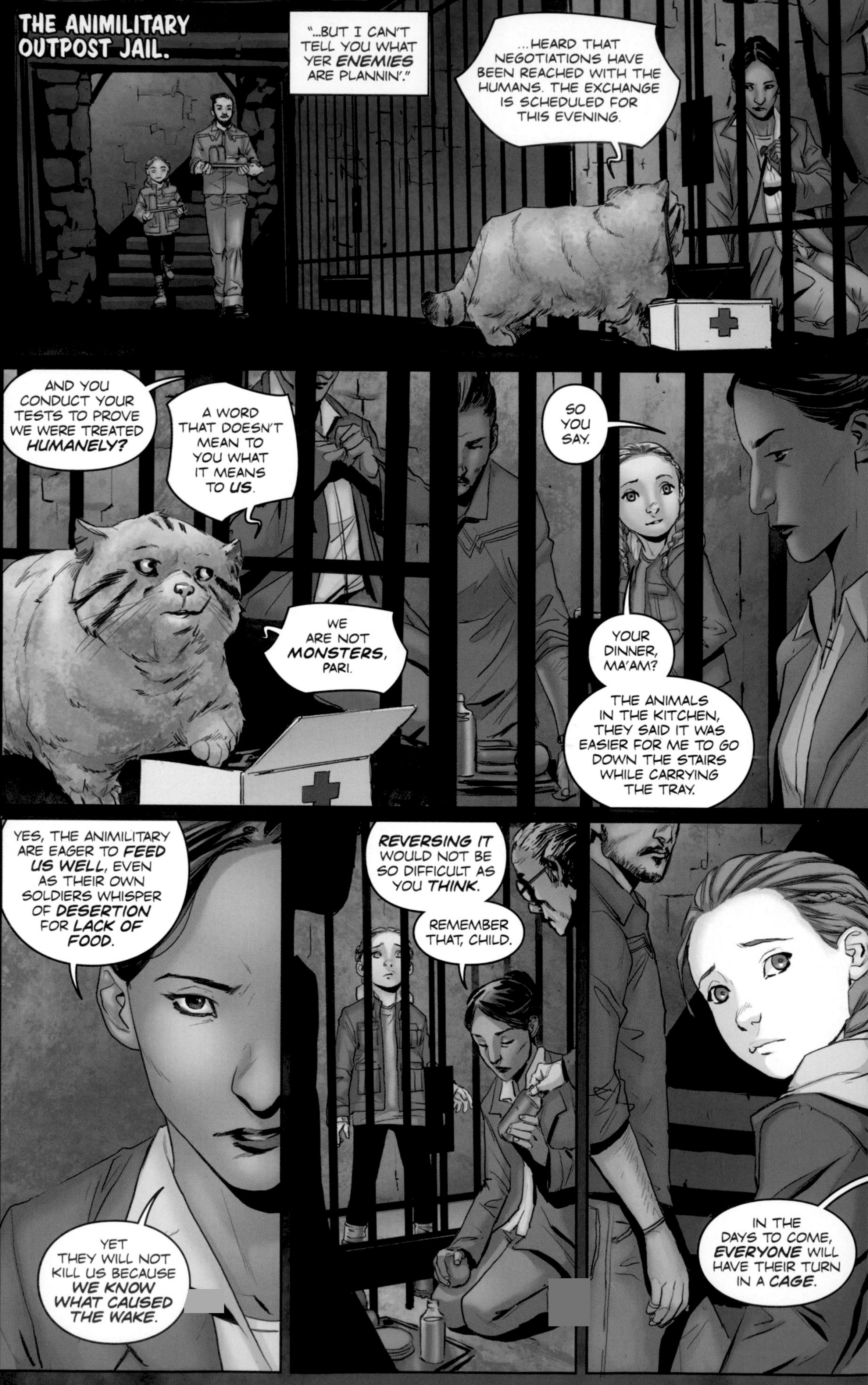
THE ANIMILITARY OUTPOST JAIL.
"...BUT I CAN'T TELL YOU WHAT YER ENEMIES ARE PLANNIN'."
...HEARD THAT NEGOTIATIONS HAVE BEEN REACHED WITH THE HUMANS. THE EXCHANGE IS SCHEDULED FOR THIS EVENING.
AND YOU CONDUCT YOUR TESTS TO PROVE WE WERE TREATED HUMANELY?
A WORD THAT DOESN'T MEAN TO YOU WHAT IT MEANS TO US.
WE ARE NOT MONSTERS, PARI.
SO YOU SAY.
YOUR DINNER, MA'AM?
THE ANIMALS IN THE KITCHEN, THEY SAID IT WAS EASIER FOR ME TO GO DOWN THE STAIRS WHILE CARRYING THE TRAY.
YES, THE ANIMILITARY ARE EAGER TO FEED US WELL, EVEN AS THEIR OWN SOLDIERS WHISPER OF DESERTION FOR LACK OF FOOD.
YET THEY WILL NOT KILL US BECAUSE WE KNOW WHAT CAUSED THE WAKE.
REVERSING IT WOULD NOT BE SO DIFFICULT AS YOU THINK.
REMEMBER THAT, CHILD.
IN THE DAYS TO COME, EVERYONE WILL HAVE THEIR TURN IN A CAGE.

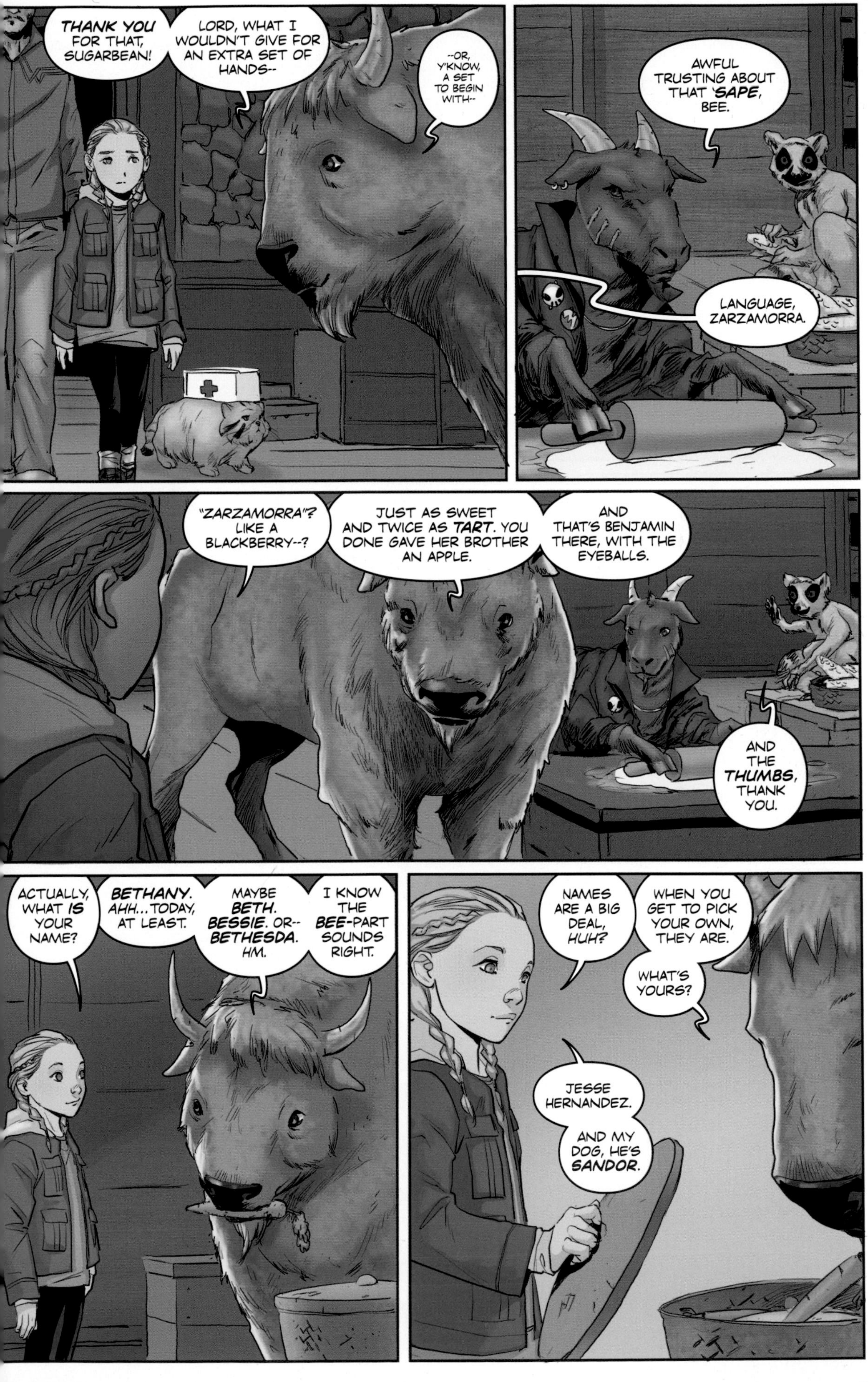
THANK YOU FOR THAT, SUGARBEAN!
LORD, WHAT I WOULDN'T GIVE FOR AN EXTRA SET OF HANDS--
--OR, Y'KNOW, A SET TO BEGIN WITH--
AWFUL TRUSTING ABOUT THAT 'SAPE, BEE.
LANGUAGE, ZARZAMORRA.
"ZARZAMORRA"? LIKE A BLACKBERRY--?
JUST AS SWEET AND TWICE AS TART. YOU DONE GAVE HER BROTHER AN APPLE.
AND THAT'S BENJAMIN THERE, WITH THE EYEBALLS.
AND THE THUMBS, THANK YOU.
ACTUALLY, WHAT IS YOUR NAME?
BETHANY. AHH...TODAY, AT LEAST.
MAYBE BETH. BESSIE. OR-- BETHESDA. HM.
I KNOW THE BEE-PART SOUNDS RIGHT.
NAMES ARE A BIG DEAL, HUH?
WHEN YOU GET TO PICK YOUR OWN, THEY ARE.
WHAT'S YOURS?
JESSE HERNANDEZ.
AND MY DOG, HE'S SANDOR.

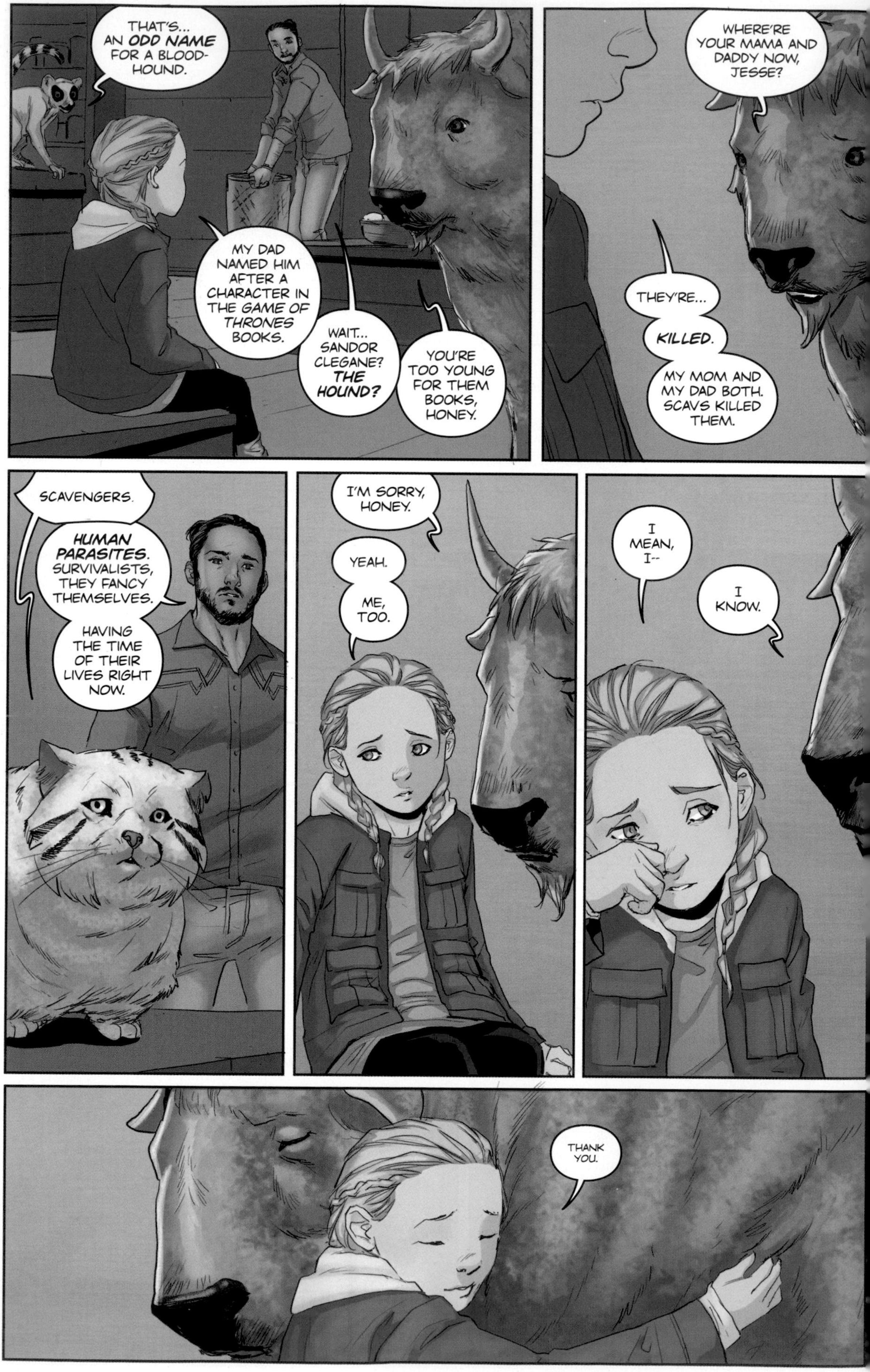

THAT'S... AN ODD NAME FOR A BLOOD-HOUND.
MY DAD NAMED HIM AFTER A CHARACTER IN THE GAME OF THRONES BOOKS.
WAIT... SANDOR CLEGANE? THE HOUND?
YOU'RE TOO YOUNG FOR THEM BOOKS, HONEY.
WHERE'RE YOUR MAMA AND DADDY NOW, JESSE?
THEY'RE...
KILLED.
MY MOM AND MY DAD BOTH. SCAVS KILLED THEM.
SCAVENGERS.
HUMAN PARASITES. SURVIVALISTS, THEY FANCY THEMSELVES.
HAVING THE TIME OF THEIR LIVES RIGHT NOW.
I'M SORRY, HONEY.
YEAH.
ME, TOO.
I MEAN, I--
I KNOW.
THANK YOU.

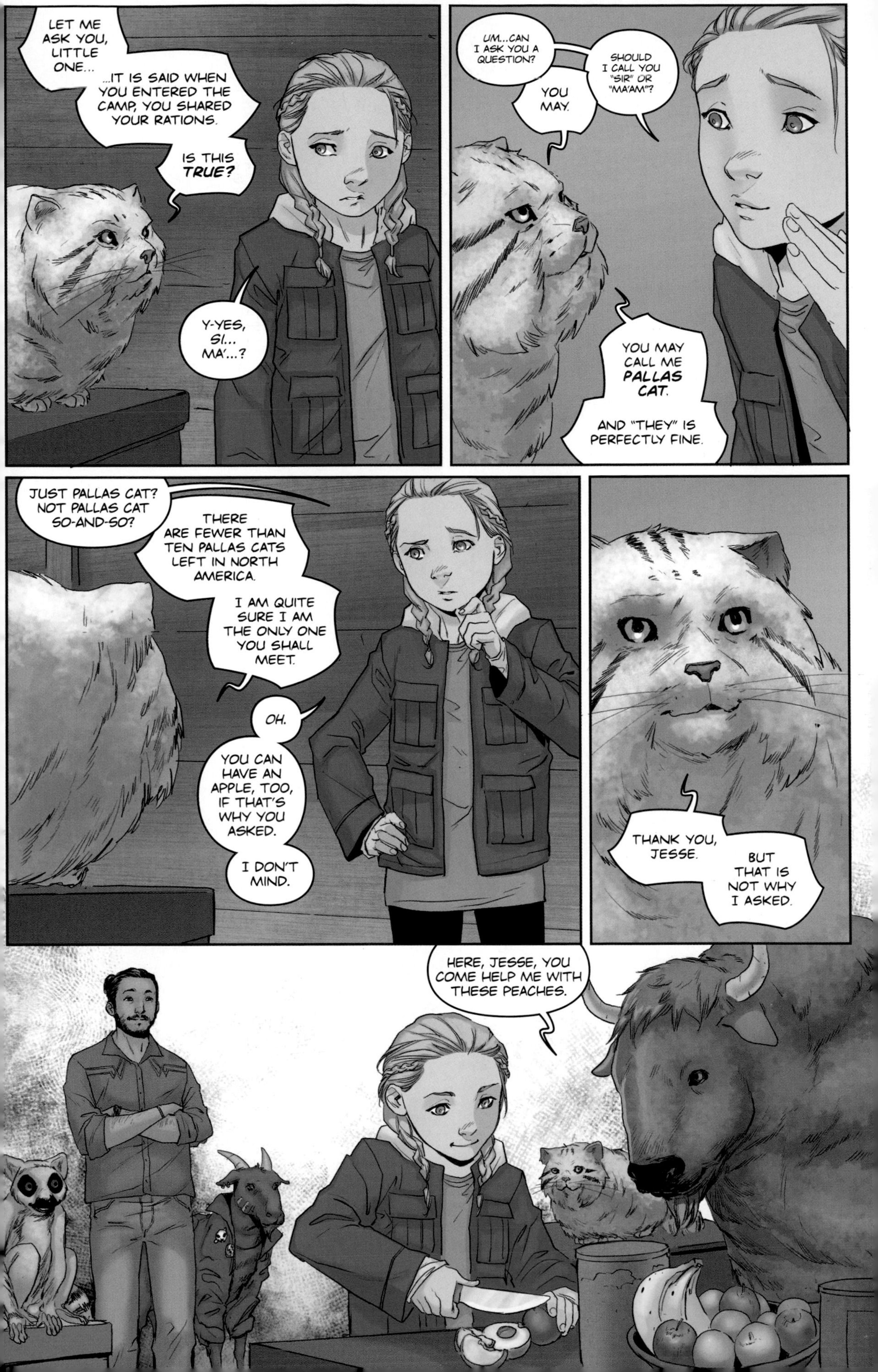
LET ME ASK YOU, LITTLE ONE...
...IT IS SAID WHEN YOU ENTERED THE CAMP, YOU SHARED YOUR RATIONS.
IS THIS TRUE?
Y-YES, SI... MA'...?
UM...CAN I ASK YOU A QUESTION?
YOU MAY.
SHOULD I CALL YOU "SIR" OR "MA'AM"?
YOU MAY CALL ME PALLAS CAT.
AND "THEY" IS PERFECTLY FINE.
JUST PALLAS CAT? NOT PALLAS CAT SO-AND-SO?
THERE ARE FEWER THAN TEN PALLAS CATS LEFT IN NORTH AMERICA.
I AM QUITE SURE I AM THE ONLY ONE YOU SHALL MEET.
OH.
YOU CAN HAVE AN APPLE, TOO, IF THAT'S WHY YOU ASKED.
I DON'T MIND.
THANK YOU, JESSE.
BUT THAT IS NOT WHY I ASKED.
HERE, JESSE, YOU COME HELP ME WITH THESE PEACHES.

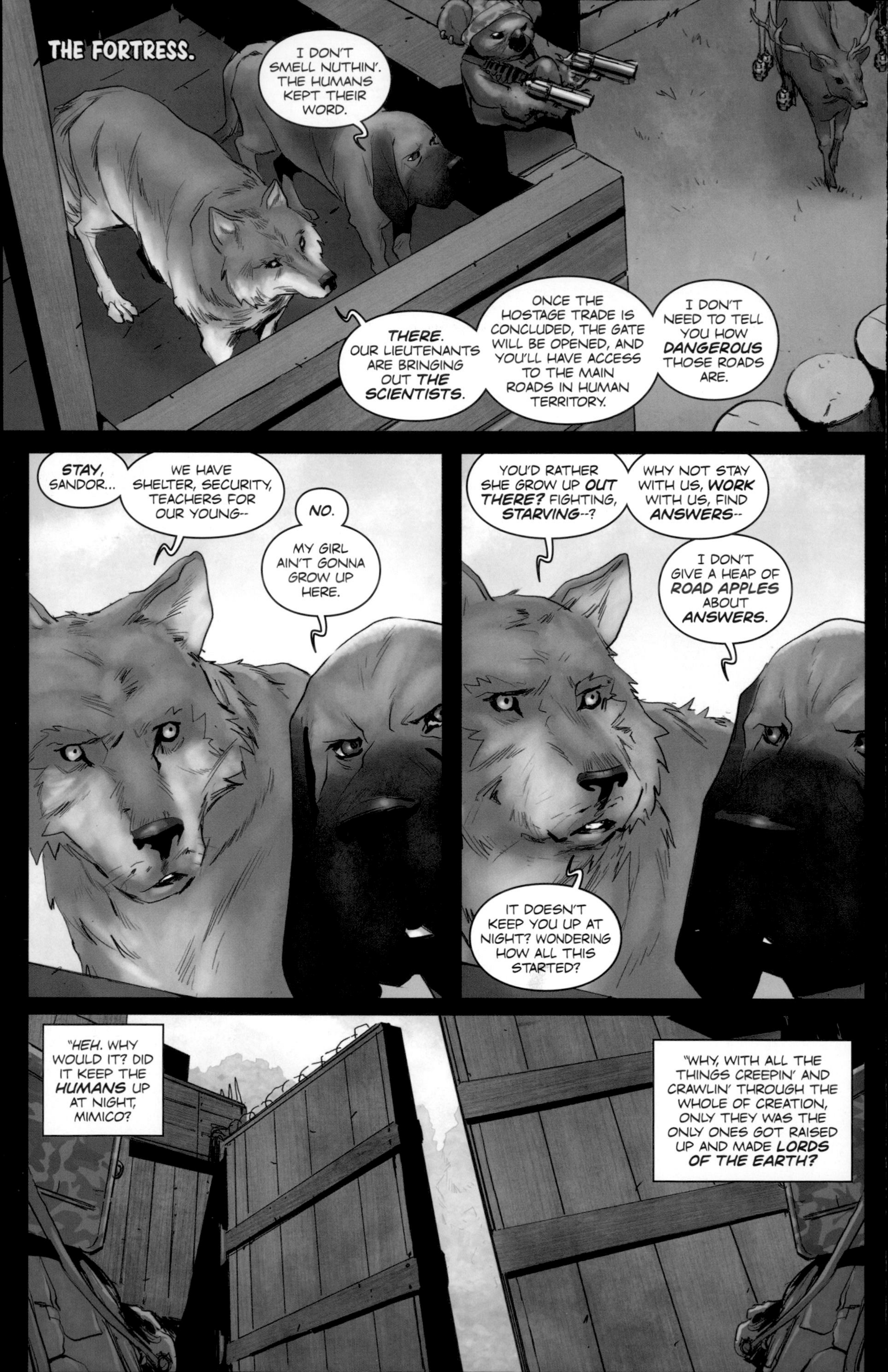
THE FORTRESS.
I DON'T SMELL NUTHIN'. THE HUMANS KEPT THEIR WORD.
THERE. OUR LIEUTENANTS ARE BRINGING OUT THE SCIENTISTS.
ONCE THE HOSTAGE TRADE IS CONCLUDED, THE GATE WILL BE OPENED, AND YOU'LL HAVE ACCESS TO THE MAIN ROADS IN HUMAN TERRITORY.
I DON'T NEED TO TELL YOU HOW DANGEROUS THOSE ROADS ARE.
STAY, SANDOR...
WE HAVE SHELTER, SECURITY, TEACHERS FOR OUR YOUNG--
NO.
MY GIRL AIN'T GONNA GROW UP HERE.
YOU'D RATHER SHE GROW UP OUT THERE? FIGHTING, STARVING--?
WHY NOT STAY WITH US, WORK WITH US, FIND ANSWERS--
I DON'T GIVE A HEAP OF ROAD APPLES ABOUT ANSWERS.
IT DOESN'T KEEP YOU UP AT NIGHT? WONDERING HOW ALL THIS STARTED?
"HEH. WHY WOULD IT? DID IT KEEP THE HUMANS UP AT NIGHT, MIMICO?
"WHY, WITH ALL THE THINGS CREEPIN' AND CRAWLIN' THROUGH THE WHOLE OF CREATION, ONLY THEY WAS THE ONLY ONES GOT RAISED UP AND MADE LORDS OF THE EARTH?

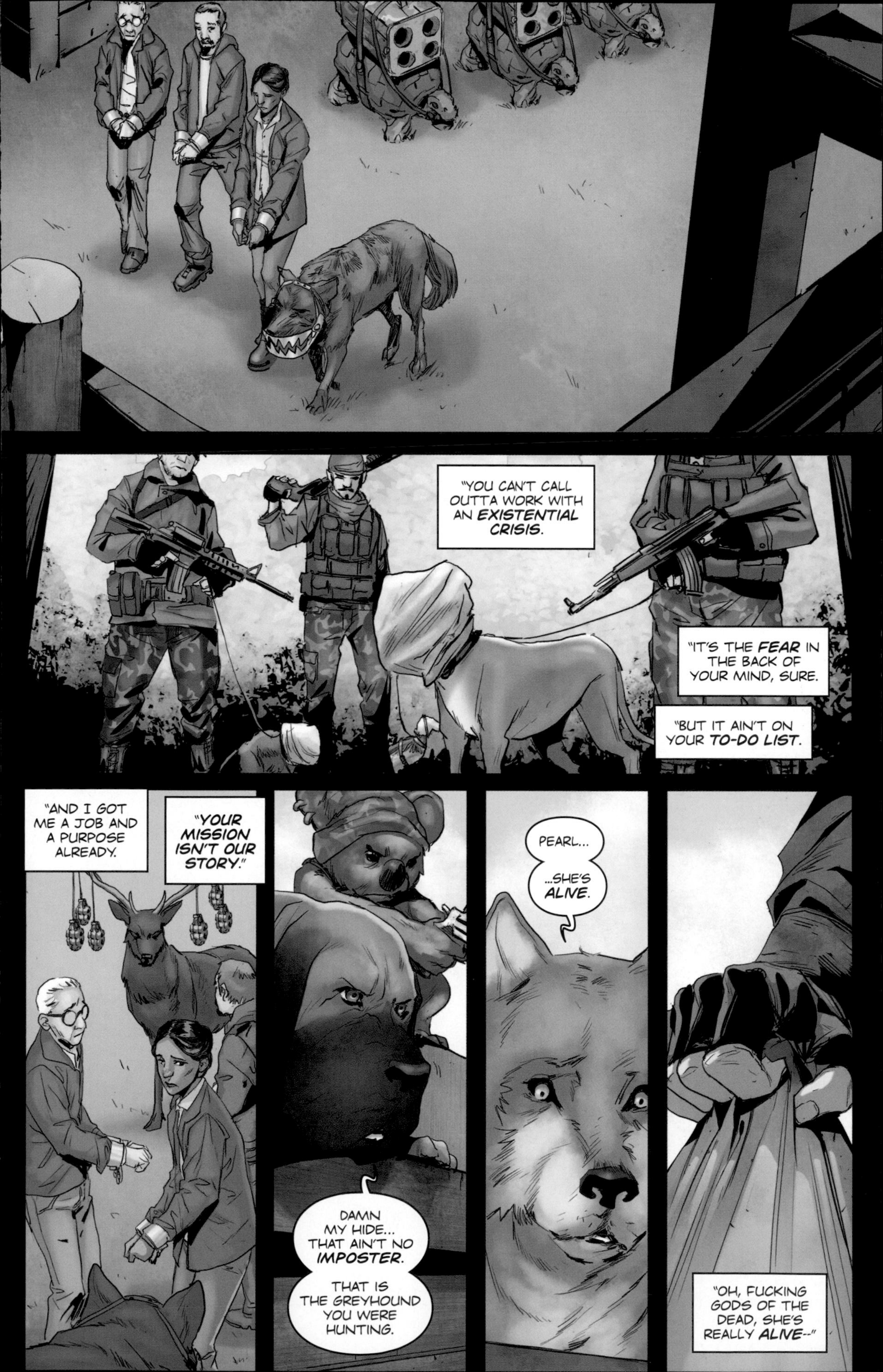
"YOU CAN'T CALL OUTTA WORK WITH AN EXISTENTIAL CRISIS.
"IT'S THE FEAR IN THE BACK OF YOUR MIND, SURE.
"BUT IT AIN'T ON YOUR TO-DO LIST.
"AND I GOT ME A JOB AND A PURPOSE ALREADY.
"YOUR MISSION ISN'T OUR STORY."
DAMN MY HIDE... THAT AIN'T NO IMPOSTER.
THAT IS THE GREYHOUND YOU WERE HUNTING.
PEARL...
...SHE'S ALIVE.
"OH, FUCKING GODS OF THE DEAD, SHE'S REALLY ALIVE--"

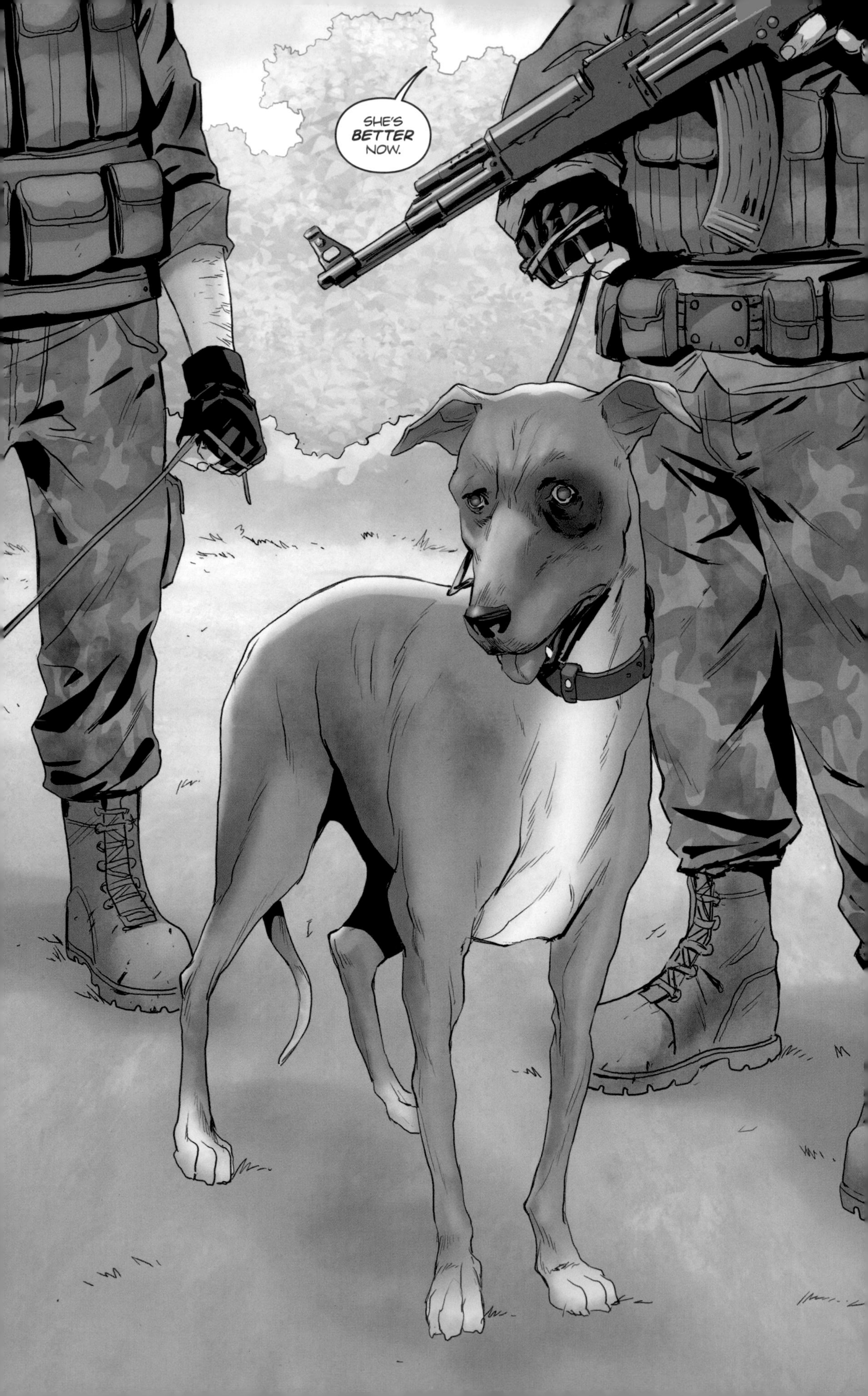
SHE'S BETTER NOW.

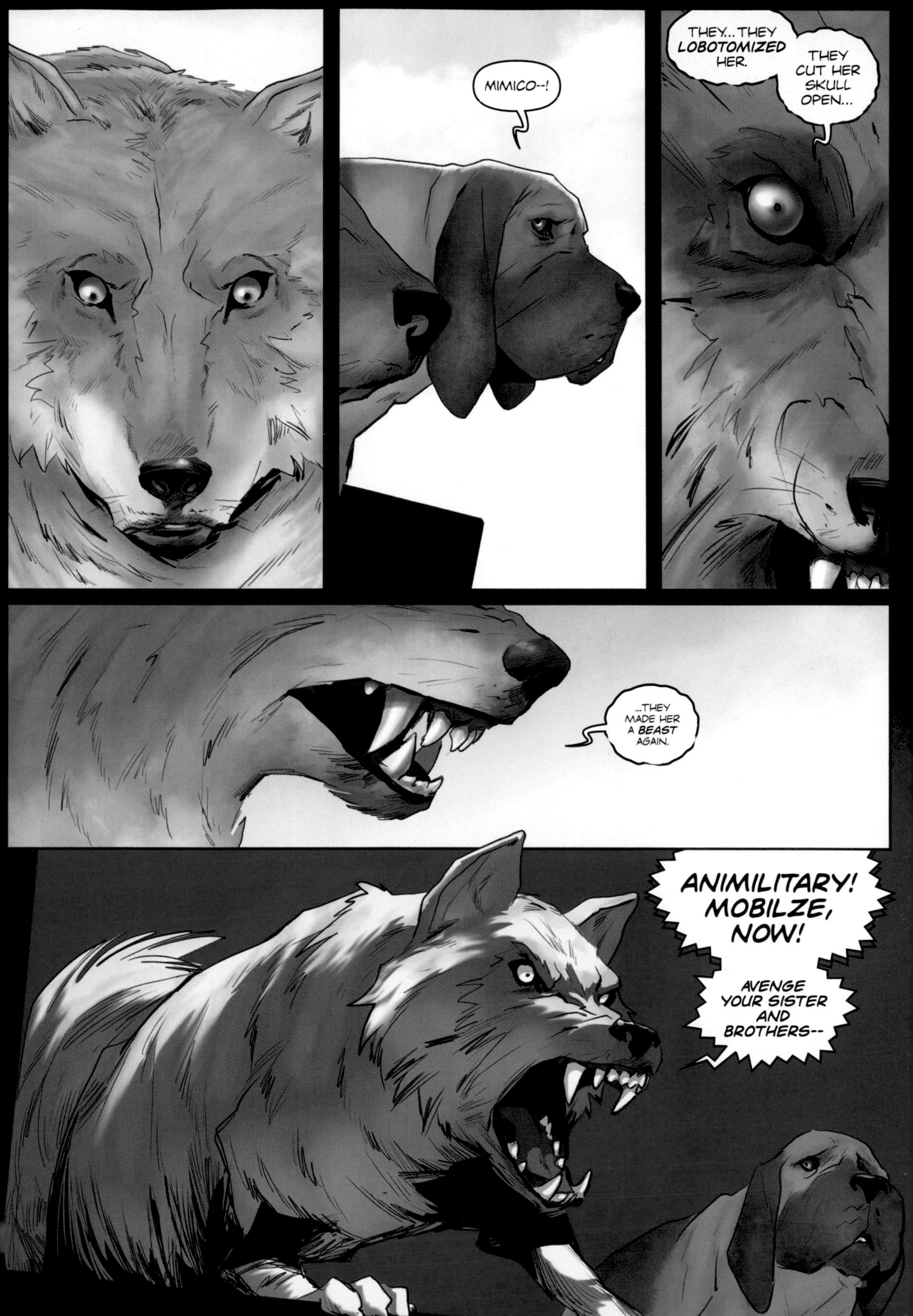
MIMICO--!
THEY... THEY LOBOTOMIZED HER.
THEY CUT HER SKULL OPEN...
...THEY MADE HER A BEAST AGAIN.
ANIMILITARY! MOBILZE, NOW!
AVENGE YOUR SISTER AND BROTHERS--

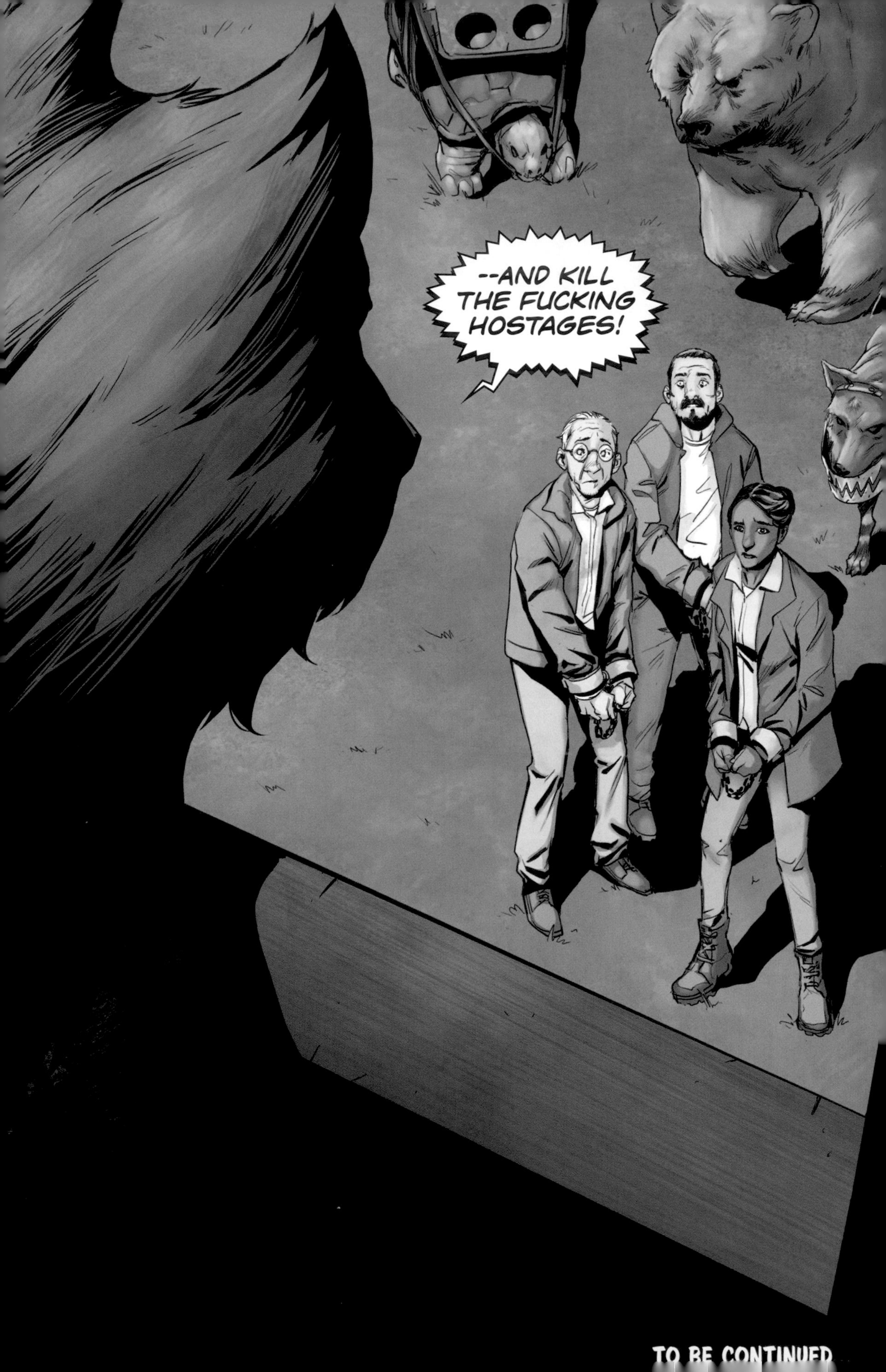
--AND KILL THE FUCKING HOSTAGES!
TO BE CONTINUED

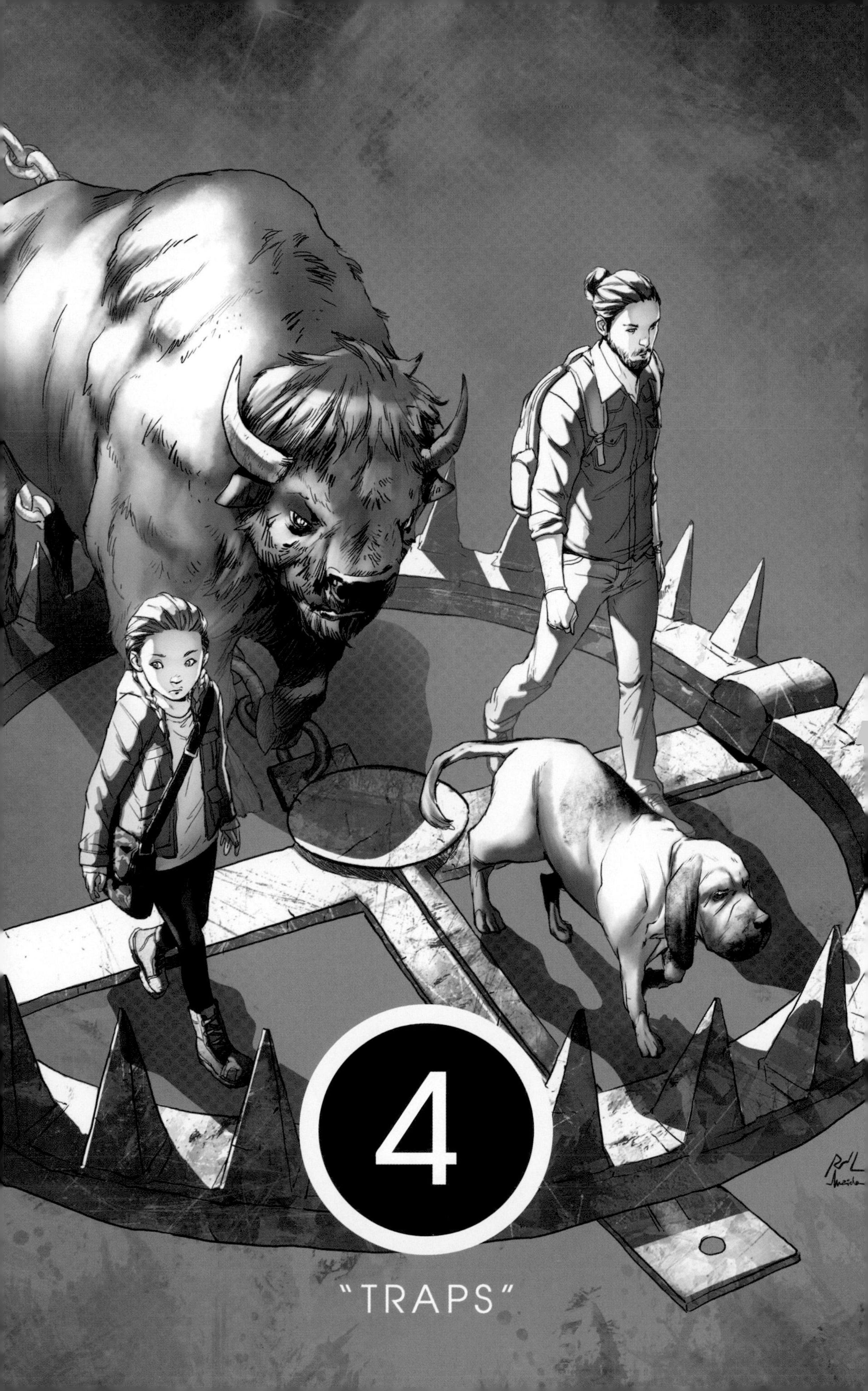
4
"TRAPS"

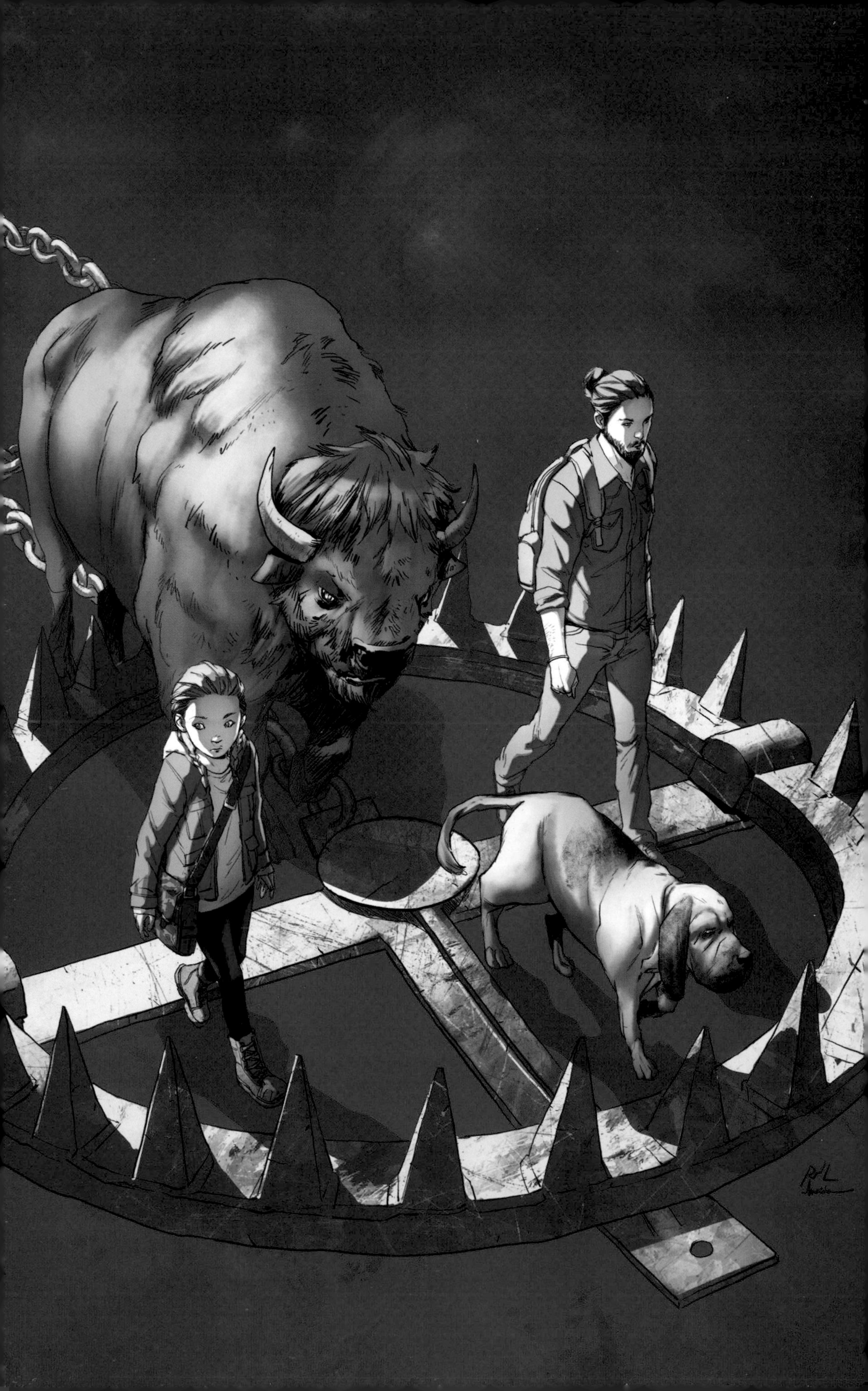

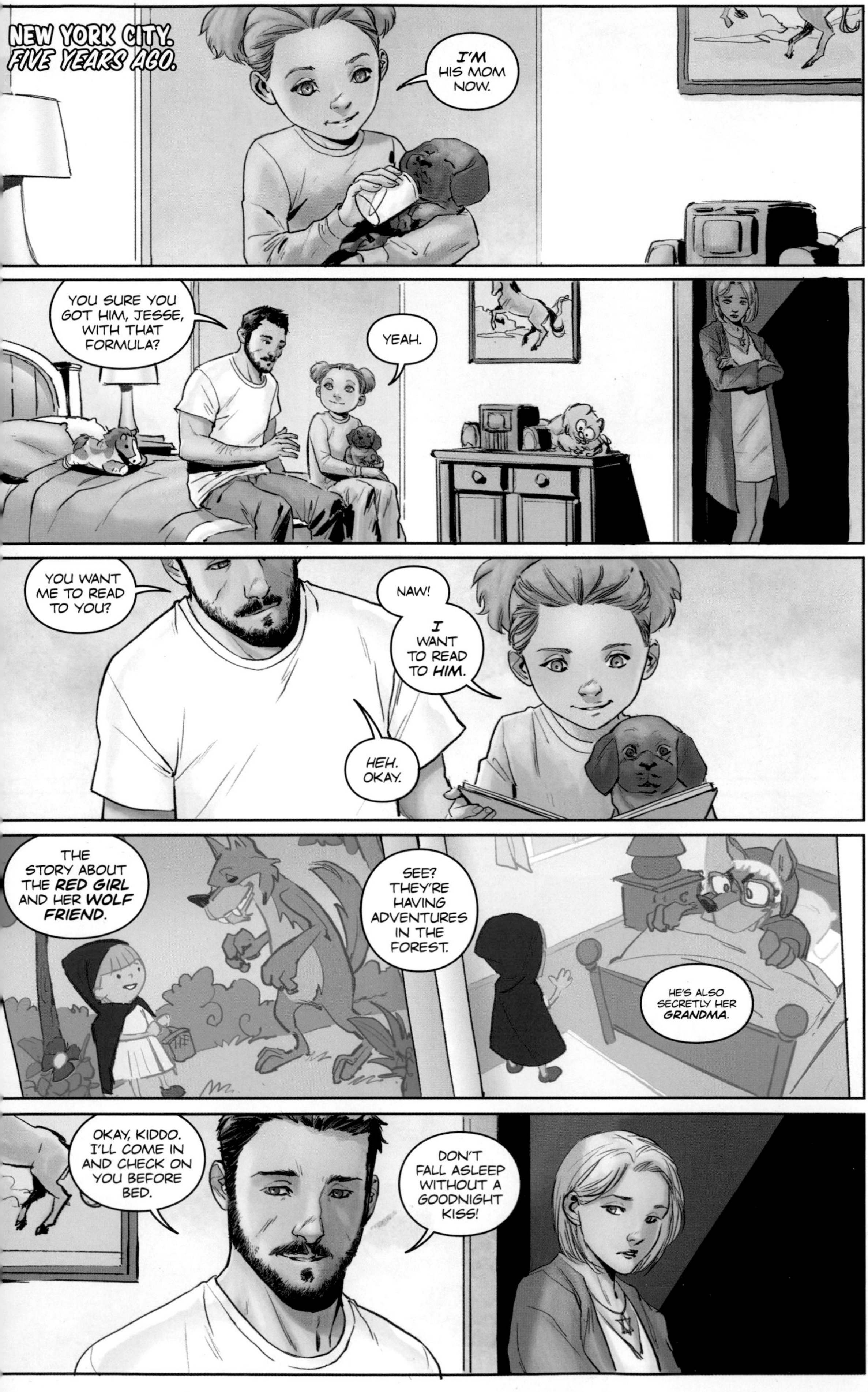
NEW YORK CITY.
FIVE YEARS AGO.
I'M HIS MOM NOW.
YOU SURE YOU GOT HIM, JESSE, WITH THAT FORMULA?
YEAH.
YOU WANT ME TO READ TO YOU?
NAW!
I WANT TO READ TO HIM.
HEH. OKAY.
THE STORY ABOUT THE RED GIRL AND HER WOLF FRIEND.
SEE? THEY'RE HAVING ADVENTURES IN THE FOREST.
HE'S ALSO SECRETLY HER GRANDMA.
OKAY, KIDDO. I'LL COME IN AND CHECK ON YOU BEFORE BED.
DON'T FALL ASLEEP WITHOUT A GOODNIGHT KISS!

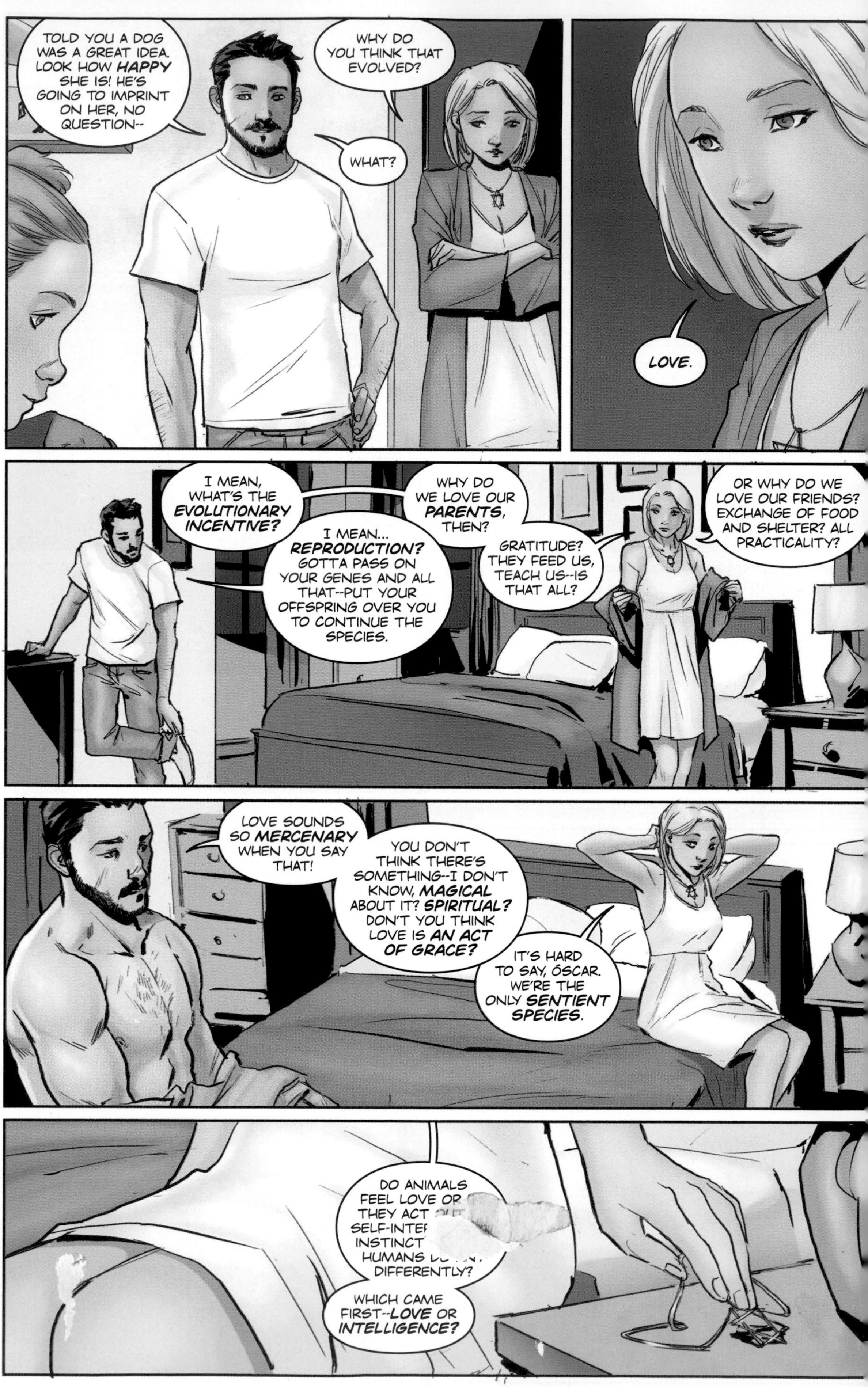

TOLD YOU A DOG WAS A GREAT IDEA. LOOK HOW HAPPY SHE IS! HE'S GOING TO IMPRINT ON HER, NO QUESTION--
WHY DO YOU THINK THAT EVOLVED?
WHAT?
LOVE.
I MEAN, WHAT'S THE EVOLUTIONARY INCENTIVE?
I MEAN... REPRODUCTION? GOTTA PASS ON YOUR GENES AND ALL THAT--PUT YOUR OFFSPRING OVER YOU TO CONTINUE THE SPECIES.
WHY DO WE LOVE OUR PARENTS, THEN?
GRATITUDE? THEY FEED US, TEACH US--IS THAT ALL?
OR WHY DO WE LOVE OUR FRIENDS? EXCHANGE OF FOOD AND SHELTER? ALL PRACTICALITY?
LOVE SOUNDS SO MERCENARY WHEN YOU SAY THAT!
YOU DON'T THINK THERE'S SOMETHING--I DON'T KNOW, MAGICAL ABOUT IT? SPIRITUAL? DON'T YOU THINK LOVE IS AN ACT OF GRACE?
IT'S HARD TO SAY, ÓSCAR. WE'RE THE ONLY SENTIENT SPECIES.
DO ANIMALS FEEL LOVE OR THEY ACT SELF-INTER INSTINCT HUMANS DIFFERENTLY?
WHICH CAME FIRST--LOVE OR INTELLIGENCE?

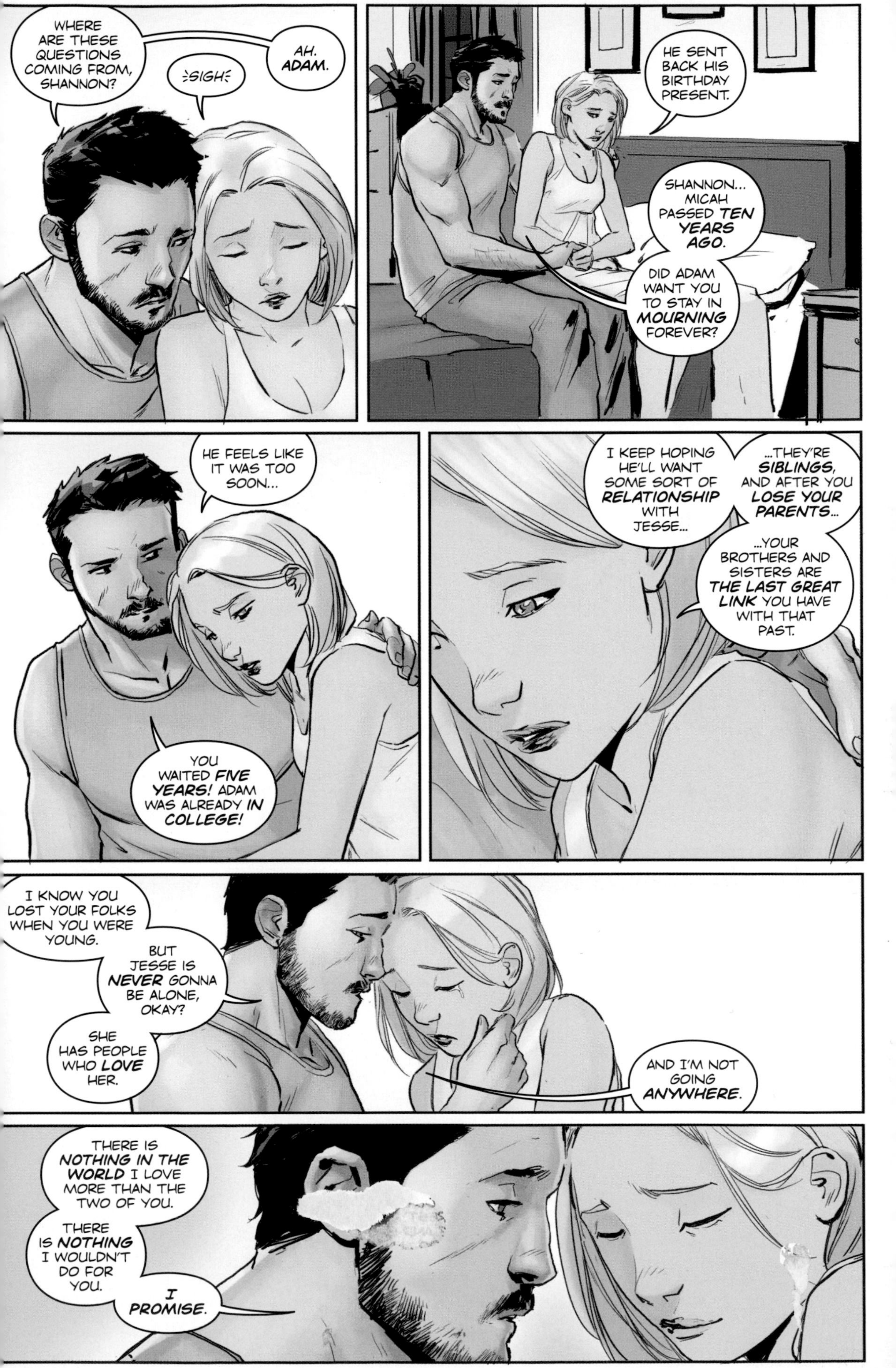
WHERE ARE THESE QUESTIONS COMING FROM, SHANNON?
SIGH
AH. ADAM.
HE SENT BACK HIS BIRTHDAY PRESENT.
SHANNON... MICAH PASSED TEN YEARS AGO.
DID ADAM WANT YOU TO STAY IN MOURNING FOREVER?
HE FEELS LIKE IT WAS TOO SOON...
YOU WAITED FIVE YEARS! ADAM WAS ALREADY IN COLLEGE!
I KEEP HOPING HE'LL WANT SOME SORT OF RELATIONSHIP WITH JESSE...
...THEY'RE SIBLINGS, AND AFTER YOU LOSE YOUR PARENTS...
...YOUR BROTHERS AND SISTERS ARE THE LAST GREAT LINK YOU HAVE WITH THAT PAST.
I KNOW YOU LOST YOUR FOLKS WHEN YOU WERE YOUNG.
BUT JESSE IS NEVER GONNA BE ALONE, OKAY?
SHE HAS PEOPLE WHO LOVE HER.
AND I'M NOT GOING ANYWHERE.
THERE IS NOTHING IN THE WORLD I LOVE MORE THAN THE TWO OF YOU.
THERE IS NOTHING I WOULDN'T DO FOR YOU.
I PROMISE.

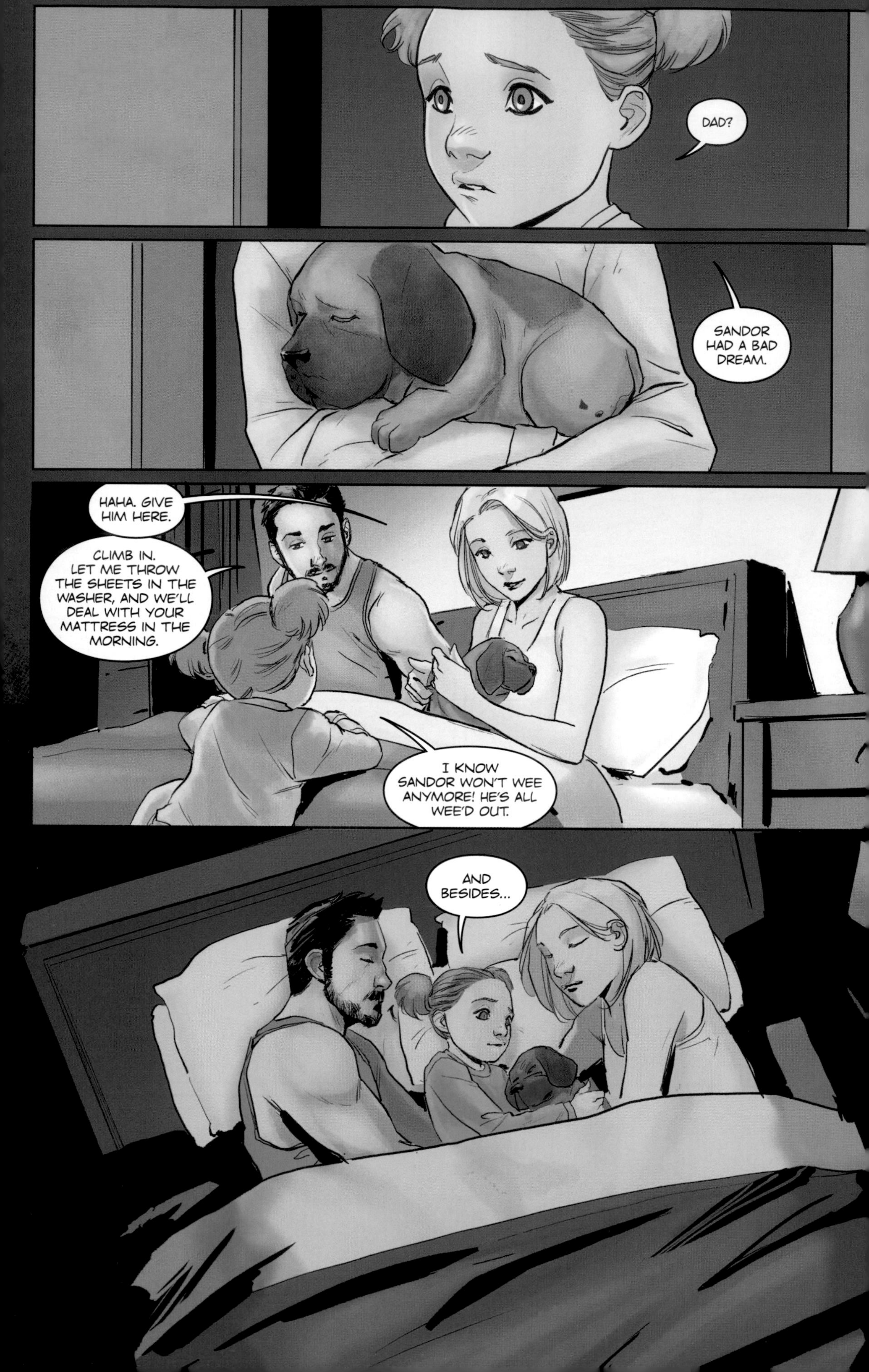
DAD?
SANDOR HAD A BAD DREAM.
HAHA. GIVE HIM HERE.
CLIMB IN. LET ME THROW THE SHEETS IN THE WASHER, AND WE'LL DEAL WITH YOUR MATTRESS IN THE MORNING.
I KNOW SANDOR WON'T WEE ANYMORE! HE'S ALL WEE'D OUT.
AND BESIDES...

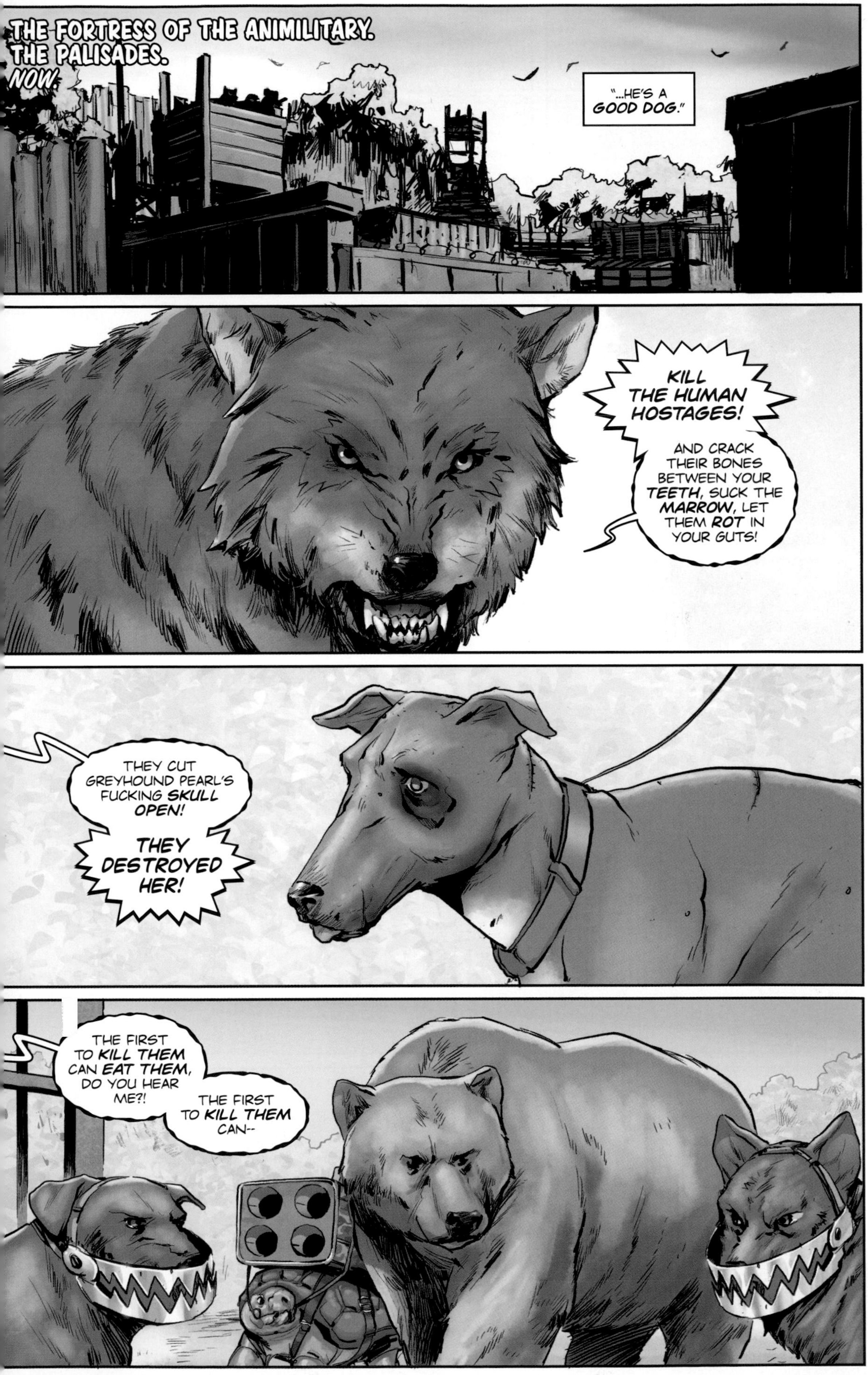
THE FORTRESS OF THE ANIMILITARY.
THE PALISADES.
NOW.
"...HE'S A GOOD DOG."
KILL THE HUMAN HOSTAGES!
AND CRACK THEIR BONES BETWEEN YOUR TEETH, SUCK THE MARROW, LET THEM ROT IN YOUR GUTS!
THEY CUT GREYHOUND PEARL'S FUCKING SKULL OPEN!
THEY DESTROYED HER!
THE FIRST TO KILL THEM CAN EAT THEM, DO YOU HEAR ME?!
THE FIRST TO KILL THEM CAN--

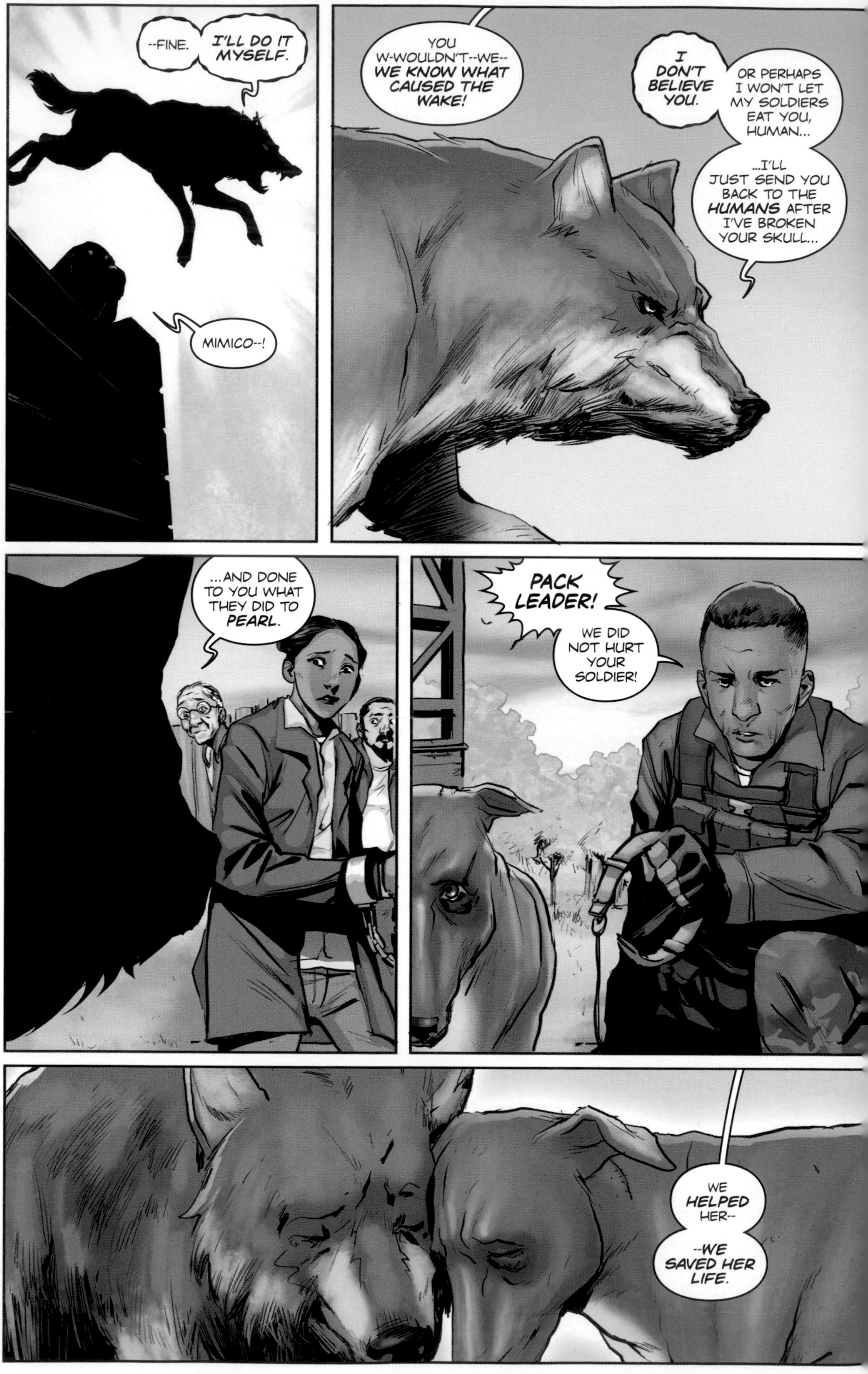
--FINE.
I'LL DO IT MYSELF.
MIMICO--!
YOU W-WOULDN'T--WE--WE KNOW WHAT CAUSED THE WAKE!
I DON'T BELIEVE YOU.
OR PERHAPS I WON'T LET MY SOLDIERS EAT YOU, HUMAN...
...I'LL JUST SEND YOU BACK TO THE HUMANS AFTER I'VE BROKEN YOUR SKULL...
...AND DONE TO YOU WHAT THEY DID TO PEARL.
PACK LEADER!
WE DID NOT HURT YOUR SOLDIER!
WE HELPED HER--
--WE SAVED HER LIFE.

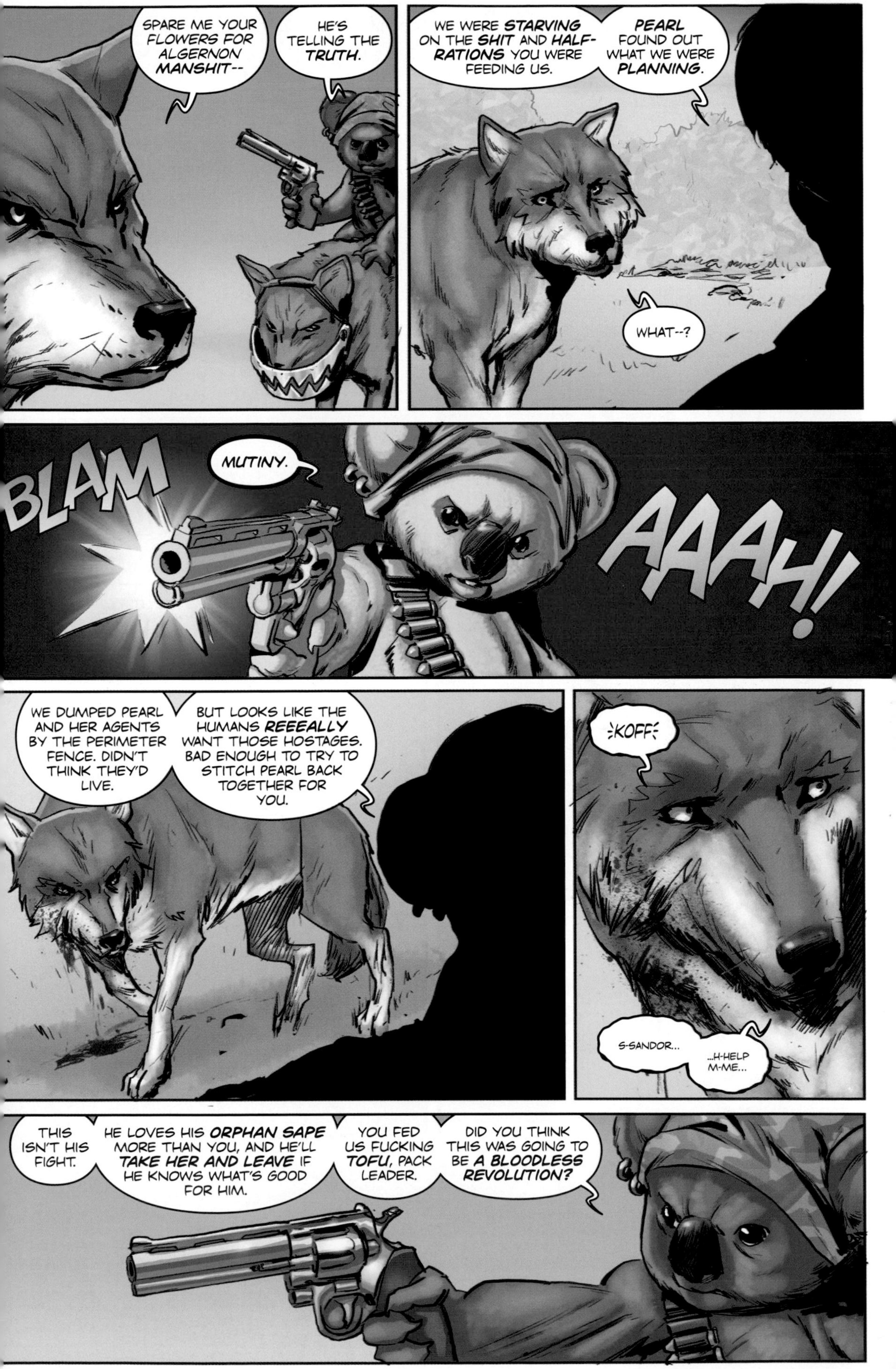
SPARE ME YOUR FLOWERS FOR ALGERNON MANSHIT--
HE'S TELLING THE TRUTH.
WE WERE STARVING ON THE SHIT AND HALF-RATIONS YOU WERE FEEDING US.
PEARL FOUND OUT WHAT WE WERE PLANNING.
WHAT--?
BLAM
MUTINY.
AAAH!
WE DUMPED PEARL AND HER AGENTS BY THE PERIMETER FENCE. DIDN'T THINK THEY'D LIVE.
BUT LOOKS LIKE THE HUMANS REEEALLY WANT THOSE HOSTAGES. BAD ENOUGH TO TRY TO STITCH PEARL BACK TOGETHER FOR YOU.
KOFF
S-SANDOR...
...H-HELP M-ME...
THIS ISN'T HIS FIGHT.
HE LOVES HIS ORPHAN SAPE MORE THAN YOU, AND HE'LL TAKE HER AND LEAVE IF HE KNOWS WHAT'S GOOD FOR HIM.
YOU FED US FUCKING TOFU, PACK LEADER.
DID YOU THINK THIS WAS GOING TO BE A BLOODLESS REVOLUTION?

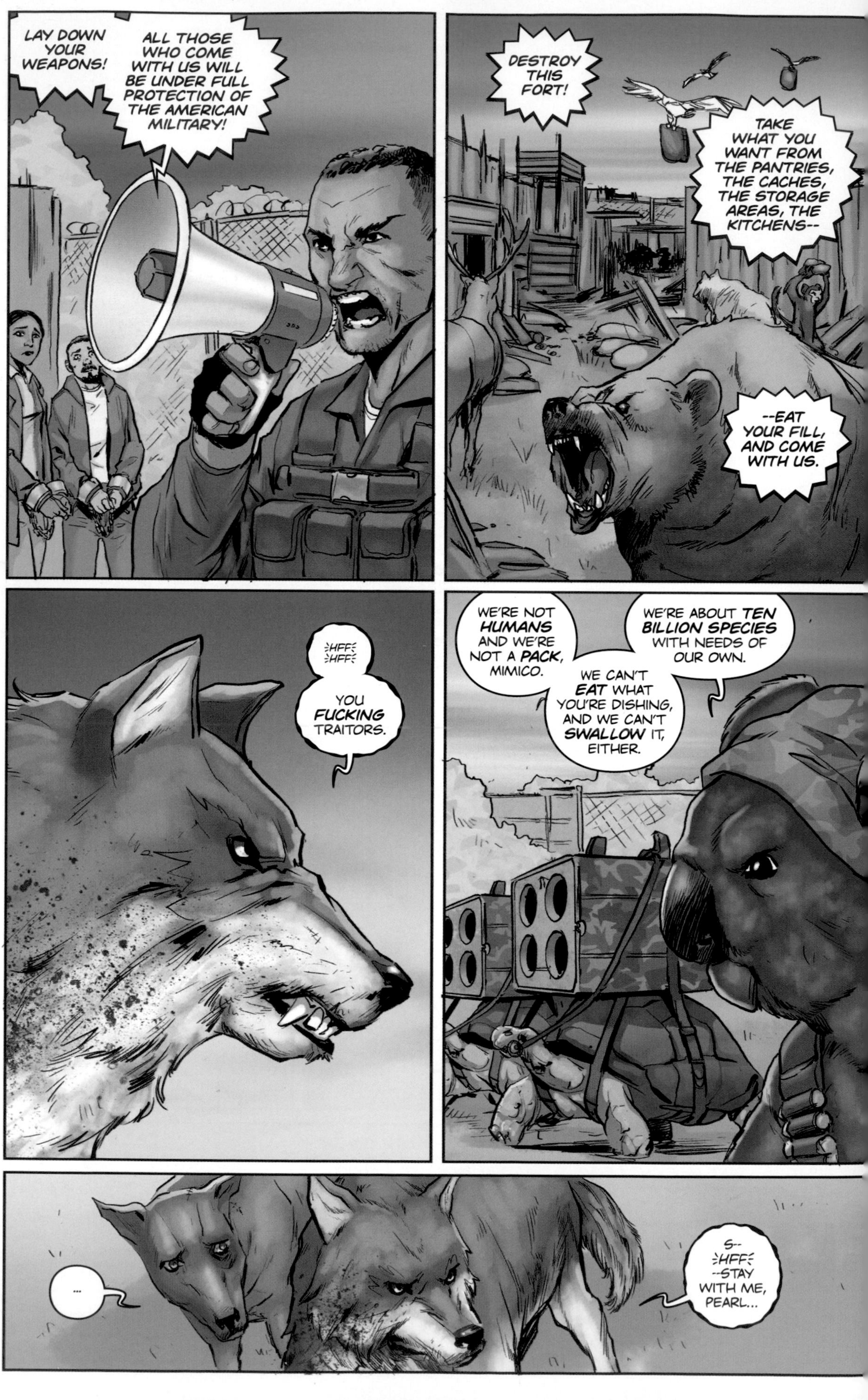
LAY DOWN YOUR WEAPONS!
ALL THOSE WHO COME WITH US WILL BE UNDER FULL PROTECTION OF THE AMERICAN MILITARY!
DESTROY THIS FORT!
TAKE WHAT YOU WANT FROM THE PANTRIES, THE CACHES, THE STORAGE AREAS, THE KITCHENS--
--EAT YOUR FILL, AND COME WITH US.
HFF HFF
YOU FUCKING TRAITORS.
WE'RE NOT HUMANS AND WE'RE NOT A PACK, MIMICO.
WE'RE ABOUT TEN BILLION SPECIES WITH NEEDS OF OUR OWN.
WE CAN'T EAT WHAT YOU'RE DISHING, AND WE CAN'T SWALLOW IT, EITHER.
...
S-- HFF --STAY WITH ME, PEARL...

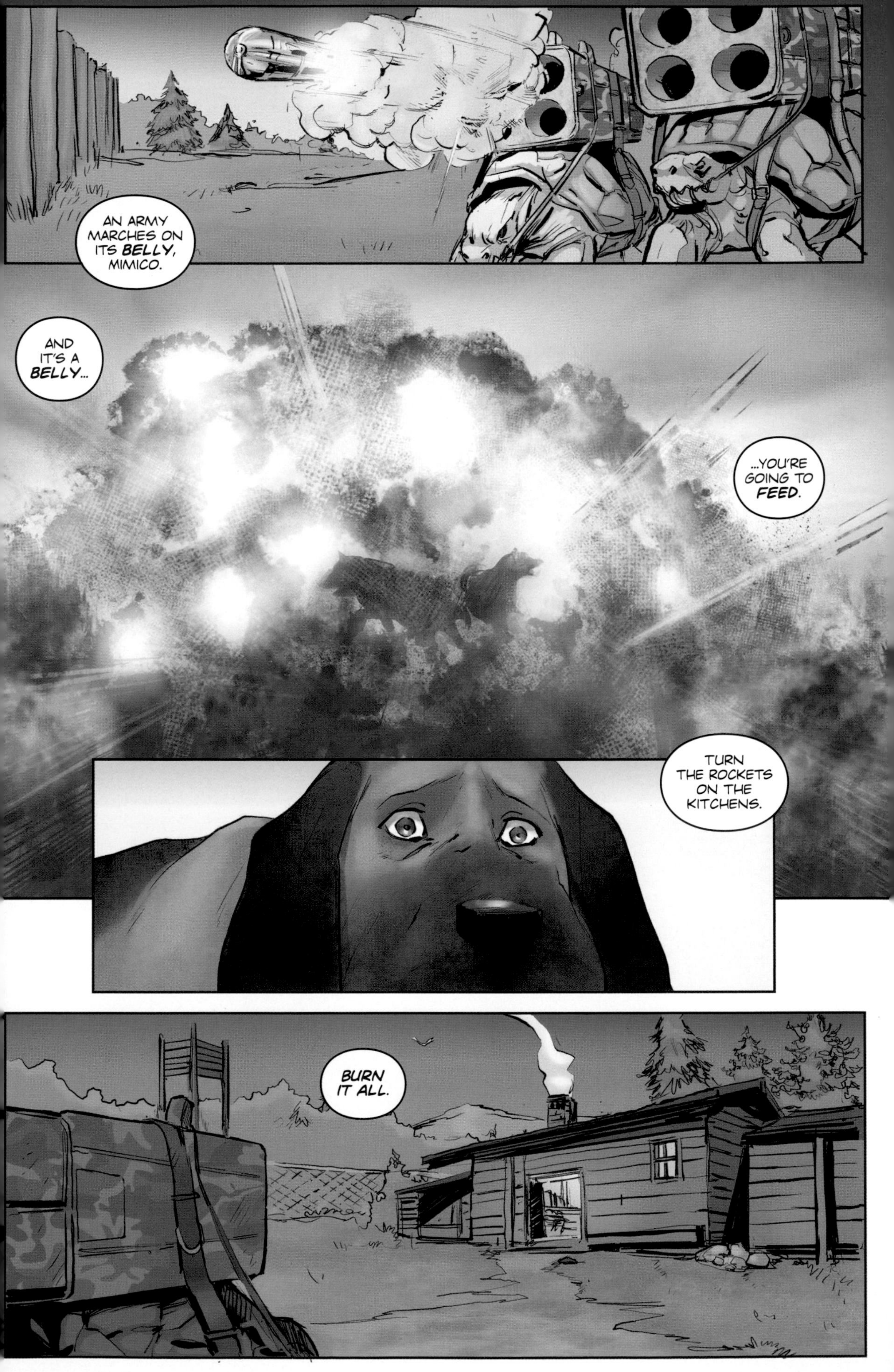
AN ARMY MARCHES ON ITS BELLY, MIMICO.
AND IT'S A BELLY...
...YOU'RE GOING TO FEED.
TURN THE ROCKETS ON THE KITCHENS.
BURN IT ALL.

THE KITCHENS.

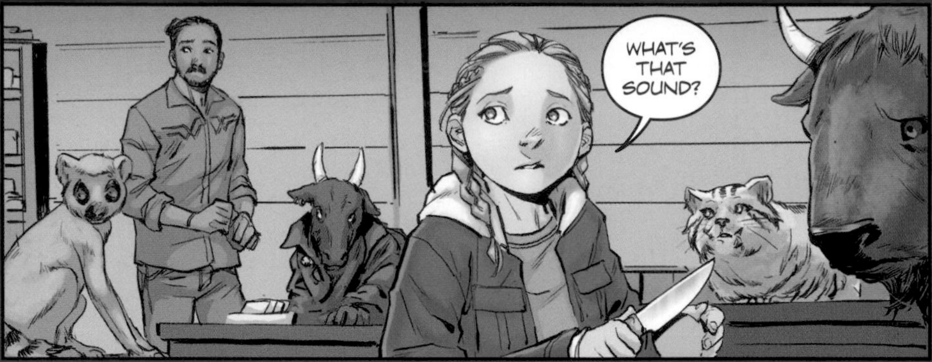
WHAT'S THAT SOUND?

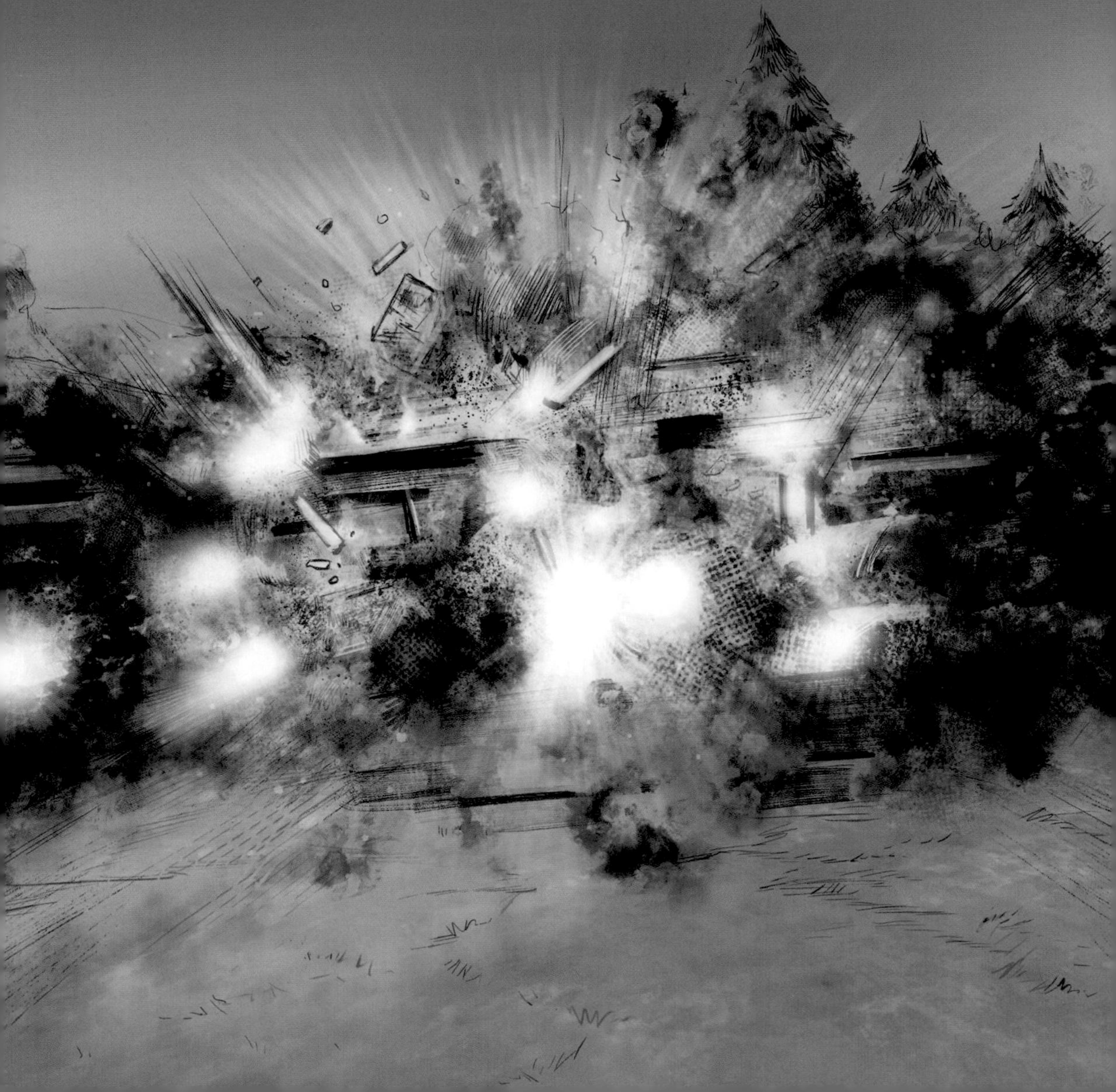

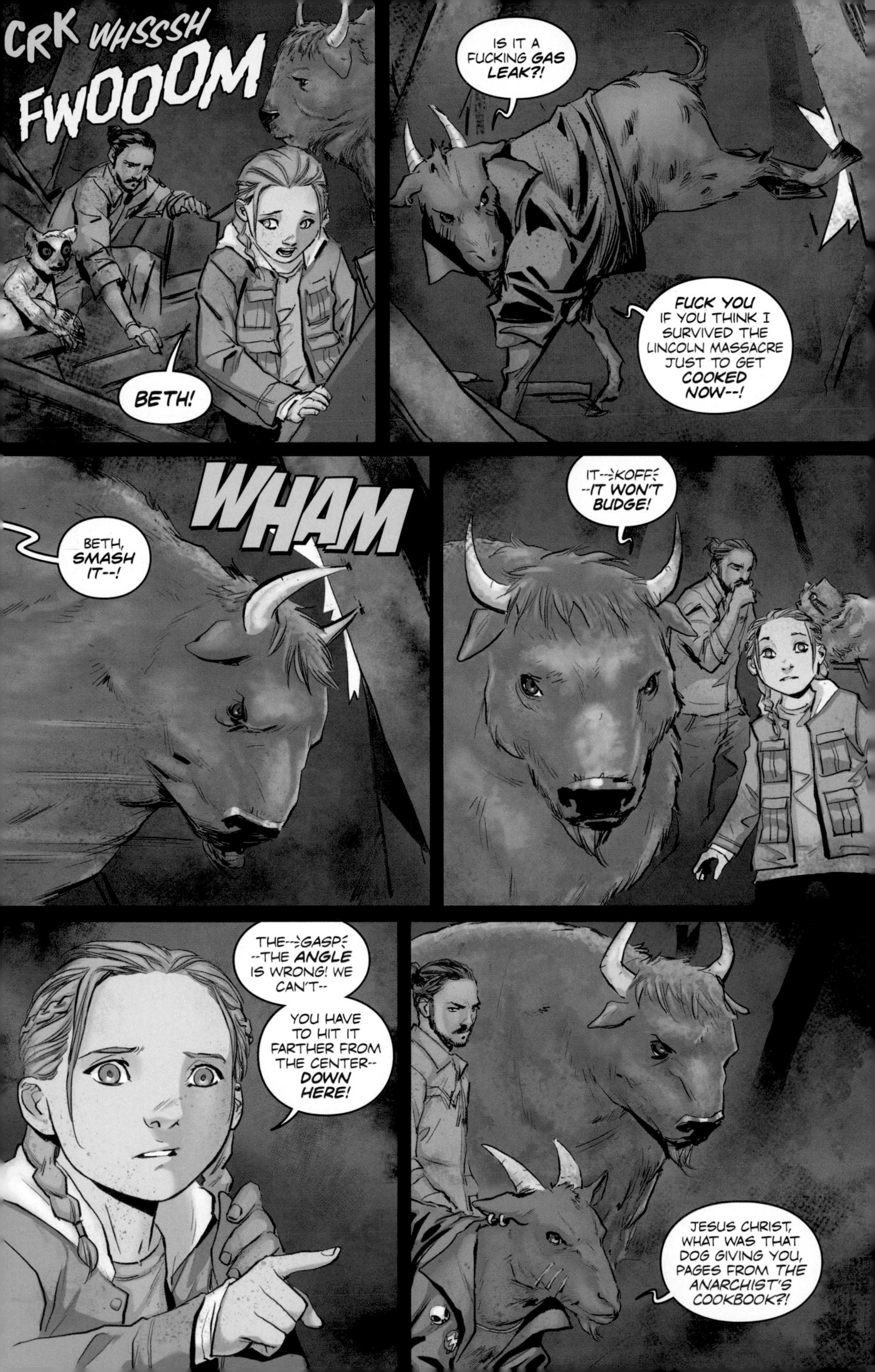
CRK WHSSSH
FWOOOM
BETH!
IS IT A FUCKING GAS LEAK?!
FUCK YOU IF YOU THINK I SURVIVED THE LINCOLN MASSACRE JUST TO GET COOKED NOW--!
WHAM
BETH, SMASH IT--!
IT--KOFF--IT WON'T BUDGE!
THE--GASP--THE ANGLE IS WRONG! WE CAN'T--
YOU HAVE TO HIT IT FARTHER FROM THE CENTER--DOWN HERE!
JESUS CHRIST, WHAT WAS THAT DOG GIVING YOU, PAGES FROM THE ANARCHIST'S COOKBOOK?!

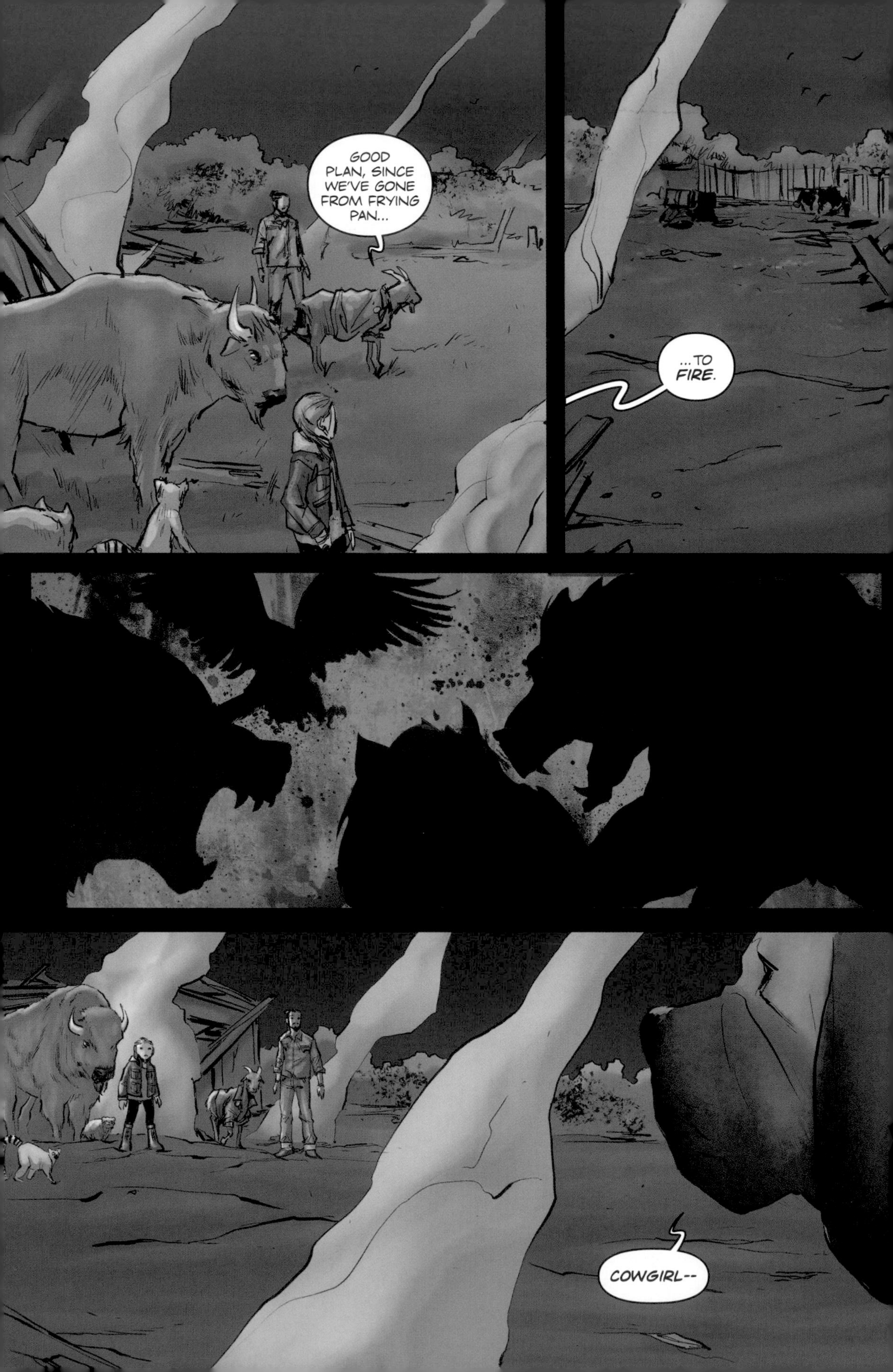
GOOD PLAN, SINCE WE'VE GONE FROM FRYING PAN...
...TO FIRE.
COWGIRL--

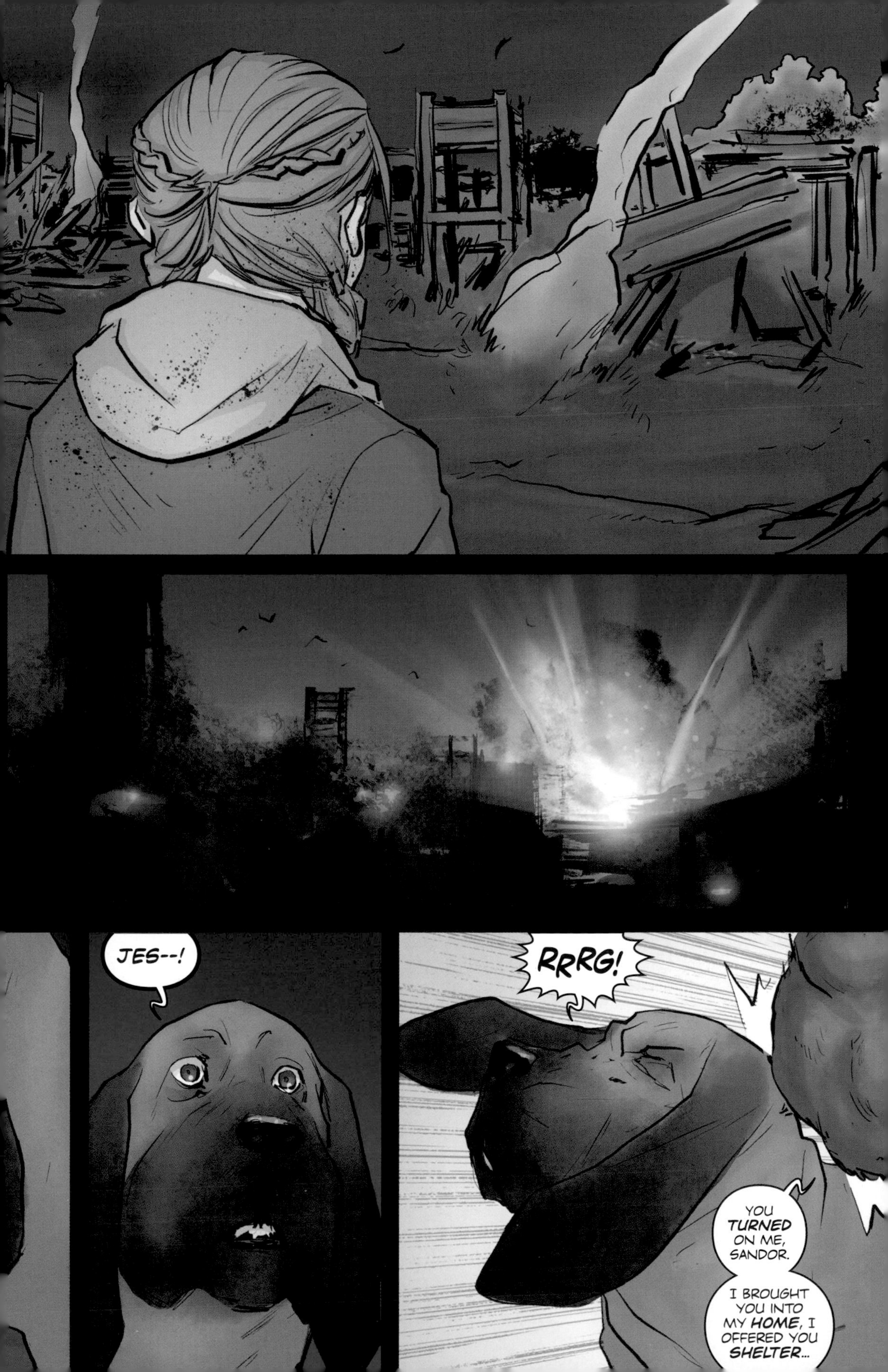
JES--!
RRRG!
YOU TURNED ON ME, SANDOR.
I BROUGHT YOU INTO MY HOME, I OFFERED YOU SHELTER...

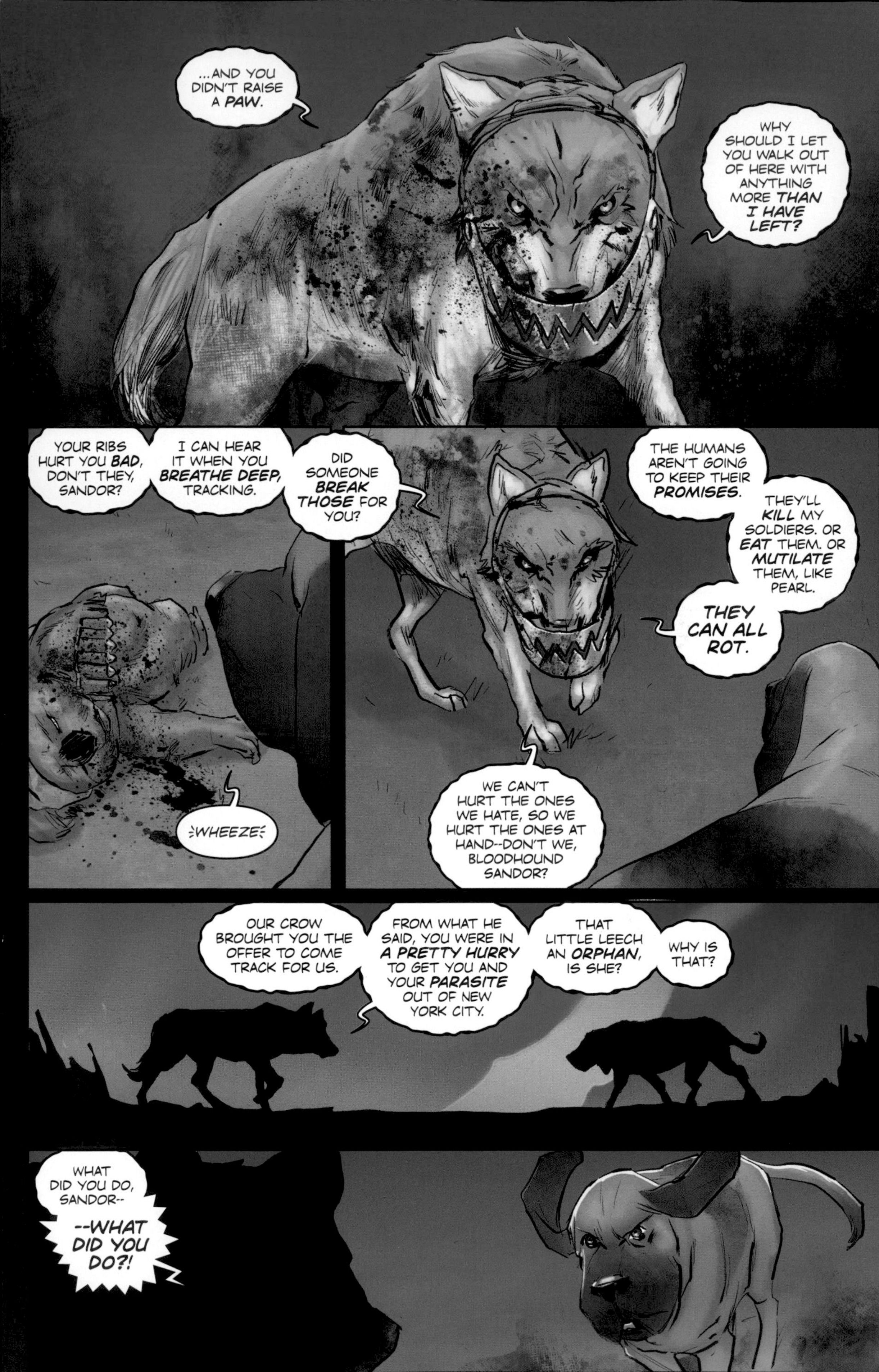
...AND YOU DIDN'T RAISE A PAW.
WHY SHOULD I LET YOU WALK OUT OF HERE WITH ANYTHING MORE THAN I HAVE LEFT?
YOUR RIBS HURT YOU BAD, DON'T THEY, SANDOR?
I CAN HEAR IT WHEN YOU BREATHE DEEP, TRACKING.
DID SOMEONE BREAK THOSE FOR YOU?
WHEEZE
THE HUMANS AREN'T GOING TO KEEP THEIR PROMISES.
THEY'LL KILL MY SOLDIERS. OR EAT THEM. OR MUTILATE THEM, LIKE PEARL.
THEY CAN ALL ROT.
WE CAN'T HURT THE ONES WE HATE, SO WE HURT THE ONES AT HAND--DON'T WE, BLOODHOUND SANDOR?
OUR CROW BROUGHT YOU THE OFFER TO COME TRACK FOR US.
FROM WHAT HE SAID, YOU WERE IN A PRETTY HURRY TO GET YOU AND YOUR PARASITE OUT OF NEW YORK CITY.
THAT LITTLE LEECH AN ORPHAN, IS SHE?
WHY IS THAT?
WHAT DID YOU DO, SANDOR--
--WHAT DID YOU DO?!

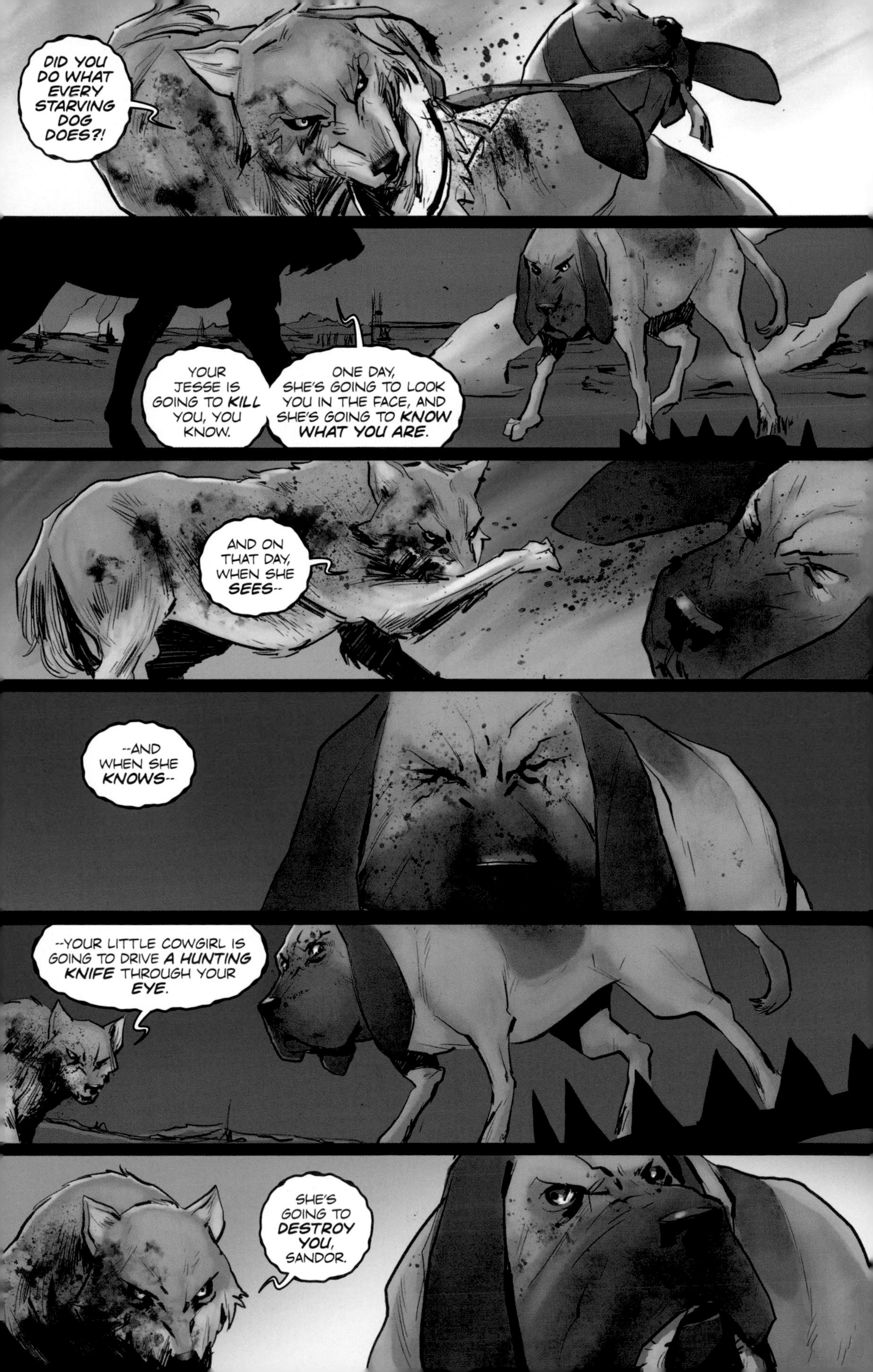
DID YOU DO WHAT EVERY STARVING DOG DOES?!
YOUR JESSE IS GOING TO KILL YOU, YOU KNOW.
ONE DAY, SHE'S GOING TO LOOK YOU IN THE FACE, AND SHE'S GOING TO KNOW WHAT YOU ARE.
AND ON THAT DAY, WHEN SHE SEES--
--AND WHEN SHE KNOWS--
--YOUR LITTLE COWGIRL IS GOING TO DRIVE A HUNTING KNIFE THROUGH YOUR EYE.
SHE'S GOING TO DESTROY YOU, SANDOR.

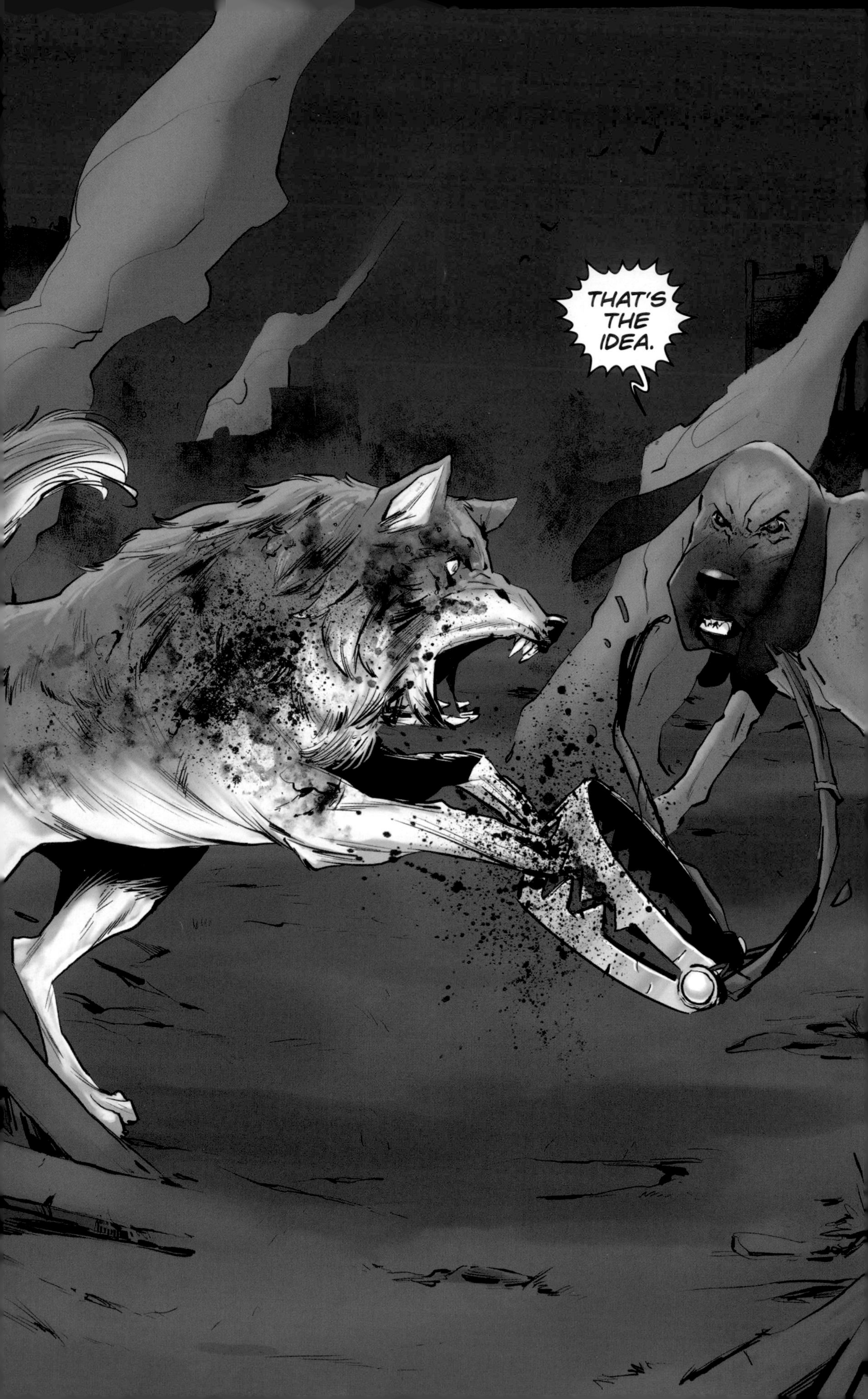
THAT'S THE IDEA.

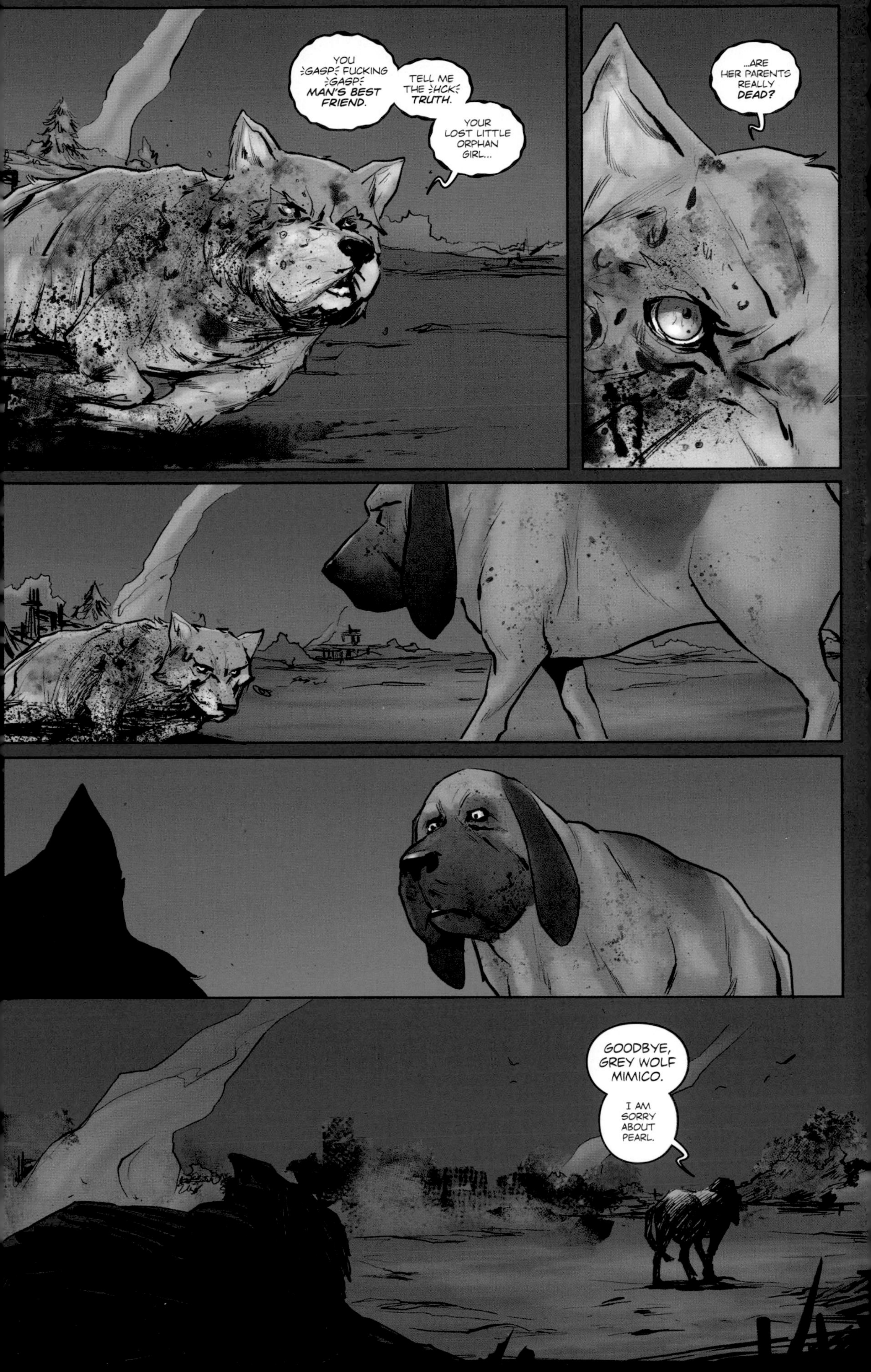
YOU ⸗GASP⸗ FUCKING ⸗GASP⸗ **MAN'S BEST FRIEND**.
TELL ME THE ⸗HCK⸗ **TRUTH**.
YOUR LOST LITTLE ORPHAN GIRL...
...ARE HER PARENTS REALLY **DEAD?**
GOODBYE, GREY WOLF MIMICO.
I AM SORRY ABOUT PEARL.

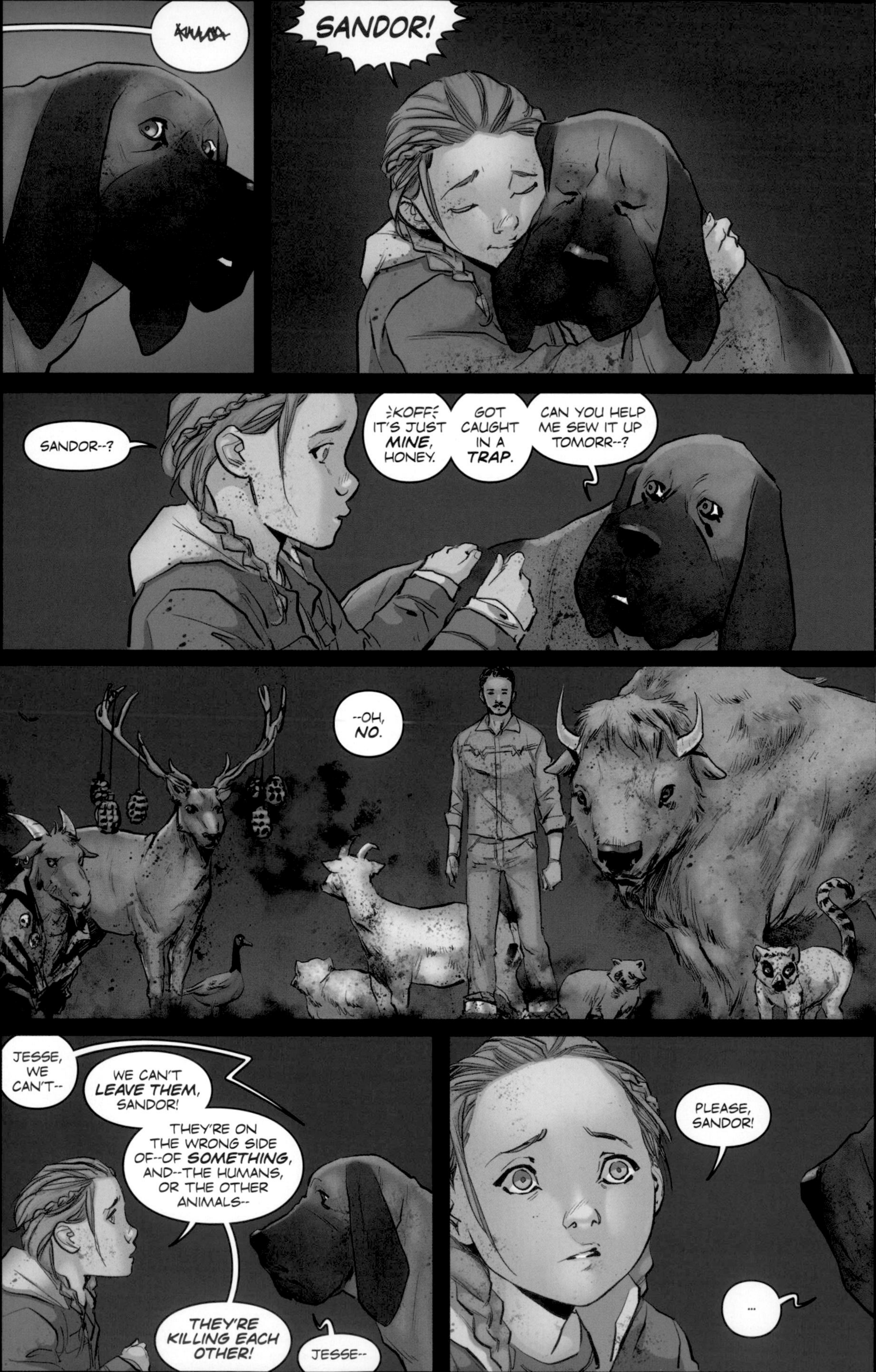
SANDOR!
SANDOR--?
KOFF IT'S JUST MINE, HONEY.
GOT CAUGHT IN A TRAP.
CAN YOU HELP ME SEW IT UP TOMORR--?
--OH, NO.
JESSE, WE CAN'T--
WE CAN'T LEAVE THEM, SANDOR!
THEY'RE ON THE WRONG SIDE OF--OF SOMETHING, AND--THE HUMANS, OR THE OTHER ANIMALS--
THEY'RE KILLING EACH OTHER!
JESSE--
PLEASE, SANDOR!
...

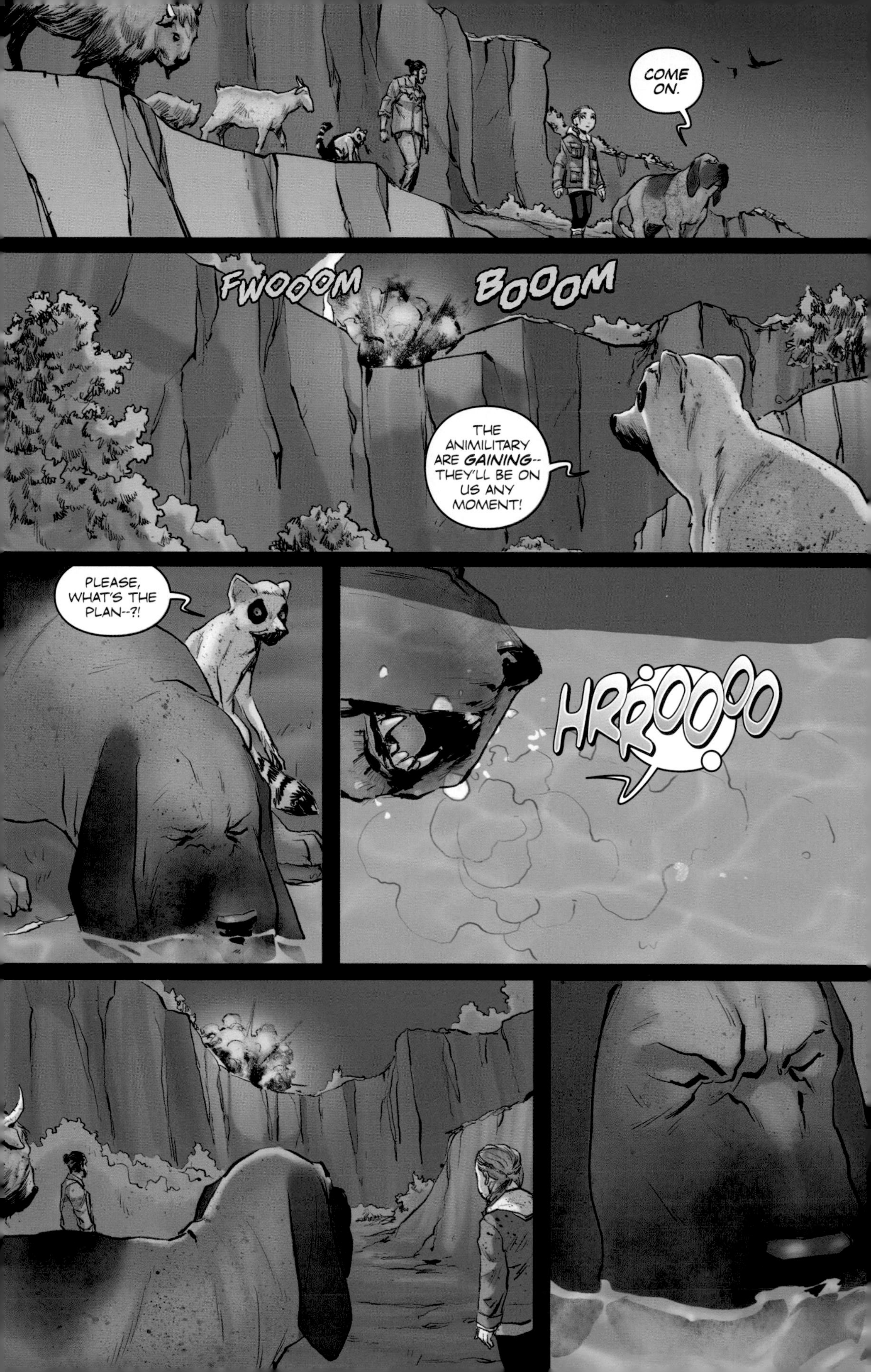
COME ON.
FWOOOM
BOOOM
THE ANIMILITARY ARE GAINING-- THEY'LL BE ON US ANY MOMENT!
PLEASE, WHAT'S THE PLAN--?!
HRROOOO

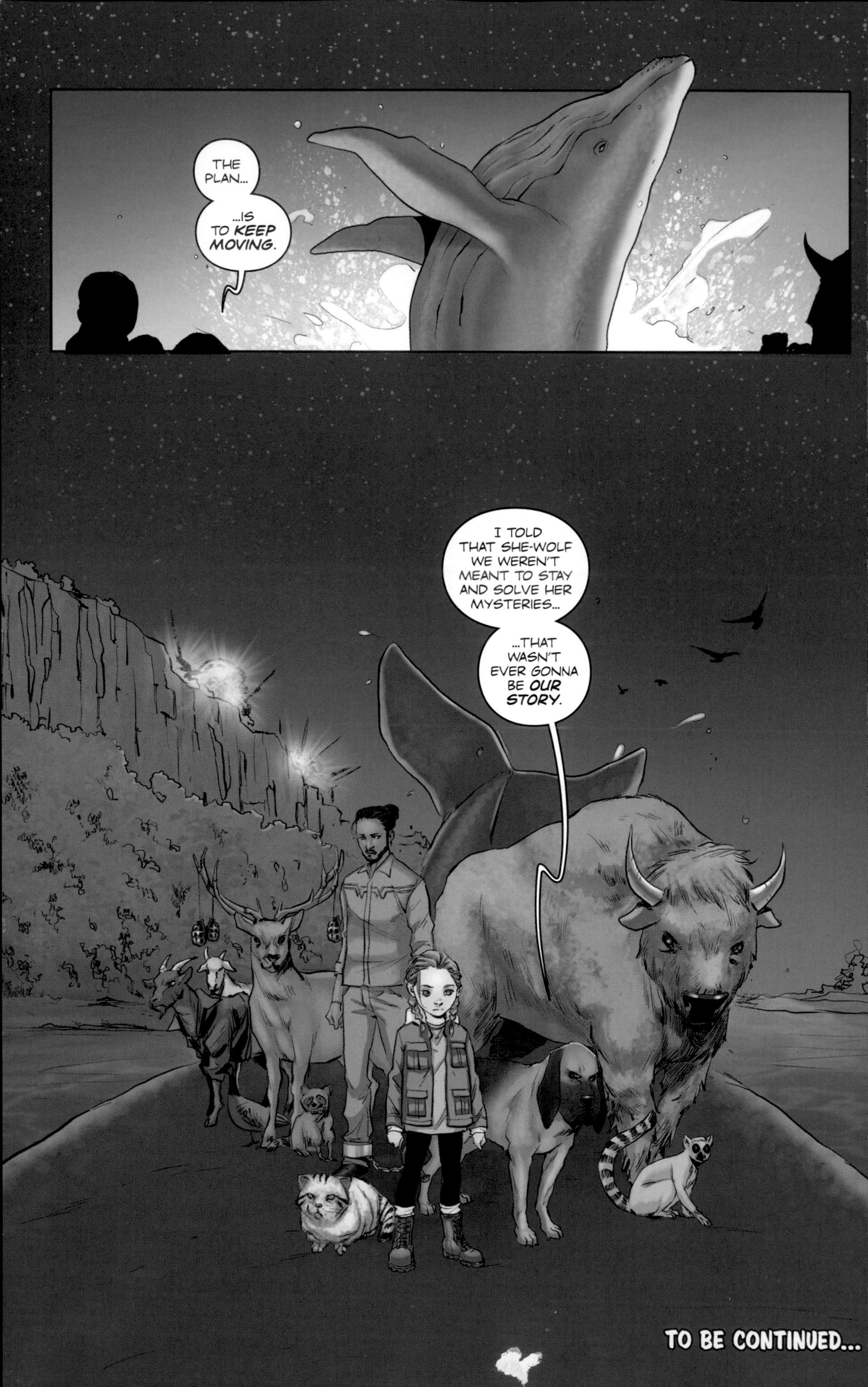
THE PLAN...
...IS TO KEEP MOVING.
I TOLD THAT SHE-WOLF WE WEREN'T MEANT TO STAY AND SOLVE HER MYSTERIES...
...THAT WASN'T EVER GONNA BE OUR STORY.
TO BE CONTINUED...

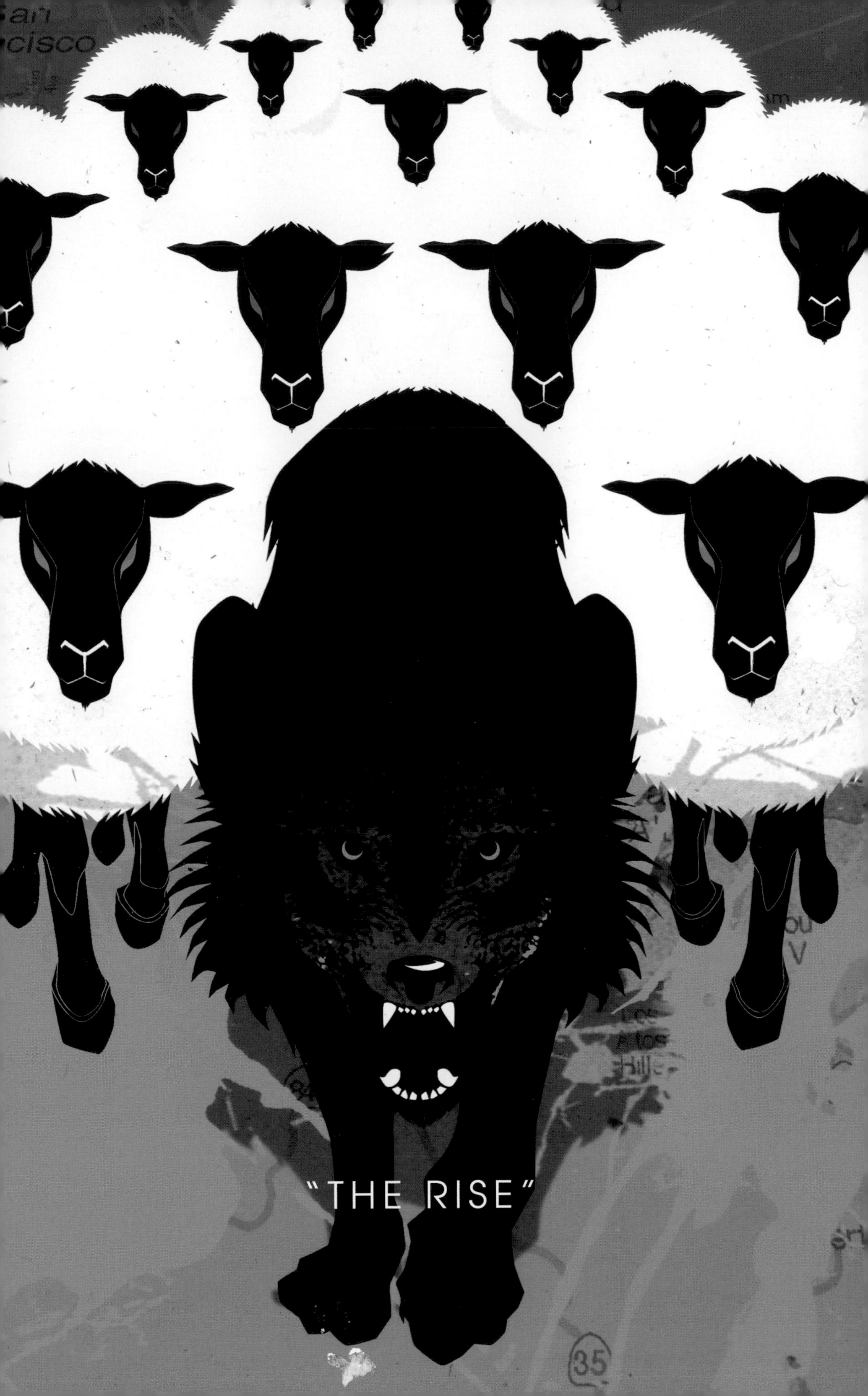
"THE RISE"

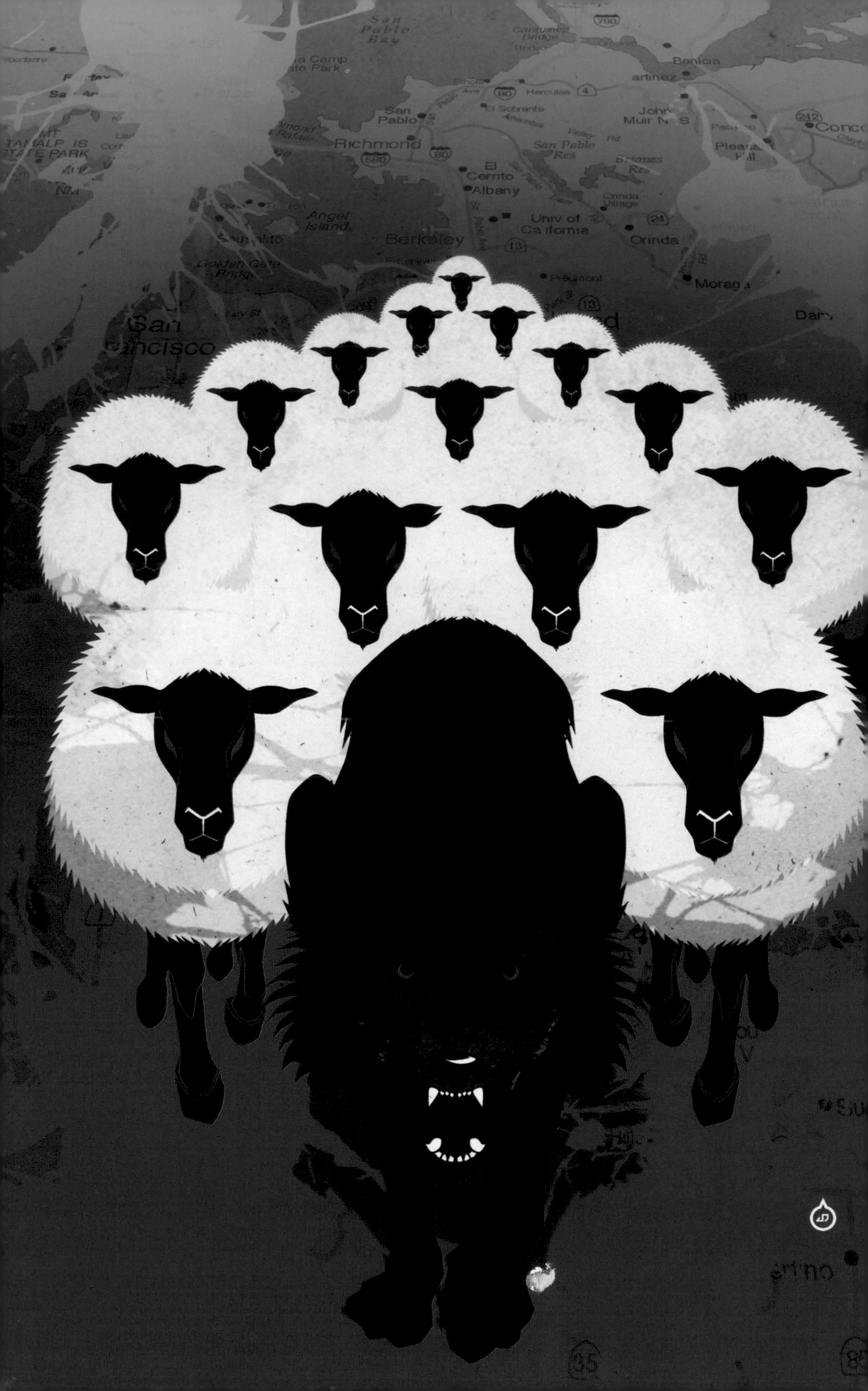
San Pablo Bay
Benicia
Richmond
San Pablo
Hercules
El Sobrante
San Pablo Res
El Cerrito
Albany
Angel Island
Berkeley
Univ of California
Orinda
Moraga
Golden Gate Bridge

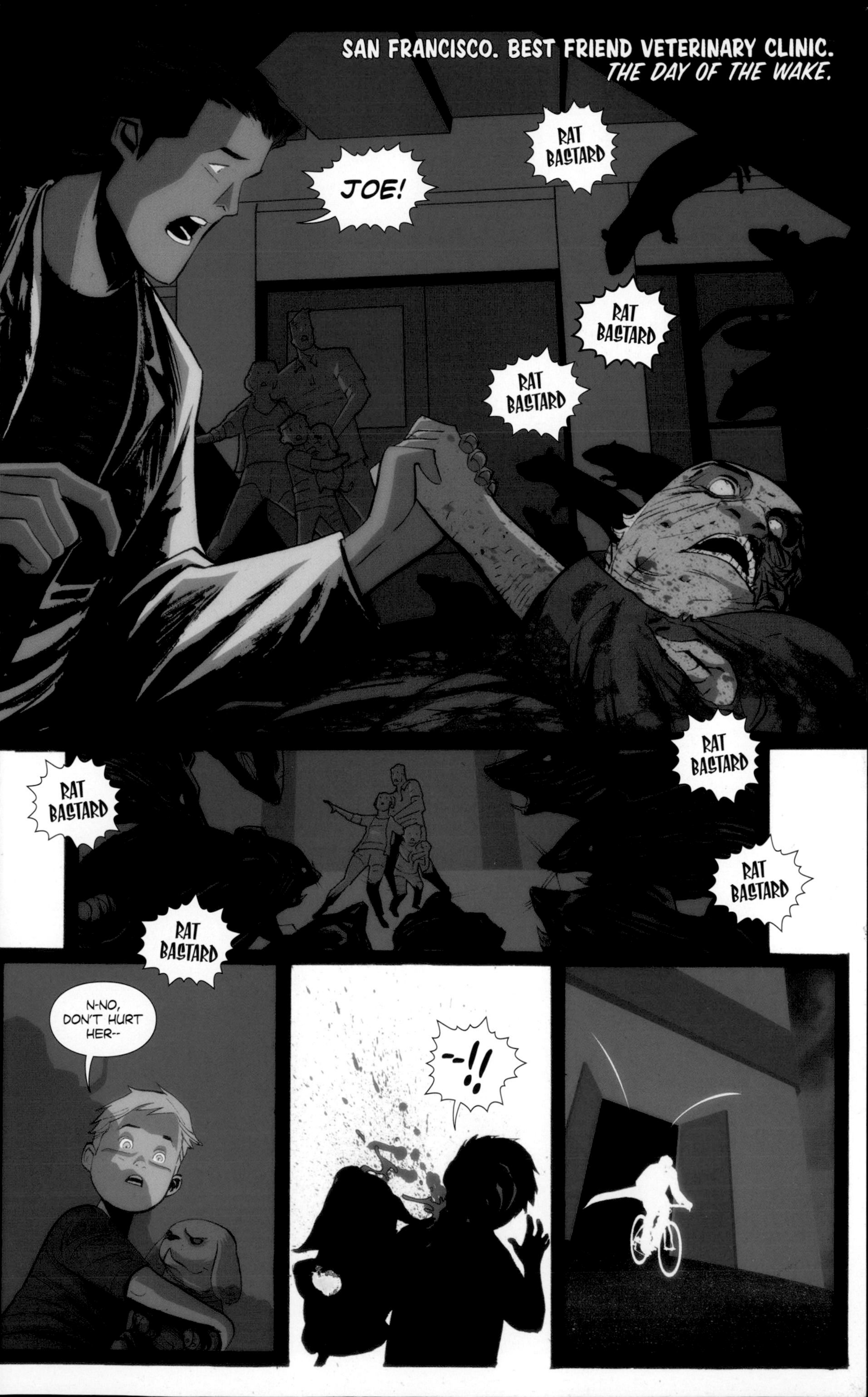
SAN FRANCISCO. BEST FRIEND VETERINARY CLINIC.
THE DAY OF THE WAKE.
JOE!
RAT BASTARD
RAT BASTARD
RAT BASTARD
RAT BASTARD
RAT BASTARD
RAT BASTARD
RAT BASTARD
N-NO, DON'T HURT HER--
--!!

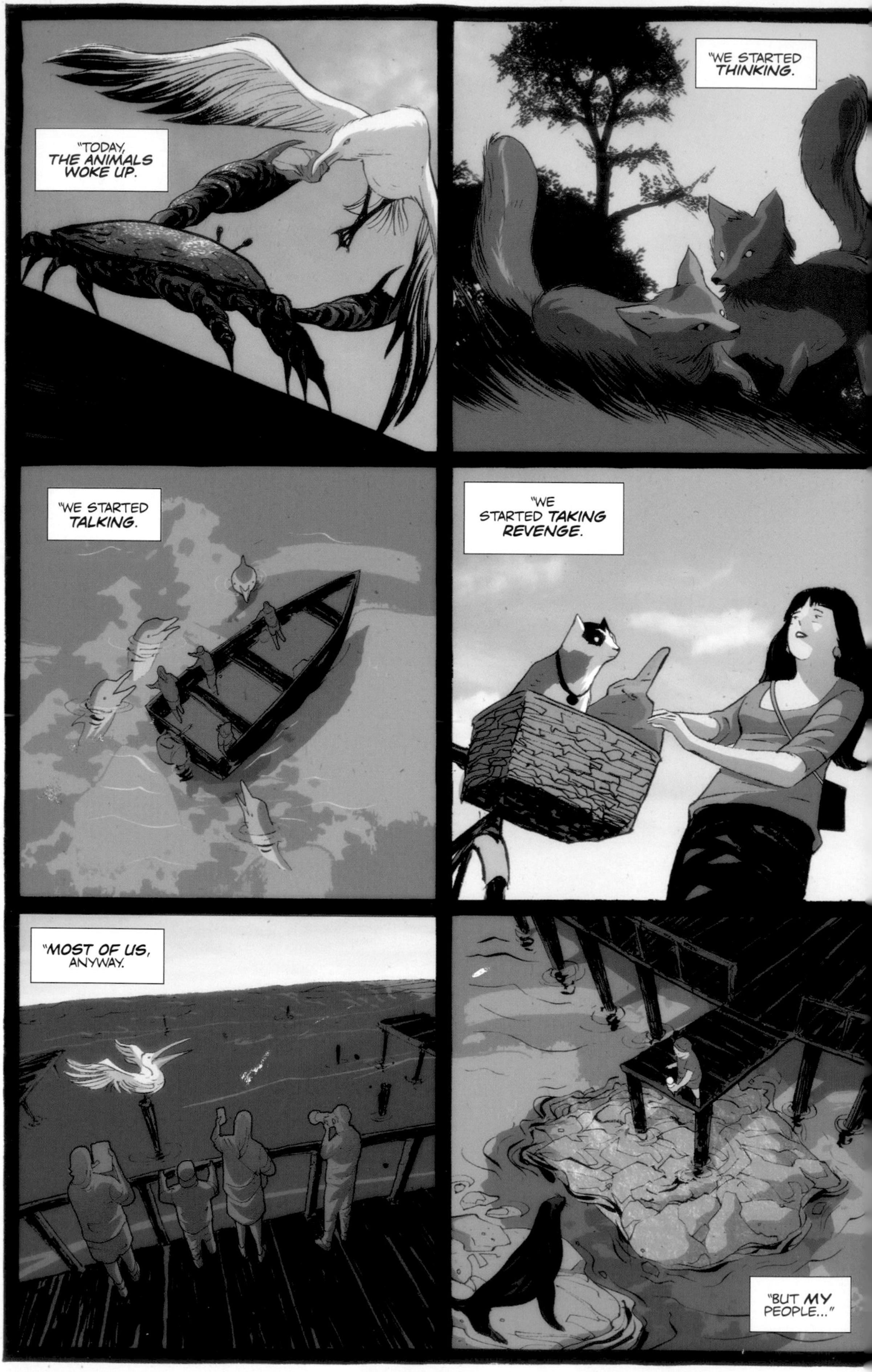
"TODAY, THE ANIMALS WOKE UP.
"WE STARTED THINKING.
"WE STARTED TALKING.
"WE STARTED TAKING REVENGE.
"MOST OF US, ANYWAY.
"BUT MY PEOPLE..."

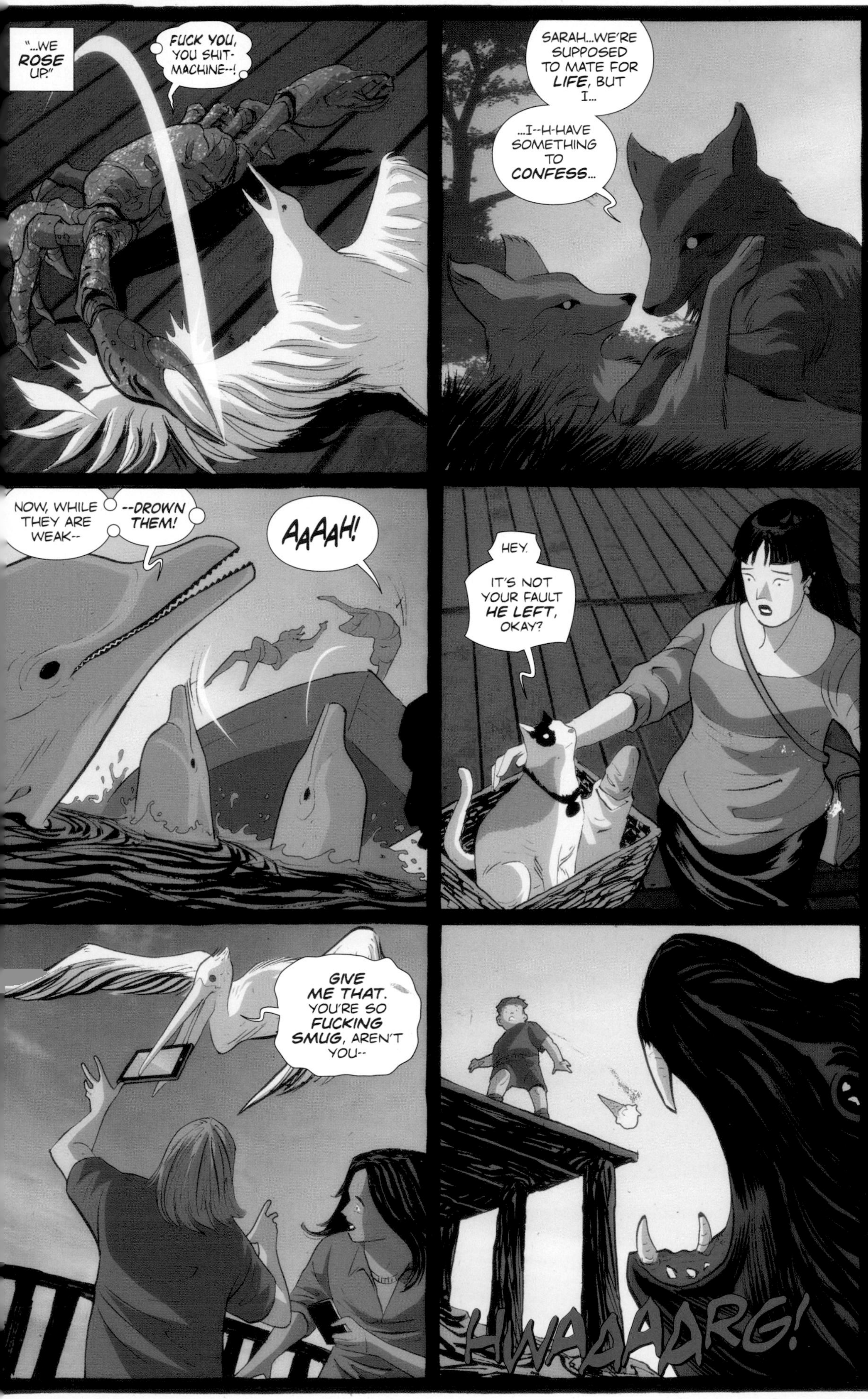
"...WE ROSE UP."
FUCK YOU, YOU SHIT-MACHINE--!
SARAH...WE'RE SUPPOSED TO MATE FOR LIFE, BUT I...
...I--H-HAVE SOMETHING TO CONFESS...
NOW, WHILE THEY ARE WEAK--
--DROWN THEM!
AAAAH!
HEY.
IT'S NOT YOUR FAULT HE LEFT, OKAY?
GIVE ME THAT. YOU'RE SO FUCKING SMUG, AREN'T YOU--
HWAAAARG!

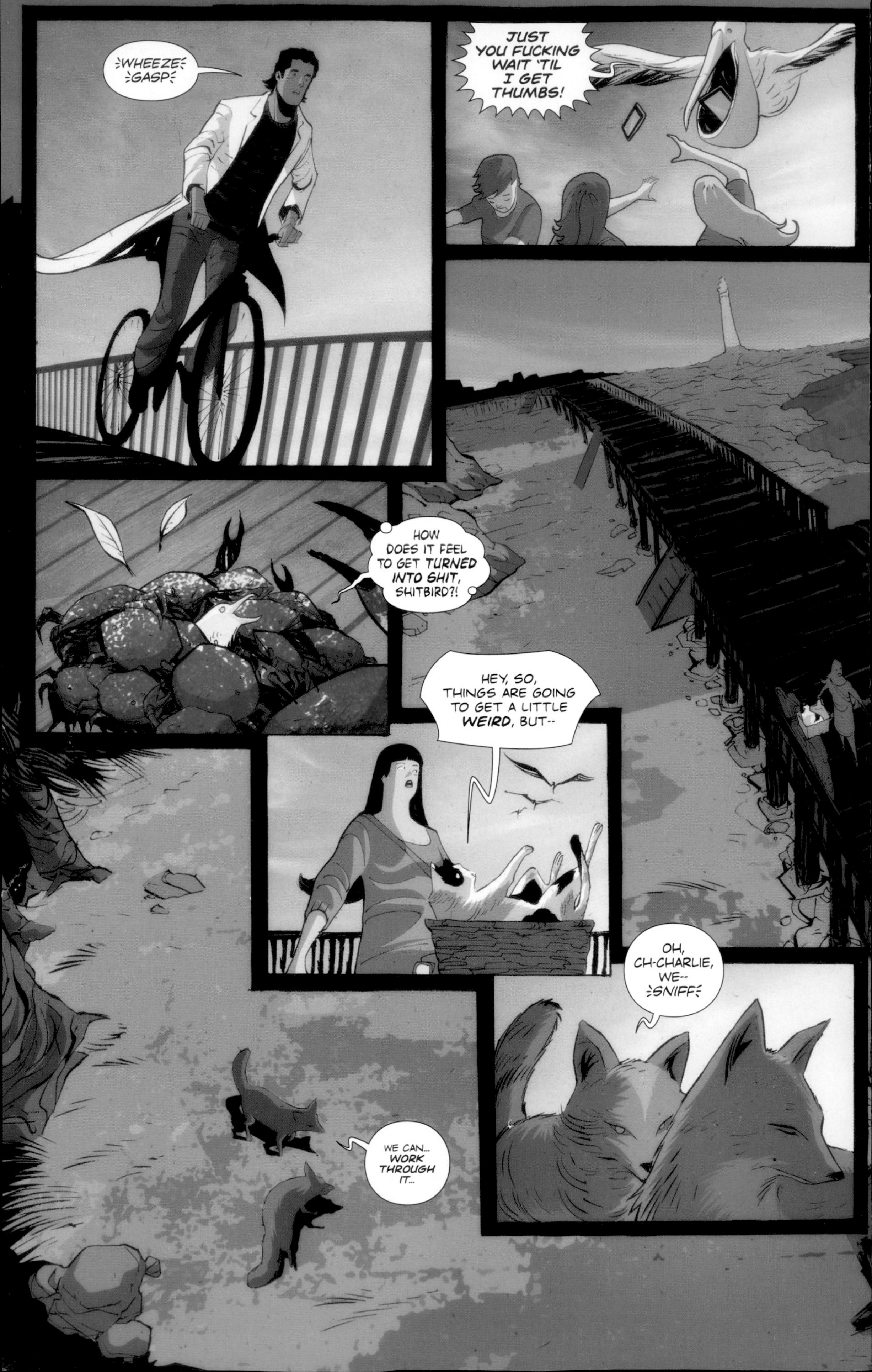
WHEEZE GASP
JUST YOU FUCKING WAIT 'TIL I GET THUMBS!
HOW DOES IT FEEL TO GET TURNED INTO SHIT, SHITBIRD?!
HEY, SO, THINGS ARE GOING TO GET A LITTLE WEIRD, BUT--
OH, CH-CHARLIE, WE-- SNIFF
WE CAN... WORK THROUGH IT...

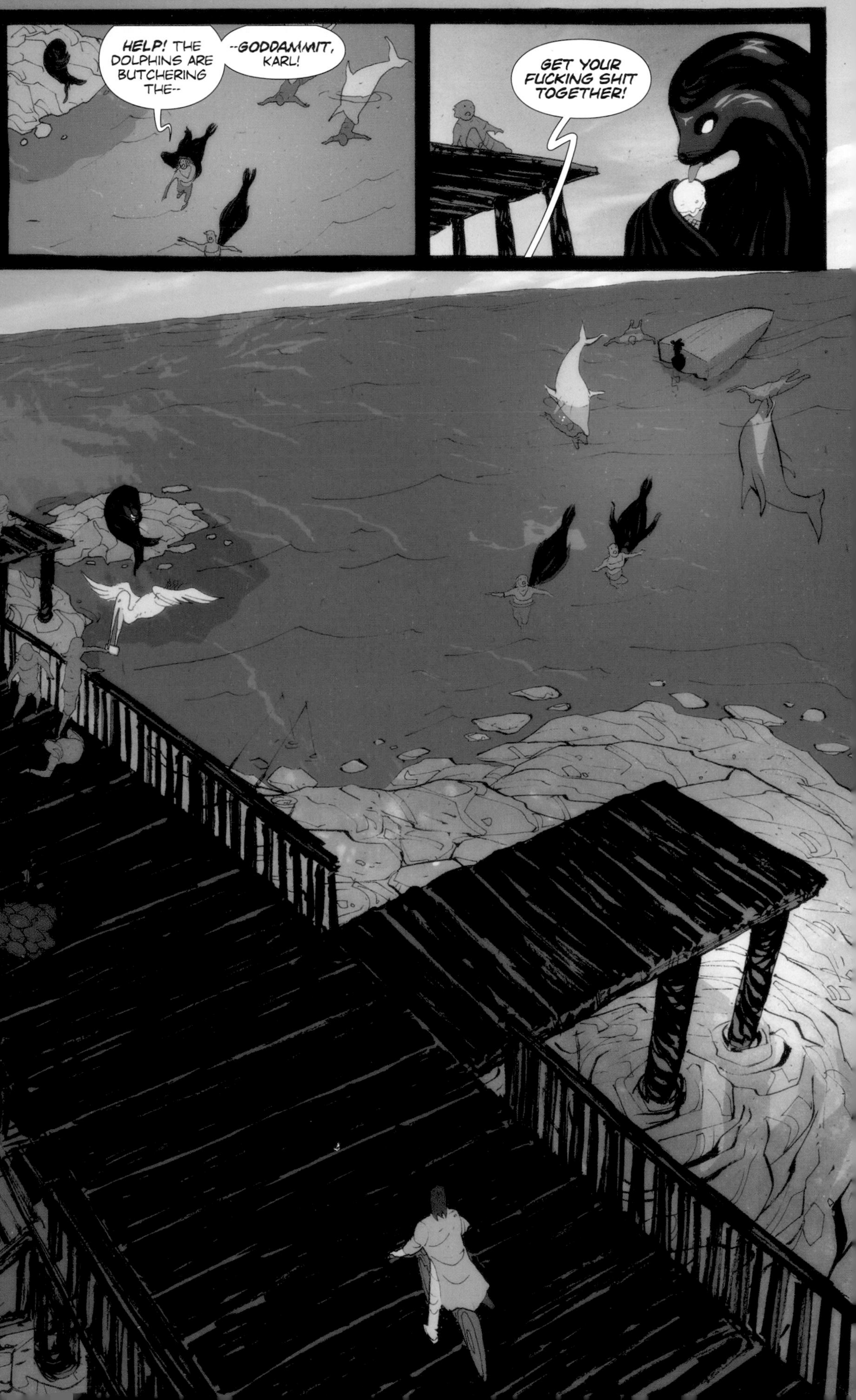
HELP! THE DOLPHINS ARE BUTCHERING THE--
--GODDAMMIT, KARL!
GET YOUR FUCKING SHIT TOGETHER!

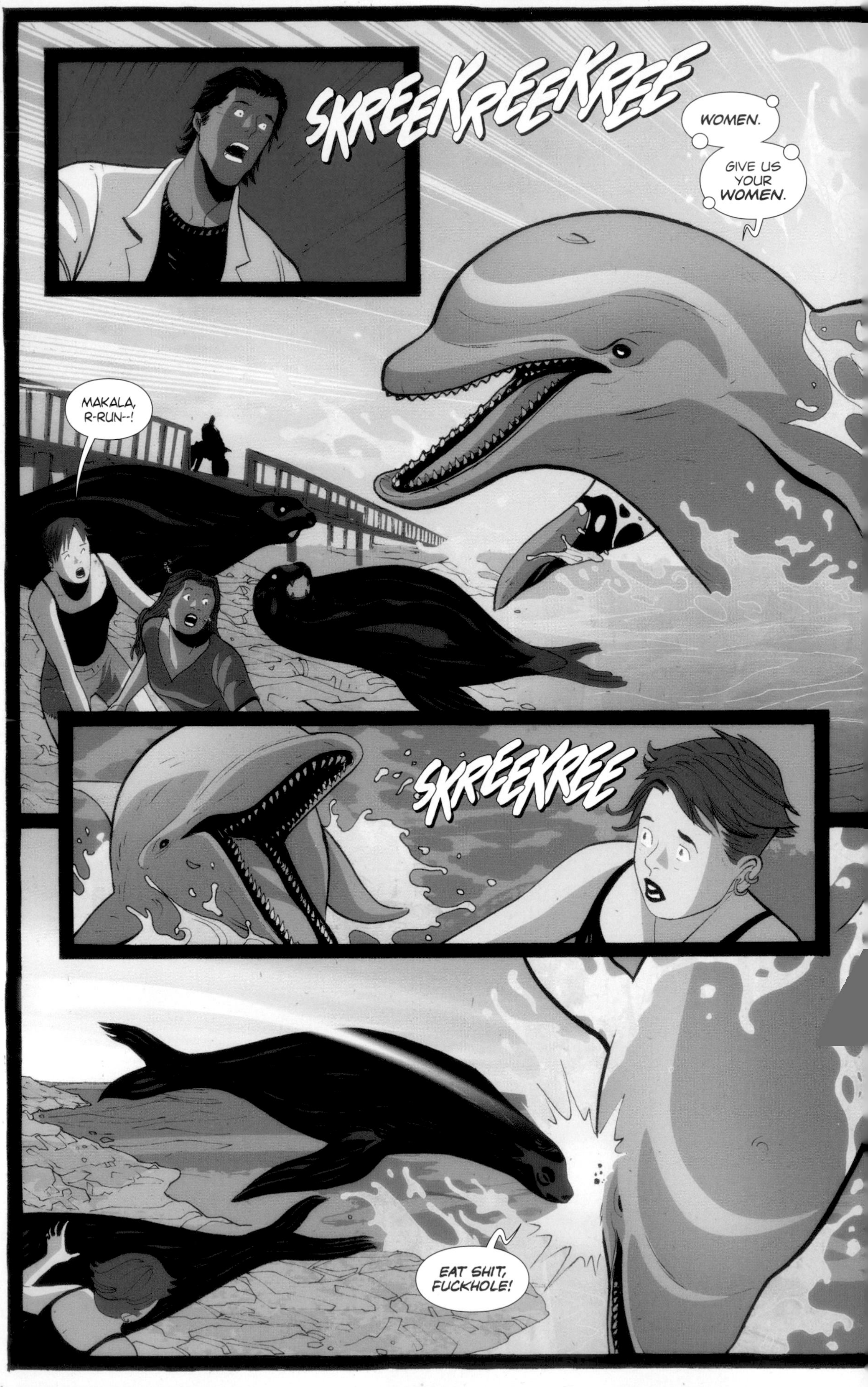
SKREEKREEKREE
WOMEN.
GIVE US YOUR WOMEN.
MAKALA, R-RUN--!
SKREEKREE
EAT SHIT, FUCKHOLE!

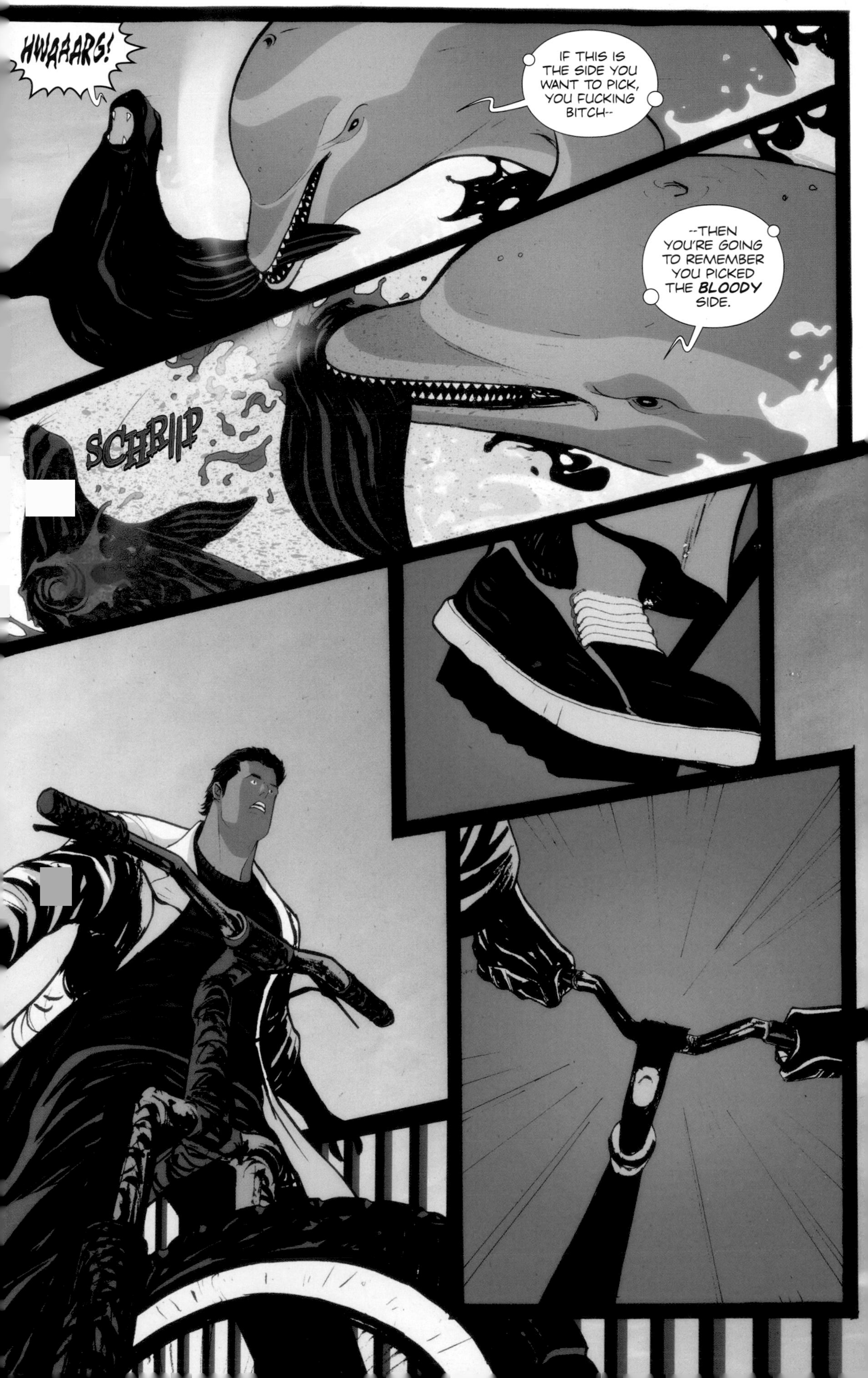
HWAAARG!
IF THIS IS THE SIDE YOU WANT TO PICK, YOU FUCKING BITCH--
--THEN YOU'RE GOING TO REMEMBER YOU PICKED THE BLOODY SIDE.
SCHRIIP

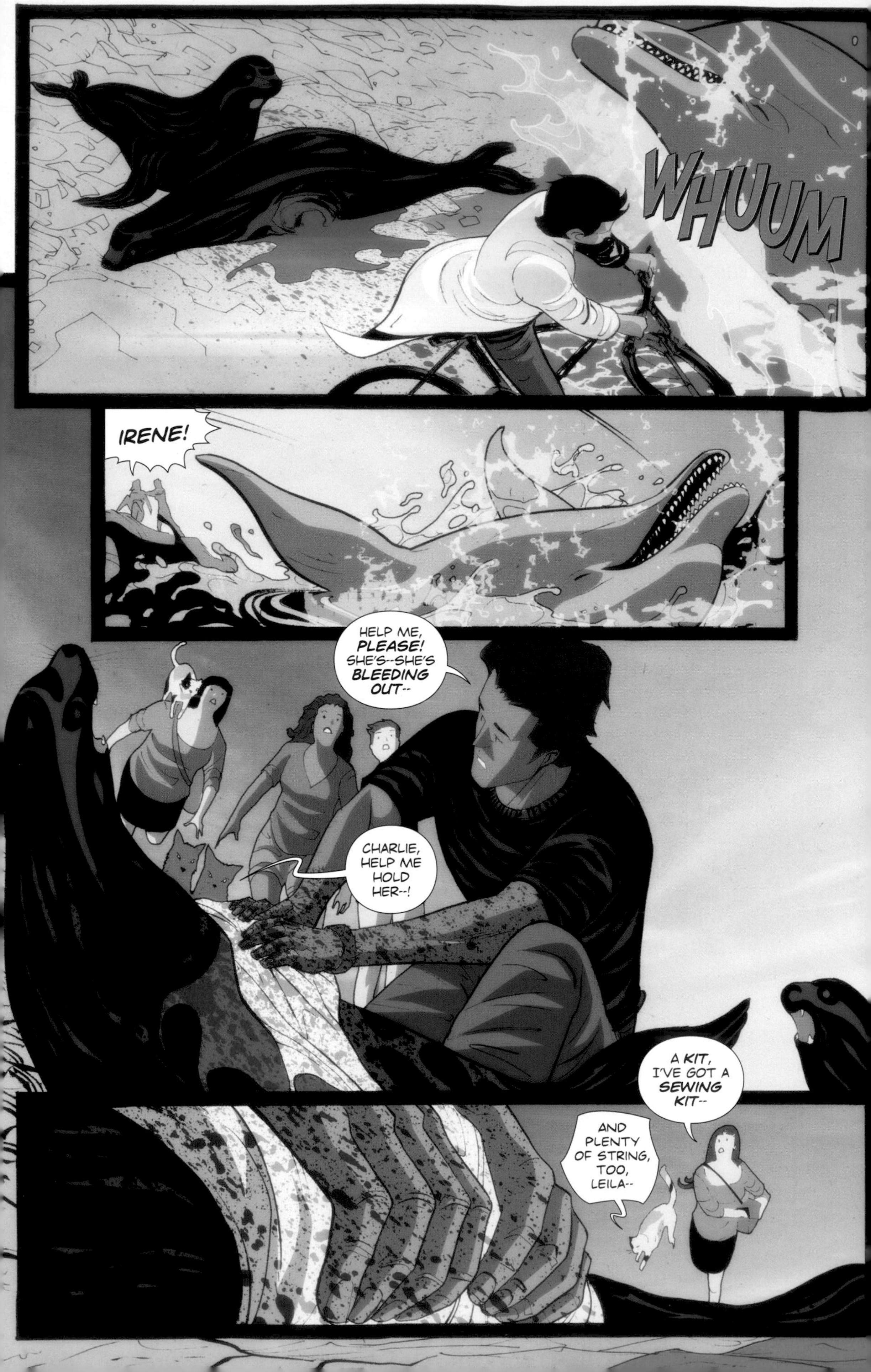
WHUUM
IRENE!
HELP ME, PLEASE! SHE'S--SHE'S BLEEDING OUT--
CHARLIE, HELP ME HOLD HER--!
A KIT, I'VE GOT A SEWING KIT--
AND PLENTY OF STRING, TOO, LEILA--

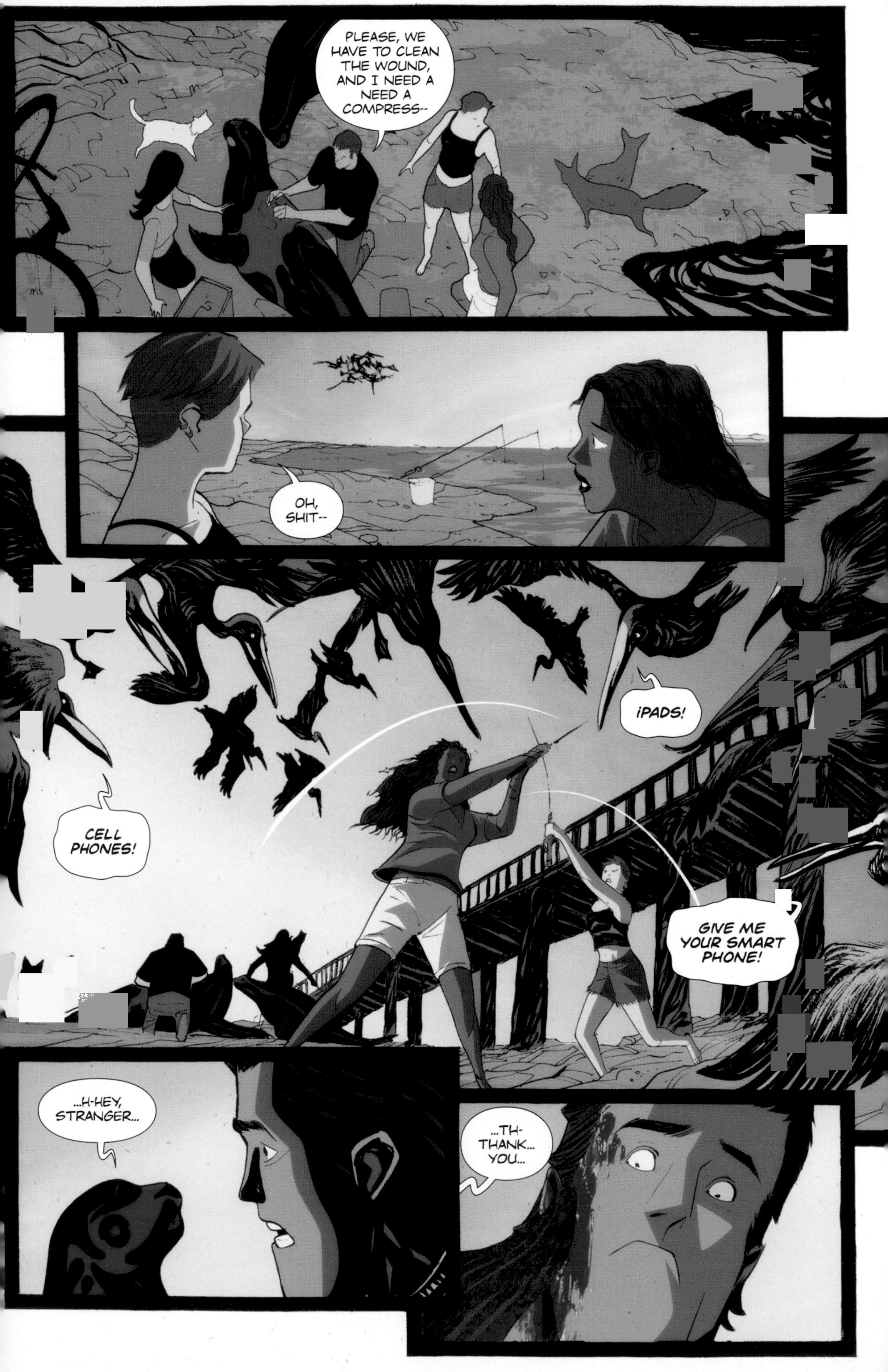
PLEASE, WE HAVE TO CLEAN THE WOUND, AND I NEED A NEED A COMPRESS--
OH, SHIT--
¡PADS!
CELL PHONES!
GIVE ME YOUR SMART PHONE!
...H-HEY, STRANGER...
...TH- THANK... YOU...

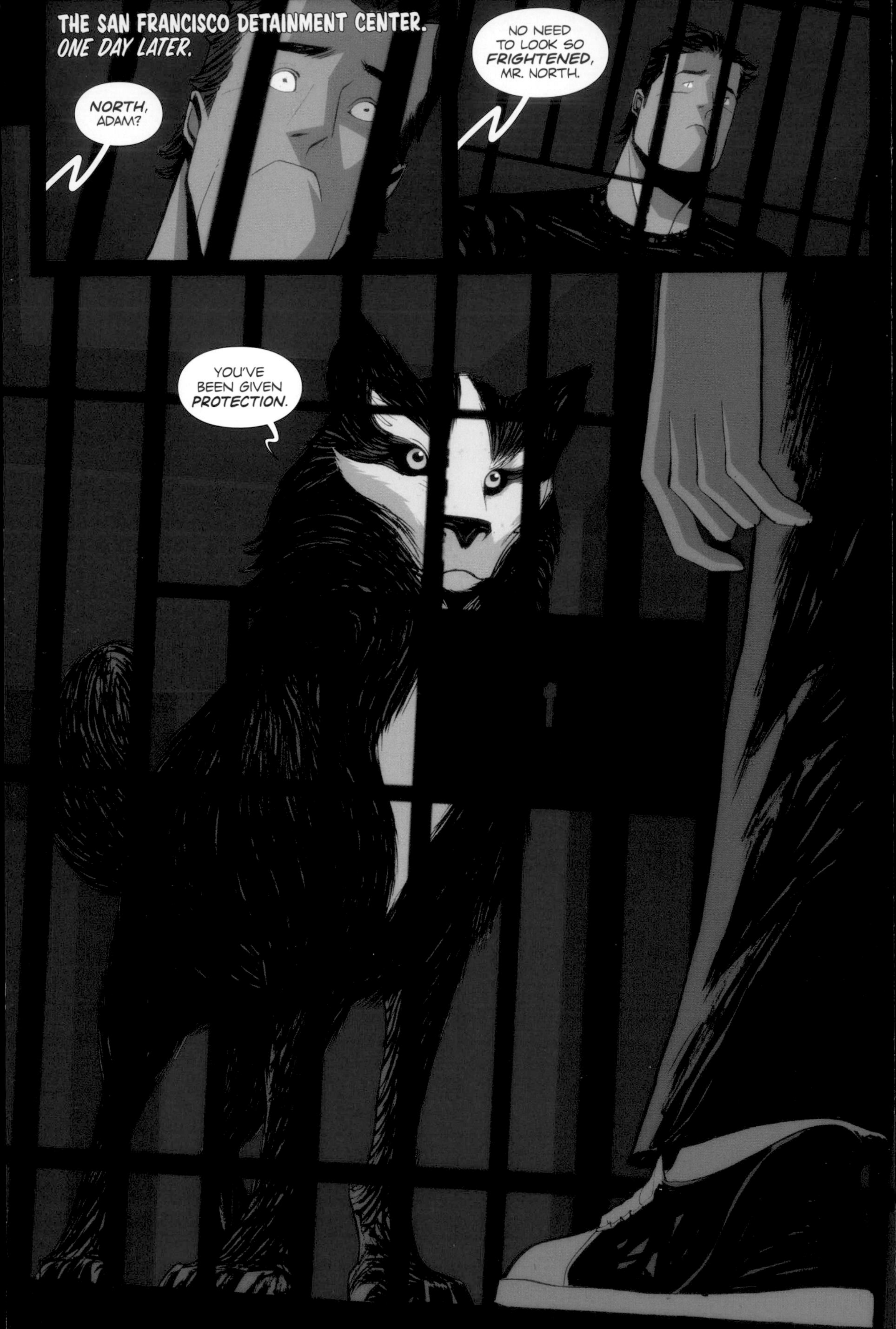
THE SAN FRANCISCO DETAINMENT CENTER.
ONE DAY LATER.
NORTH, ADAM?
NO NEED TO LOOK SO FRIGHTENED, MR. NORTH.
YOU'VE BEEN GIVEN PROTECTION.

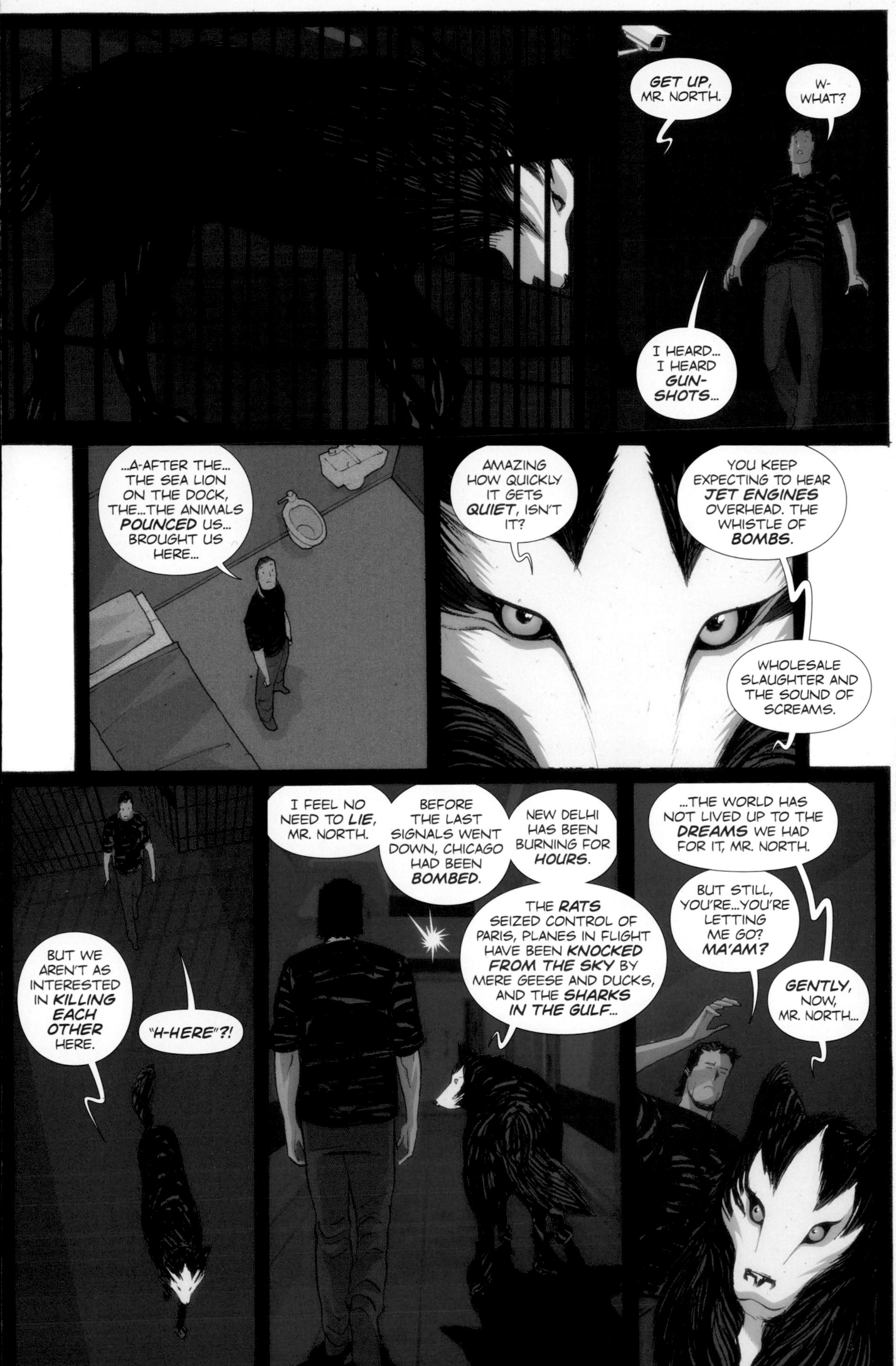
GET UP, MR. NORTH.
W-WHAT?
I HEARD... I HEARD GUN-SHOTS...
...A-AFTER THE... THE SEA LION ON THE DOCK, THE...THE ANIMALS POUNCED US... BROUGHT US HERE...
AMAZING HOW QUICKLY IT GETS QUIET, ISN'T IT?
YOU KEEP EXPECTING TO HEAR JET ENGINES OVERHEAD. THE WHISTLE OF BOMBS.
WHOLESALE SLAUGHTER AND THE SOUND OF SCREAMS.
BUT WE AREN'T AS INTERESTED IN KILLING EACH OTHER HERE.
"H-HERE"?!
I FEEL NO NEED TO LIE, MR. NORTH.
BEFORE THE LAST SIGNALS WENT DOWN, CHICAGO HAD BEEN BOMBED.
NEW DELHI HAS BEEN BURNING FOR HOURS.
THE RATS SEIZED CONTROL OF PARIS, PLANES IN FLIGHT HAVE BEEN KNOCKED FROM THE SKY BY MERE GEESE AND DUCKS, AND THE SHARKS IN THE GULF...
...THE WORLD HAS NOT LIVED UP TO THE DREAMS WE HAD FOR IT, MR. NORTH.
BUT STILL, YOU'RE...YOU'RE LETTING ME GO? MA'AM?
GENTLY, NOW, MR. NORTH...

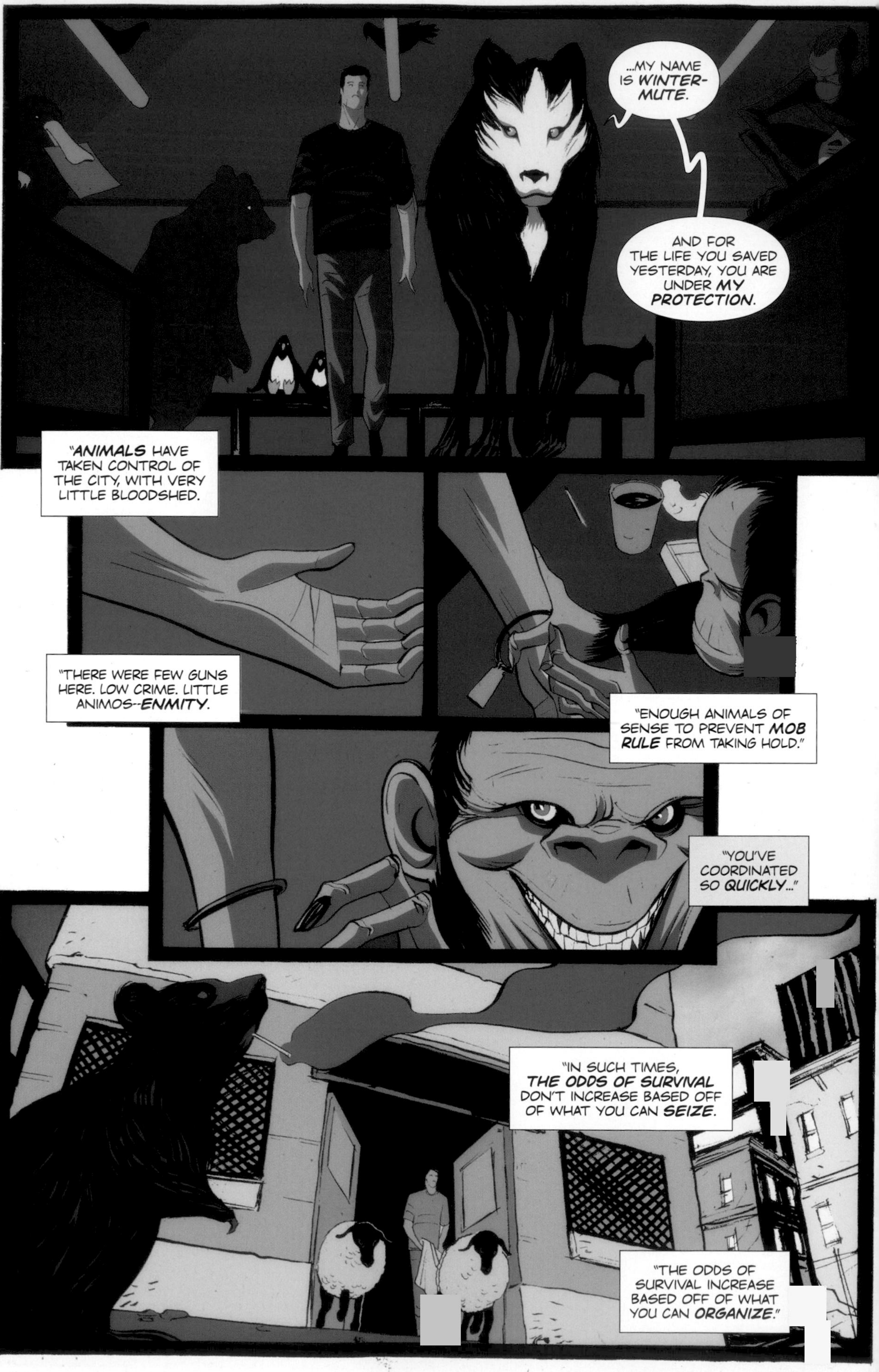
...MY NAME IS WINTERMUTE.
AND FOR THE LIFE YOU SAVED YESTERDAY, YOU ARE UNDER MY PROTECTION.
"ANIMALS HAVE TAKEN CONTROL OF THE CITY, WITH VERY LITTLE BLOODSHED.
"THERE WERE FEW GUNS HERE. LOW CRIME. LITTLE ANIMOS--ENMITY.
"ENOUGH ANIMALS OF SENSE TO PREVENT MOB RULE FROM TAKING HOLD."
"YOU'VE COORDINATED SO QUICKLY..."
"IN SUCH TIMES, THE ODDS OF SURVIVAL DON'T INCREASE BASED OFF OF WHAT YOU CAN SEIZE.
"THE ODDS OF SURVIVAL INCREASE BASED OFF OF WHAT YOU CAN ORGANIZE."

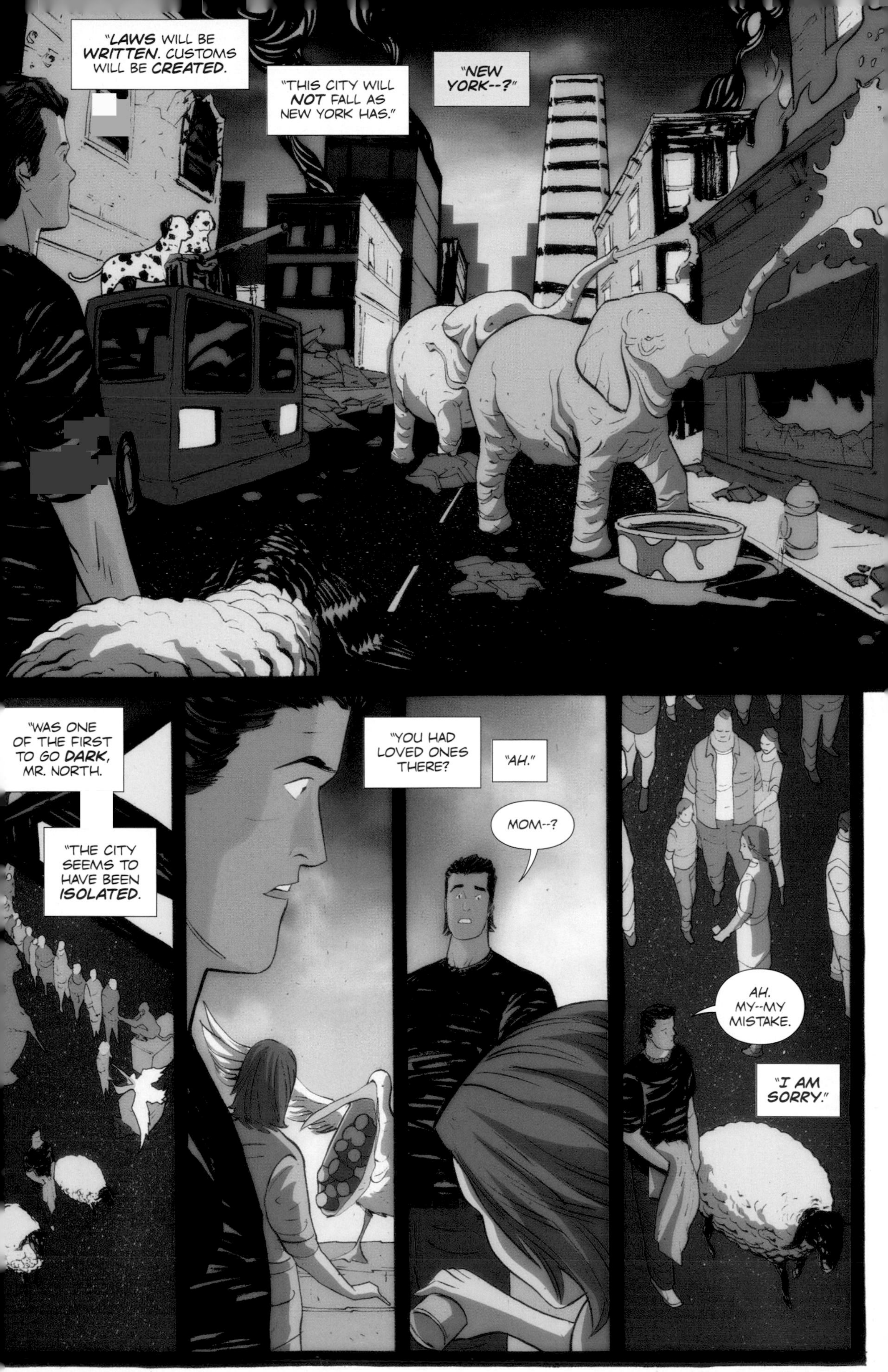
"LAWS WILL BE WRITTEN. CUSTOMS WILL BE CREATED.
"THIS CITY WILL NOT FALL AS NEW YORK HAS."
"NEW YORK--?"
"WAS ONE OF THE FIRST TO GO DARK, MR. NORTH.
"THE CITY SEEMS TO HAVE BEEN ISOLATED.
"YOU HAD LOVED ONES THERE?
"AH."
MOM--?
AH. MY--MY MISTAKE.
"I AM SORRY."

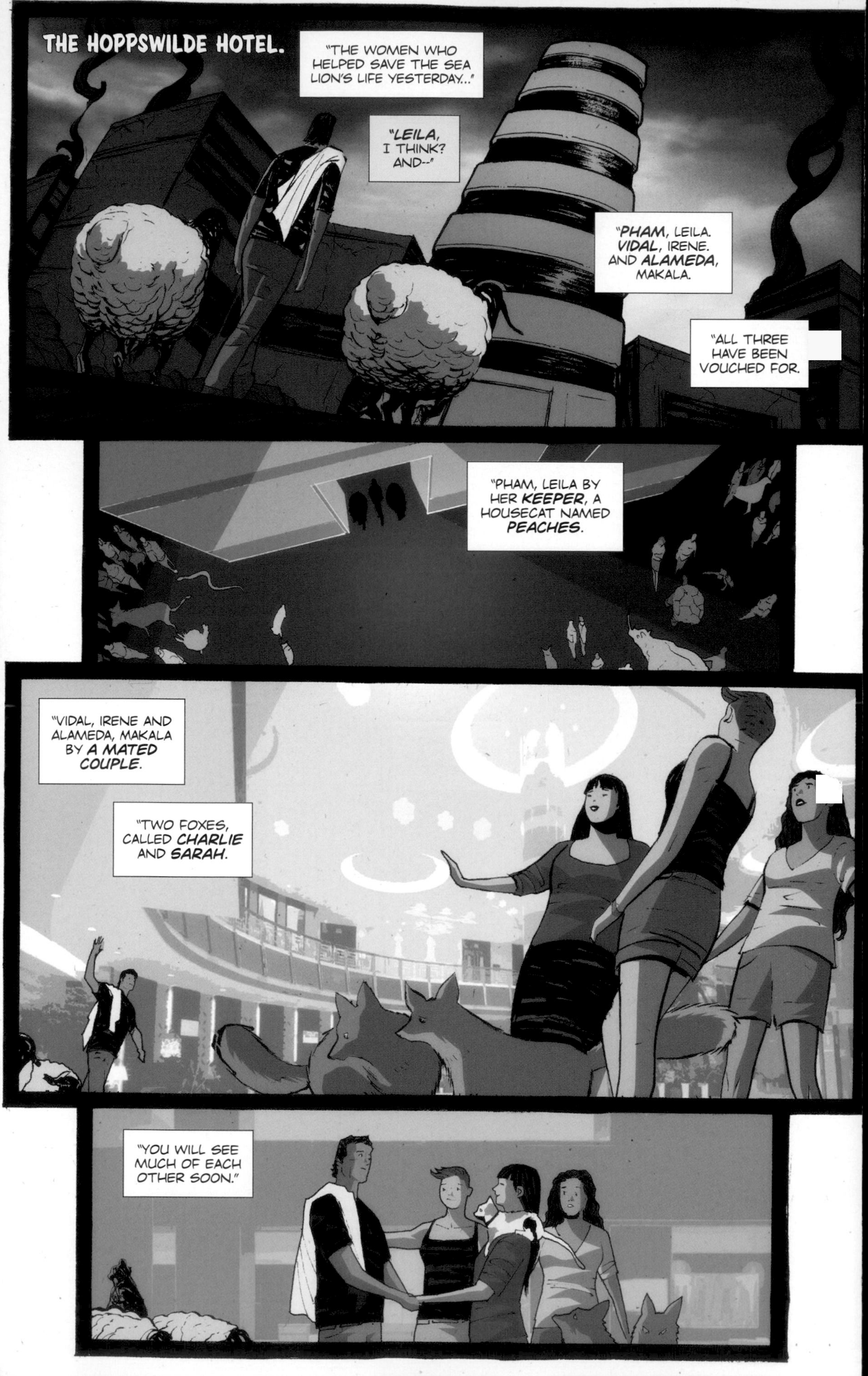
THE HOPPSWILDE HOTEL.
"THE WOMEN WHO HELPED SAVE THE SEA LION'S LIFE YESTERDAY..."
"LEILA, I THINK? AND--"
"PHAM, LEILA. VIDAL, IRENE. AND ALAMEDA, MAKALA.
"ALL THREE HAVE BEEN VOUCHED FOR.
"PHAM, LEILA BY HER KEEPER, A HOUSECAT NAMED PEACHES.
"VIDAL, IRENE AND ALAMEDA, MAKALA BY A MATED COUPLE.
"TWO FOXES, CALLED CHARLIE AND SARAH.
"YOU WILL SEE MUCH OF EACH OTHER SOON."

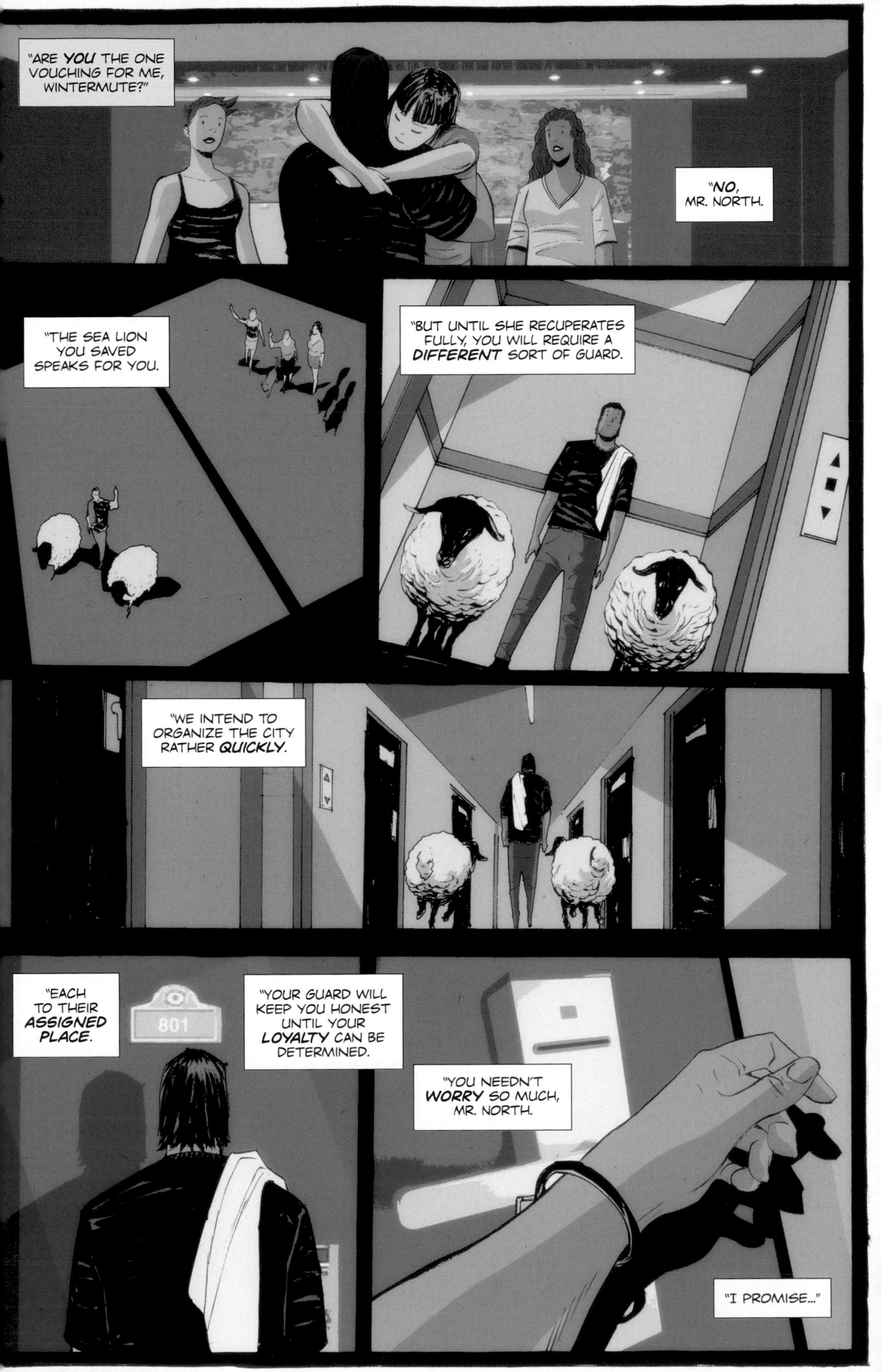
"ARE YOU THE ONE VOUCHING FOR ME, WINTERMUTE?"
"NO, MR. NORTH.
"THE SEA LION YOU SAVED SPEAKS FOR YOU.
"BUT UNTIL SHE RECUPERATES FULLY, YOU WILL REQUIRE A DIFFERENT SORT OF GUARD.
"WE INTEND TO ORGANIZE THE CITY RATHER QUICKLY.
"EACH TO THEIR ASSIGNED PLACE.
801
"YOUR GUARD WILL KEEP YOU HONEST UNTIL YOUR LOYALTY CAN BE DETERMINED.
"YOU NEEDN'T WORRY SO MUCH, MR. NORTH.
"I PROMISE..."

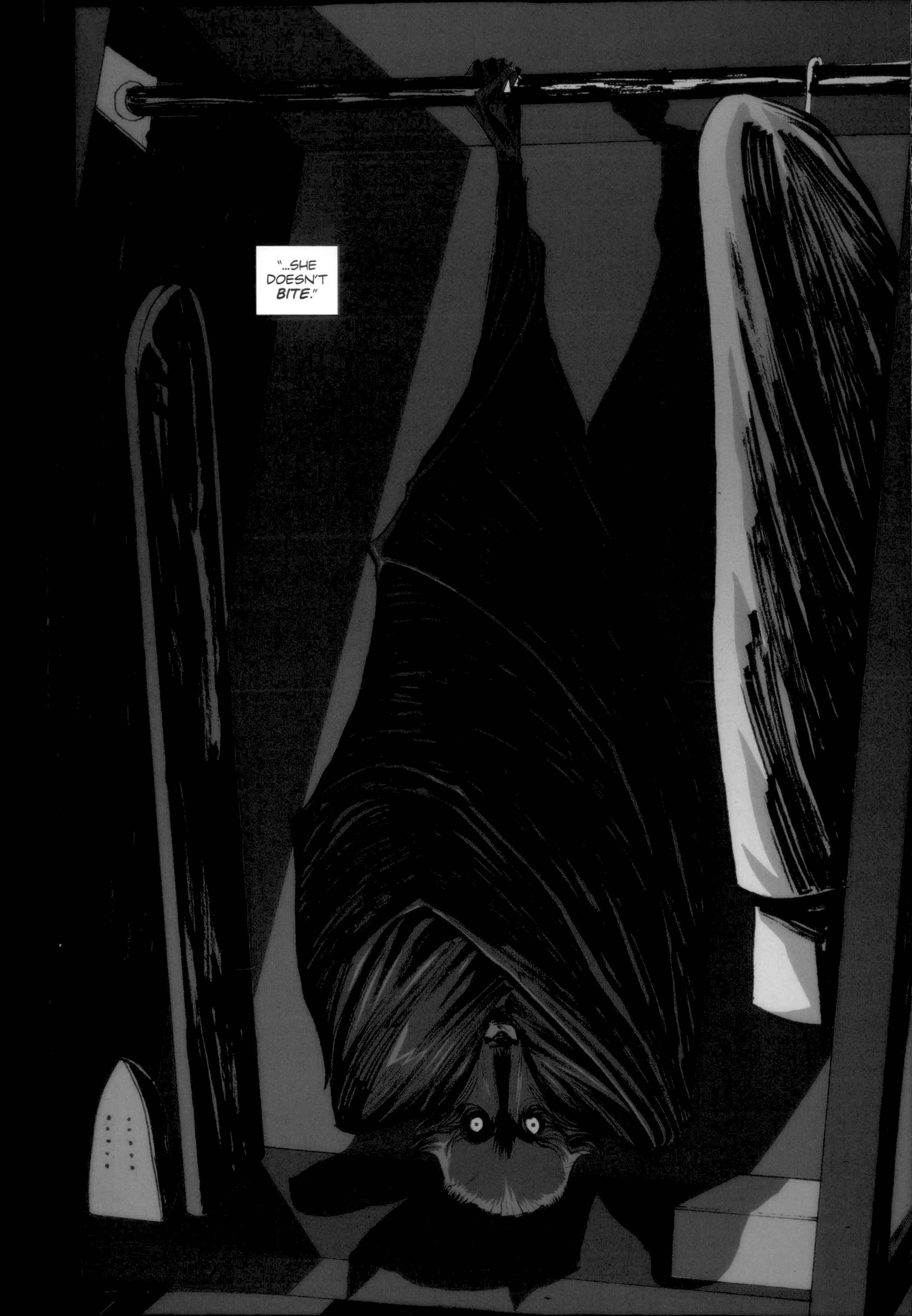
"...SHE DOESN'T BITE."

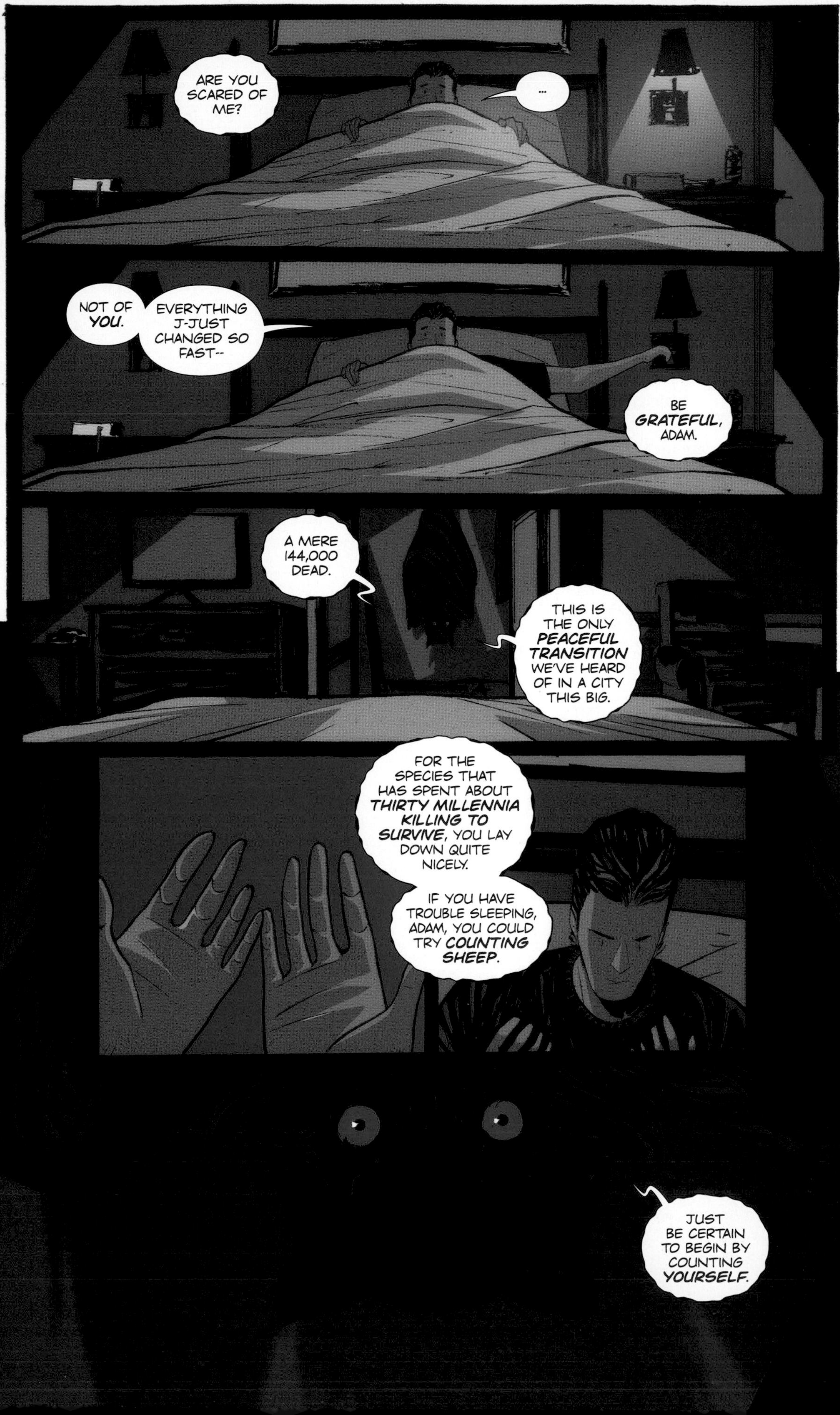
ARE YOU SCARED OF ME?
...
NOT OF YOU.
EVERYTHING J-JUST CHANGED SO FAST--
BE GRATEFUL, ADAM.
A MERE 144,000 DEAD.
THIS IS THE ONLY PEACEFUL TRANSITION WE'VE HEARD OF IN A CITY THIS BIG.
FOR THE SPECIES THAT HAS SPENT ABOUT THIRTY MILLENNIA KILLING TO SURVIVE, YOU LAY DOWN QUITE NICELY.
IF YOU HAVE TROUBLE SLEEPING, ADAM, YOU COULD TRY COUNTING SHEEP.
JUST BE CERTAIN TO BEGIN BY COUNTING YOURSELF.

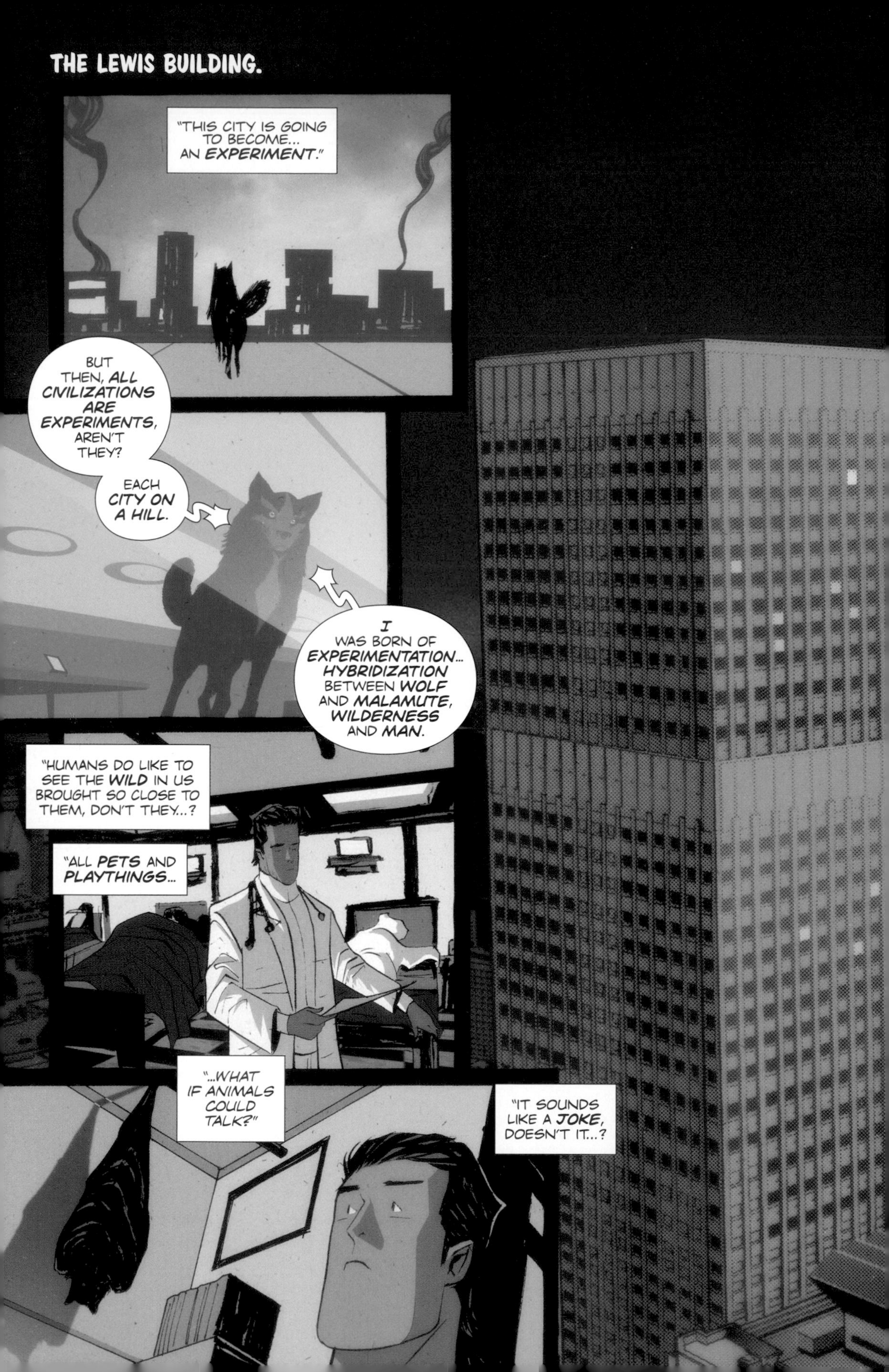
THE LEWIS BUILDING.
"THIS CITY IS GOING TO BECOME... AN EXPERIMENT."
BUT THEN, ALL CIVILIZATIONS ARE EXPERIMENTS, AREN'T THEY?
EACH CITY ON A HILL.
I WAS BORN OF EXPERIMENTATION... HYBRIDIZATION BETWEEN WOLF AND MALAMUTE, WILDERNESS AND MAN.
"HUMANS DO LIKE TO SEE THE WILD IN US BROUGHT SO CLOSE TO THEM, DON'T THEY...?
"ALL PETS AND PLAYTHINGS...
"...WHAT IF ANIMALS COULD TALK?"
"IT SOUNDS LIKE A JOKE, DOESN'T IT...?

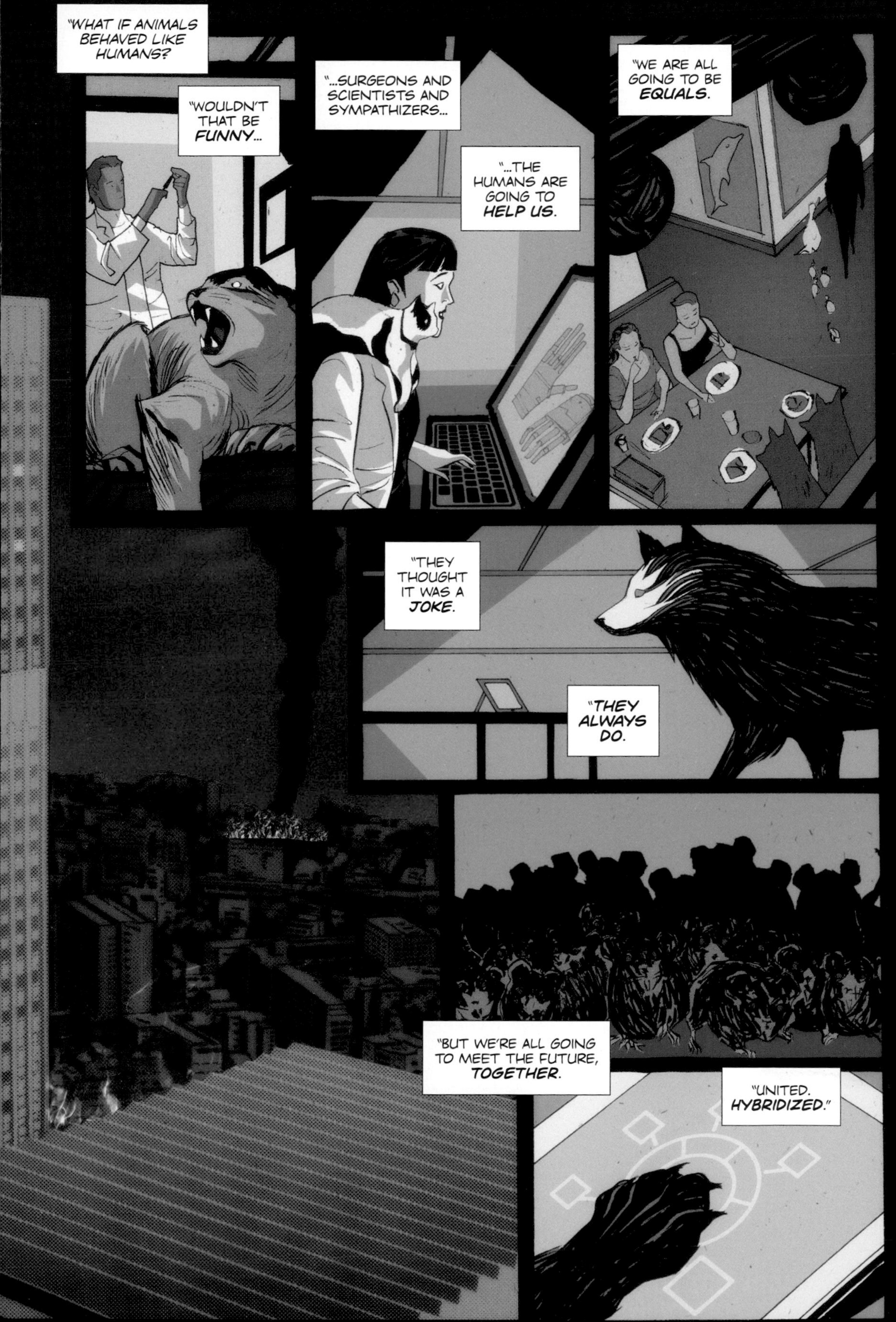
"WHAT IF ANIMALS BEHAVED LIKE HUMANS?
"WOULDN'T THAT BE FUNNY...
"...SURGEONS AND SCIENTISTS AND SYMPATHIZERS...
"...THE HUMANS ARE GOING TO HELP US.
"WE ARE ALL GOING TO BE EQUALS.
"THEY THOUGHT IT WAS A JOKE.
"THEY ALWAYS DO.
"BUT WE'RE ALL GOING TO MEET THE FUTURE, TOGETHER.
"UNITED. HYBRIDIZED."

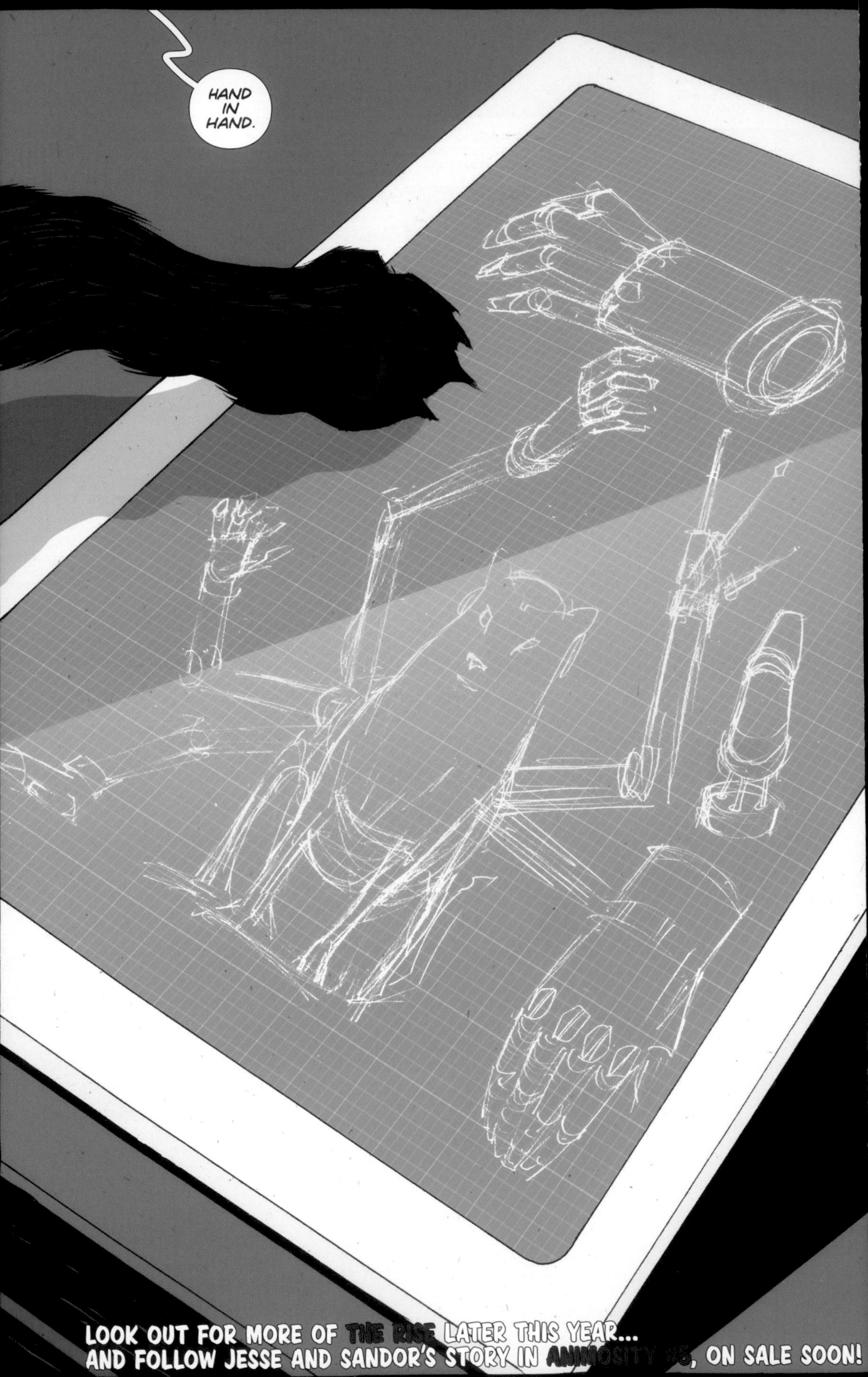
HAND IN HAND.
LOOK OUT FOR MORE OF THE RISE LATER THIS YEAR...
AND FOLLOW JESSE AND SANDOR'S STORY IN ANIMOSITY #5, ON SALE SOON!

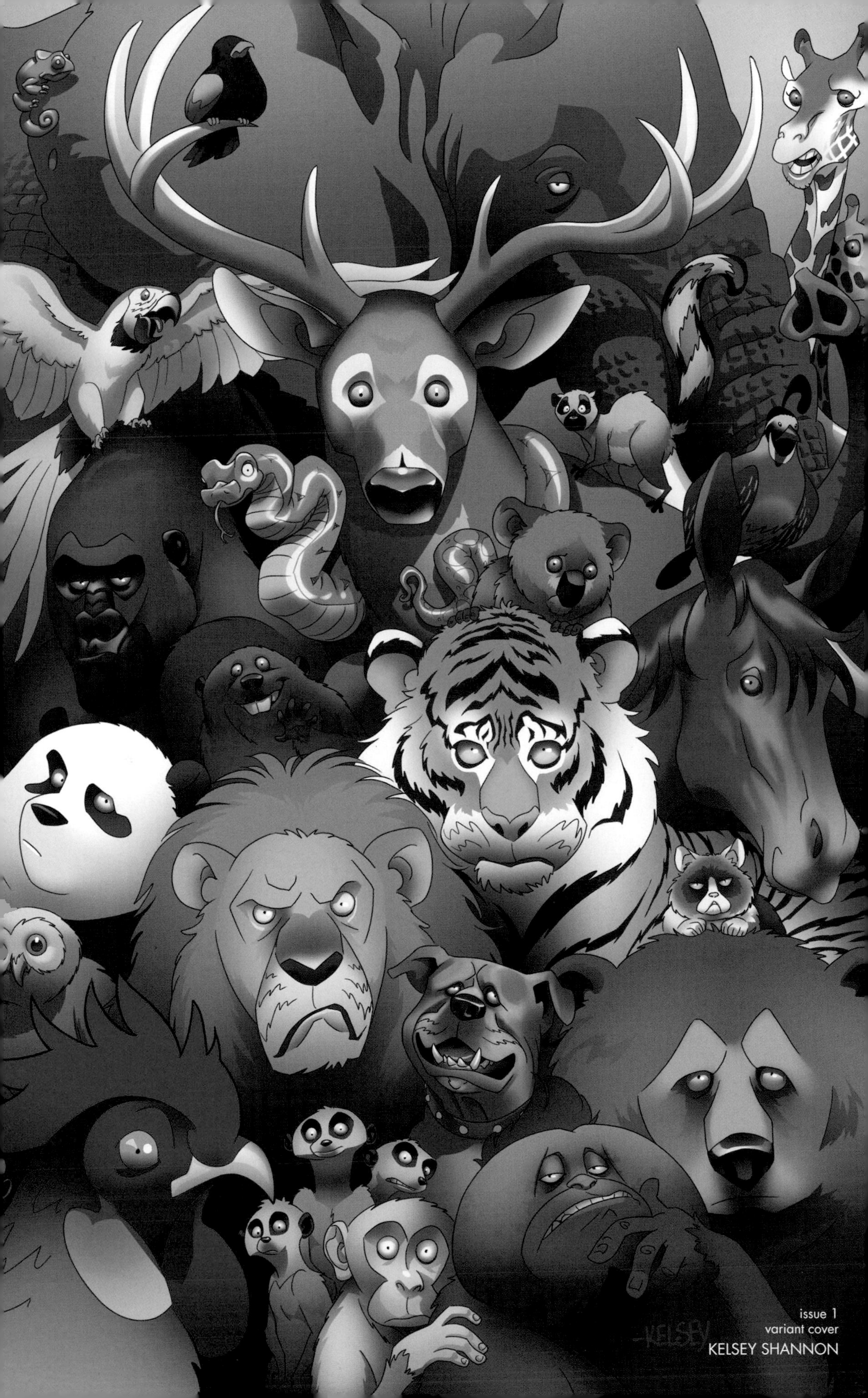

issue 1
variant cover
KELSEY SHANNON

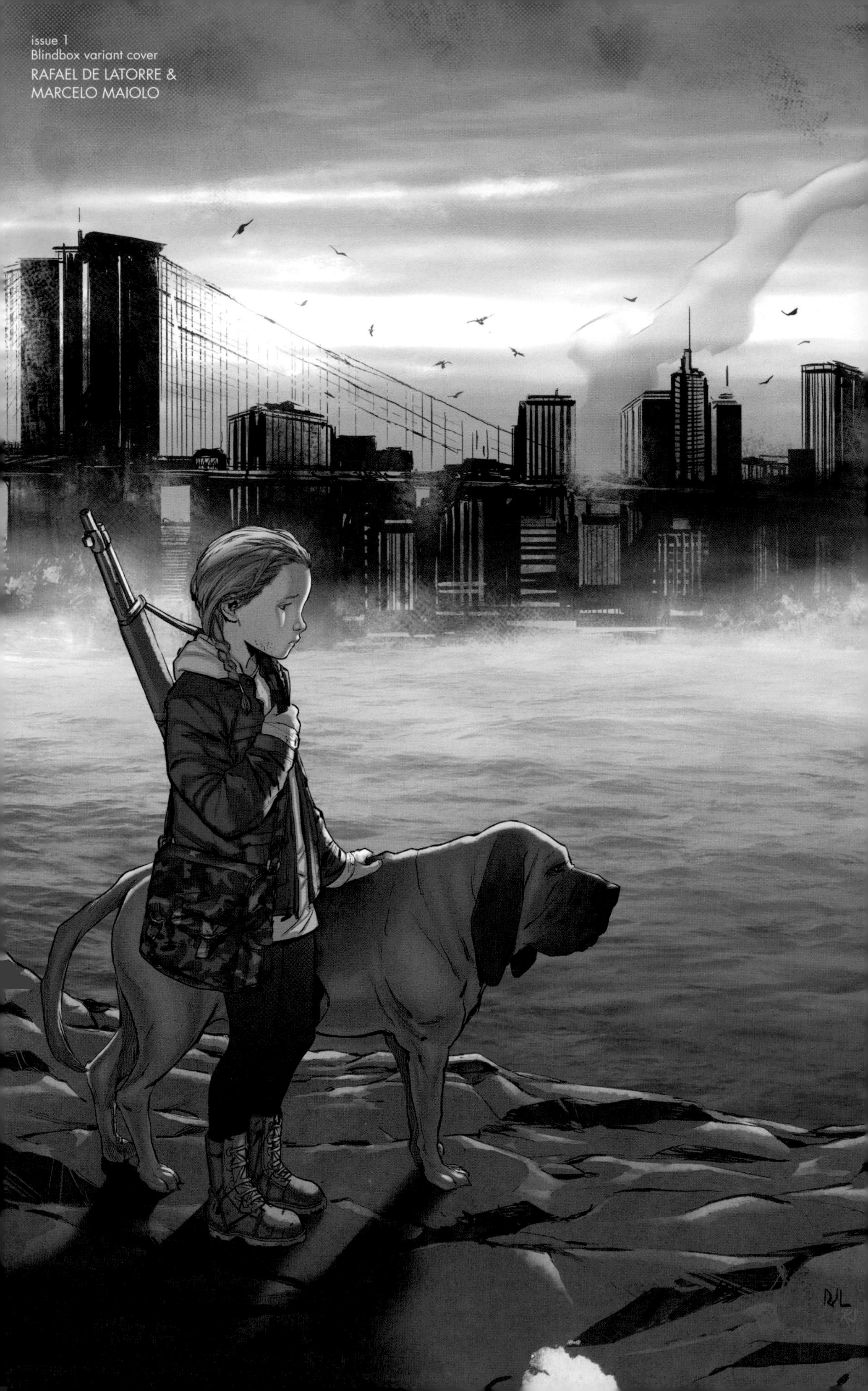

issue 1
Blindbox variant cover
RAFAEL DE LATORRE &
MARCELO MAIOLO

issue 1
Frankie's Comics variant cover
MICHAEL GAYDOS

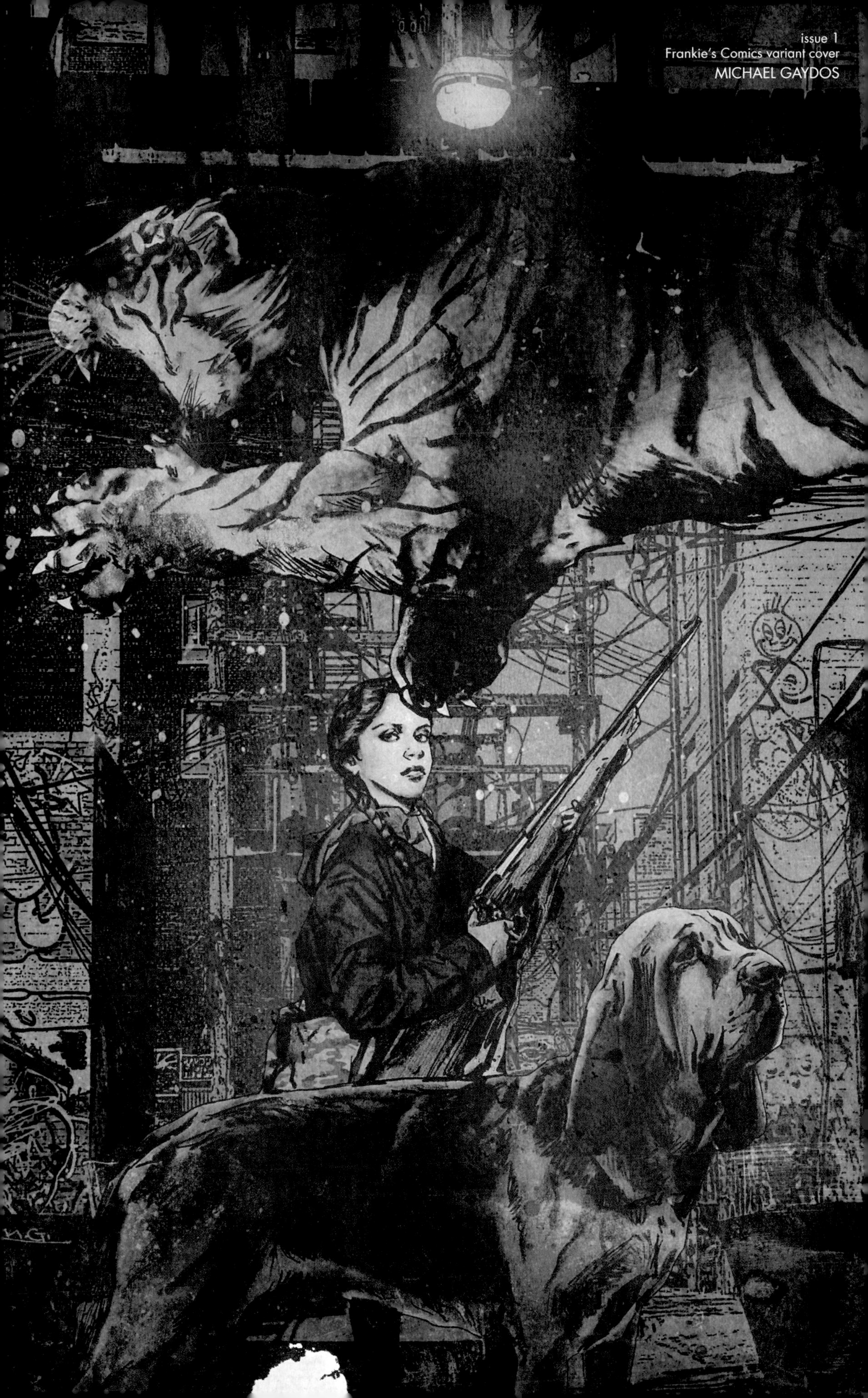
M.G.

issue 1
Blindbox variant cover
KELSEY SHANNON

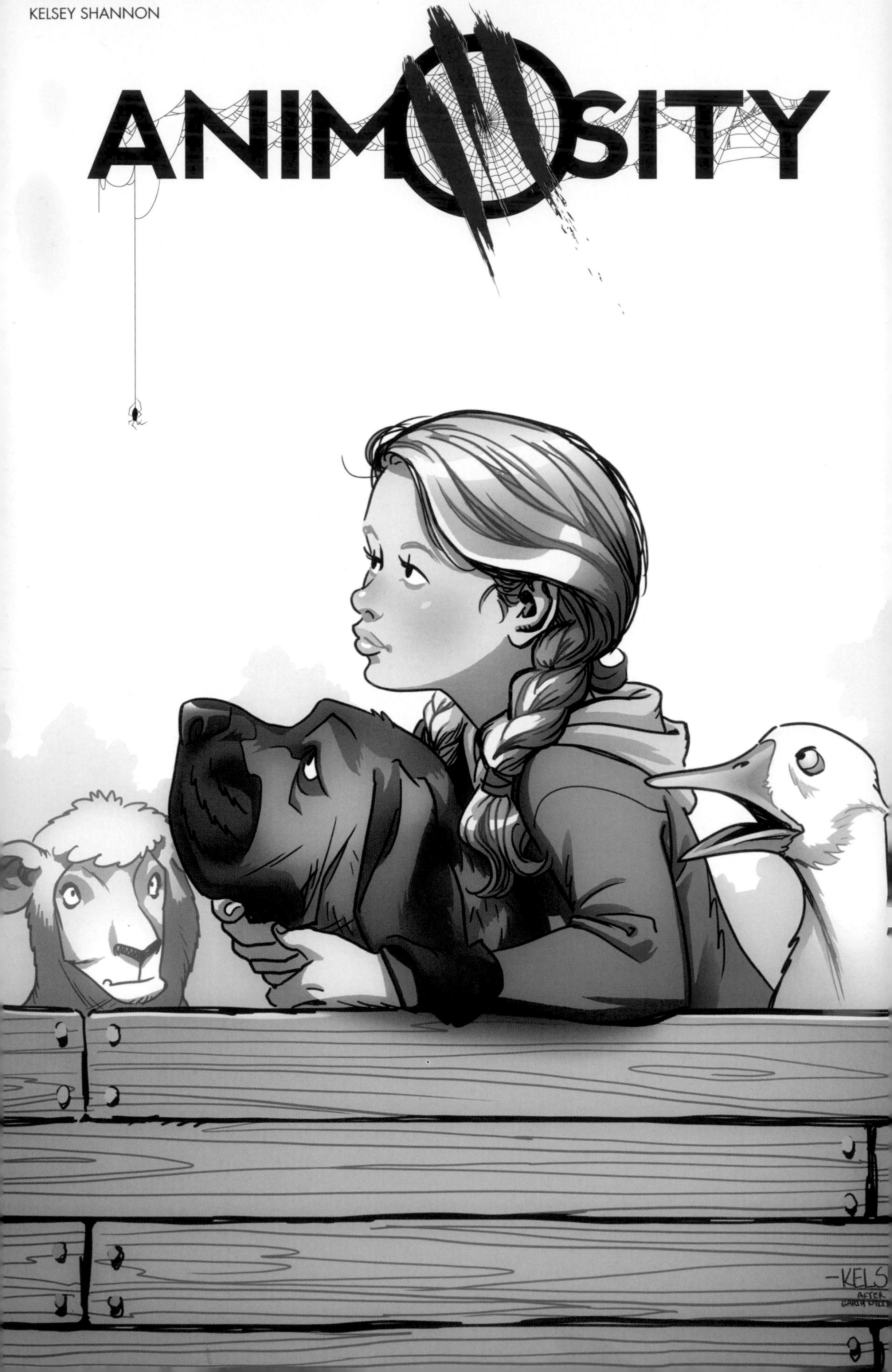
ANIMOSITY
-KELS
AFTER

issue 1
Hip Hopf variant cover
MIKE ROOTH

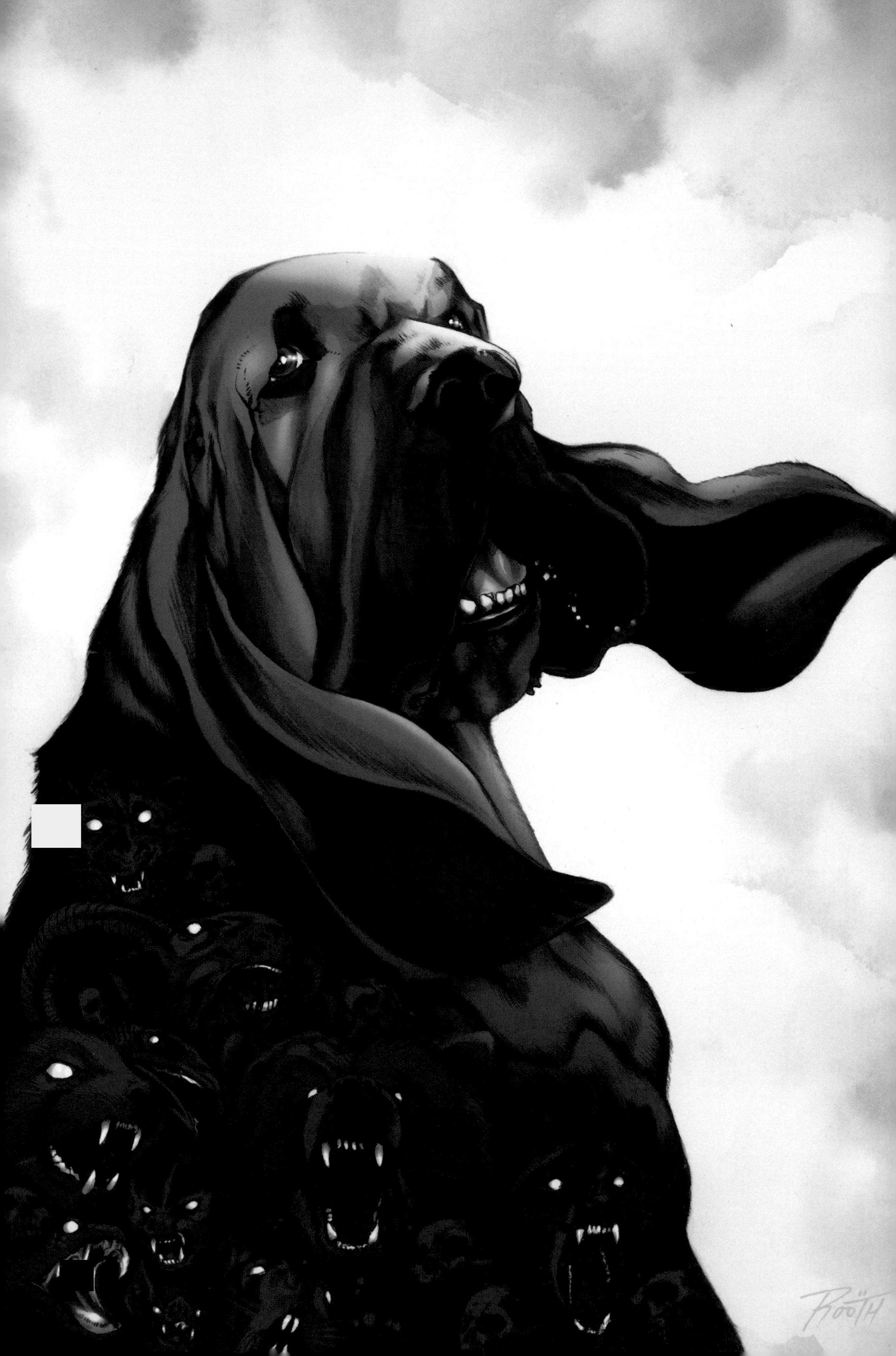

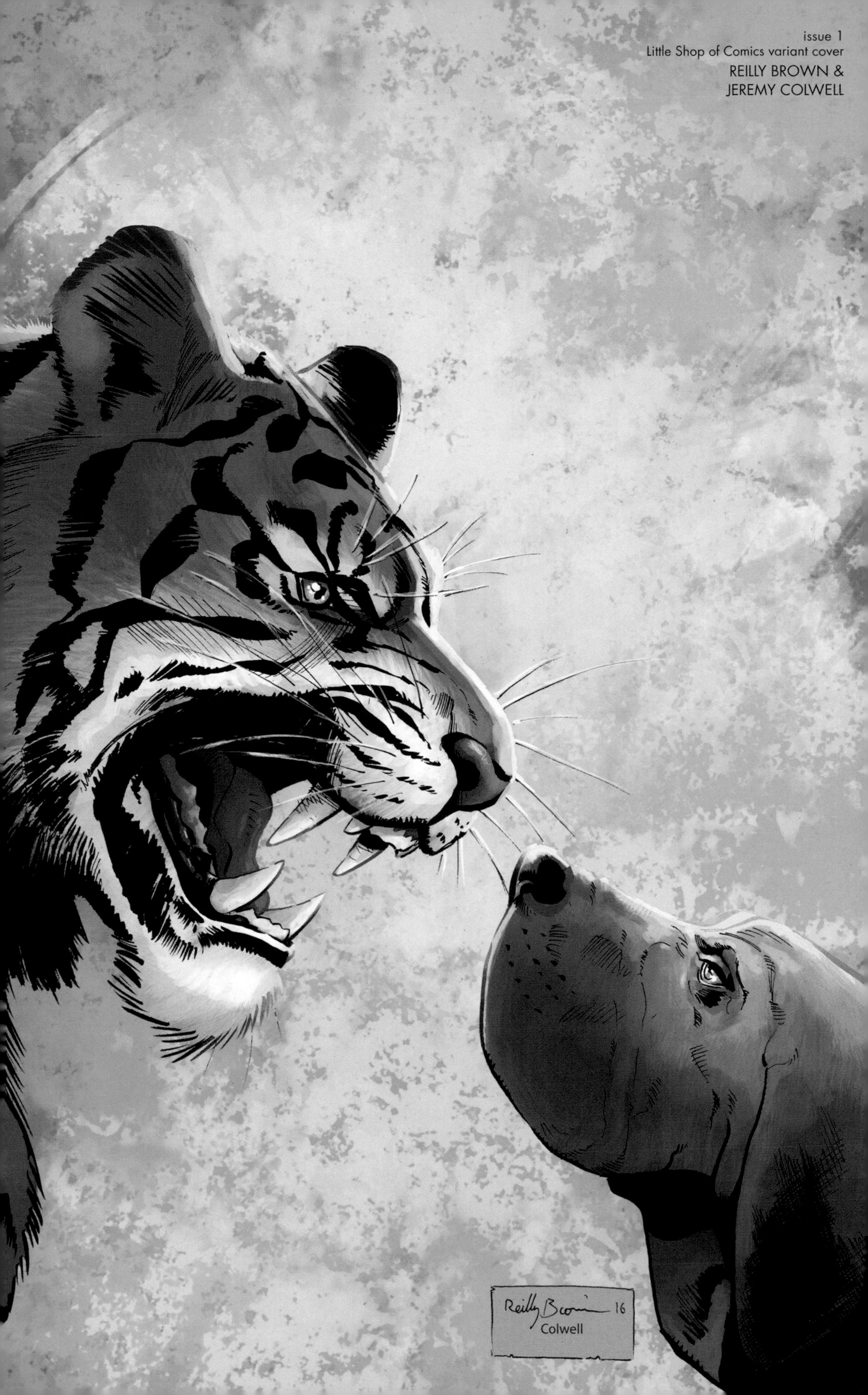

issue 1
Little Shop of Comics variant cover
REILLY BROWN &
JEREMY COLWELL

issue 1
The Comic Mint variant cover
JOHN McCREA

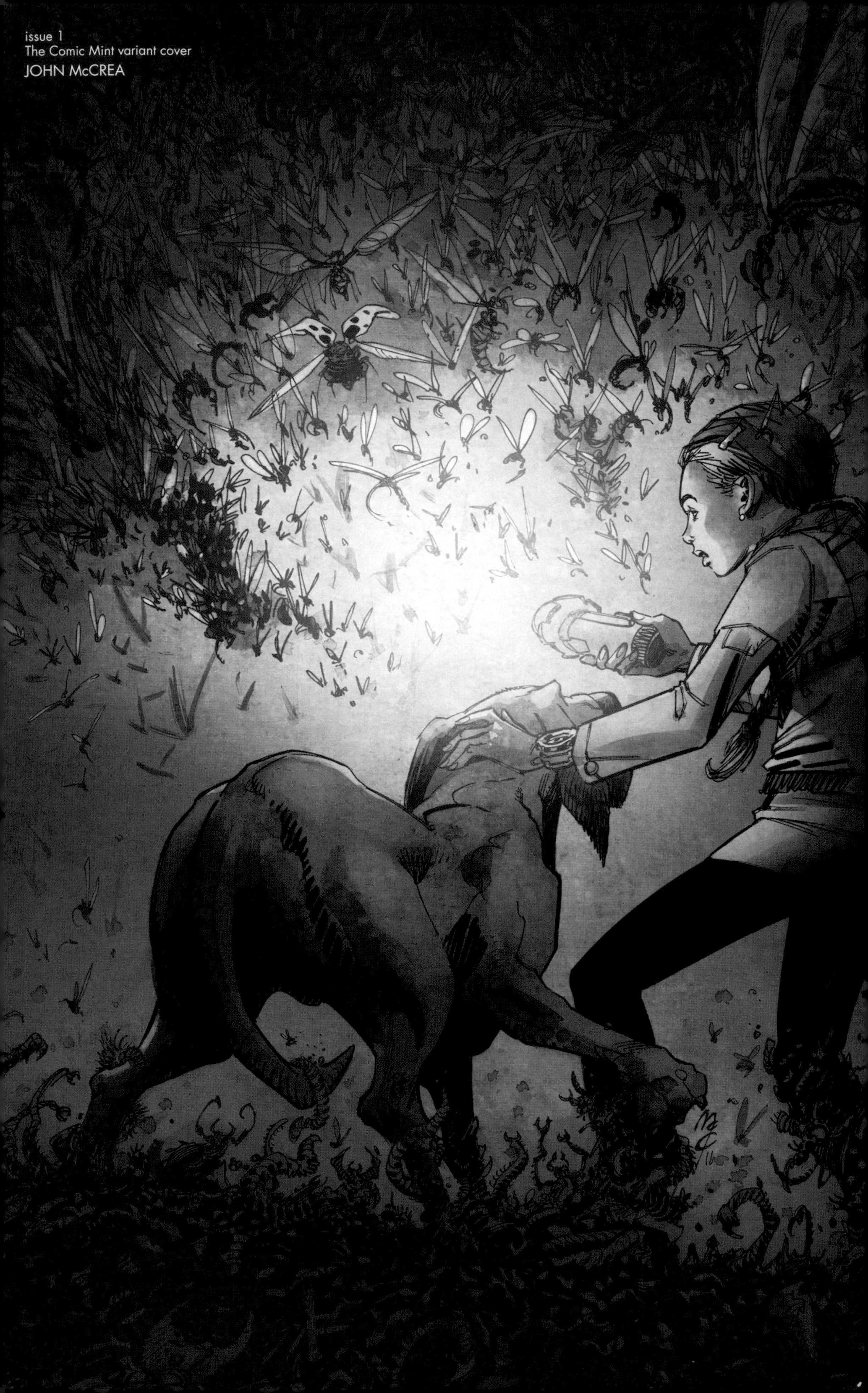

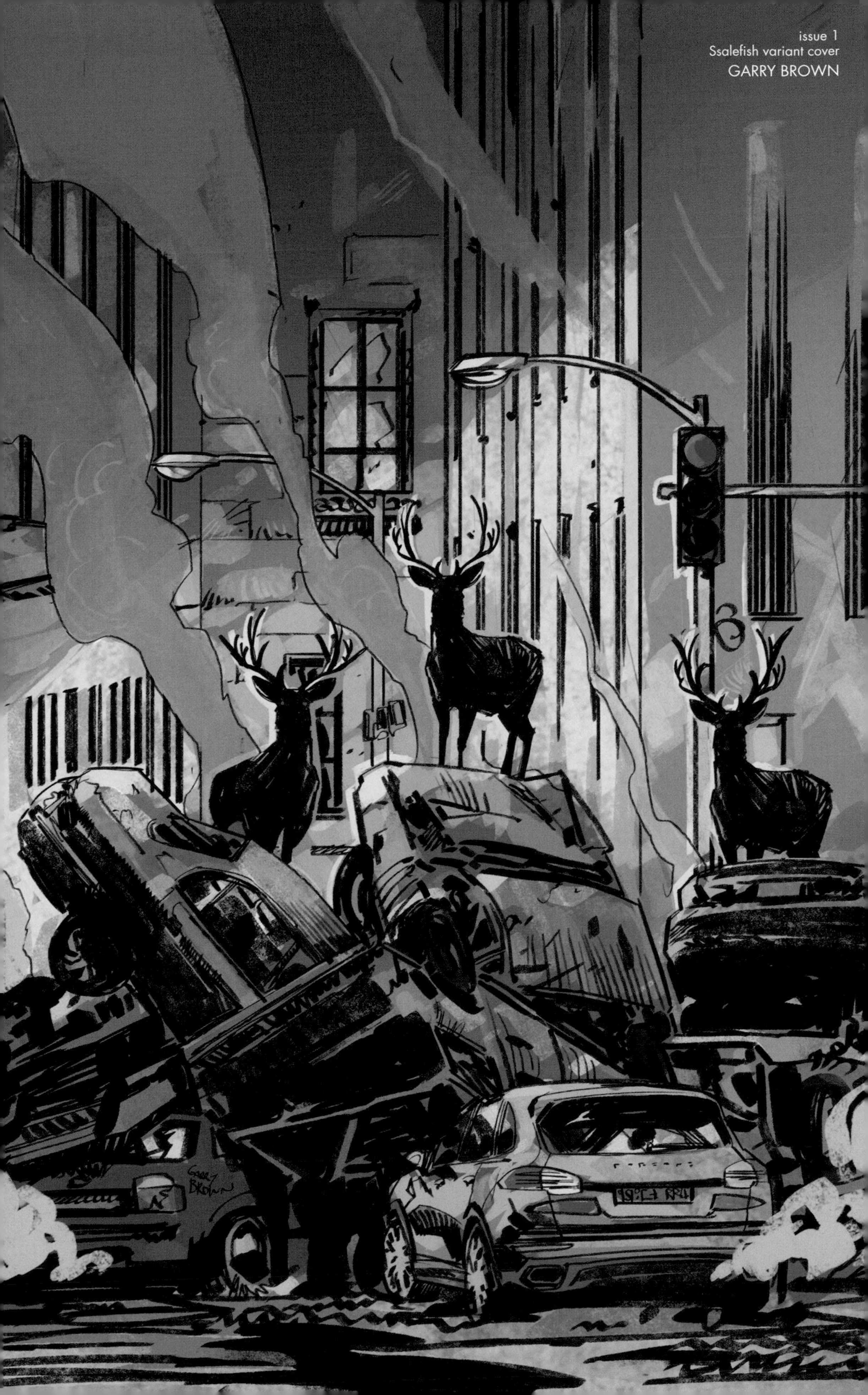
GARRY BROWN

issue 1
Ssalefish variant cover
GARRY BROWN

issue 1
Frankie's Comics fifth printing cover
HOYT SILVA

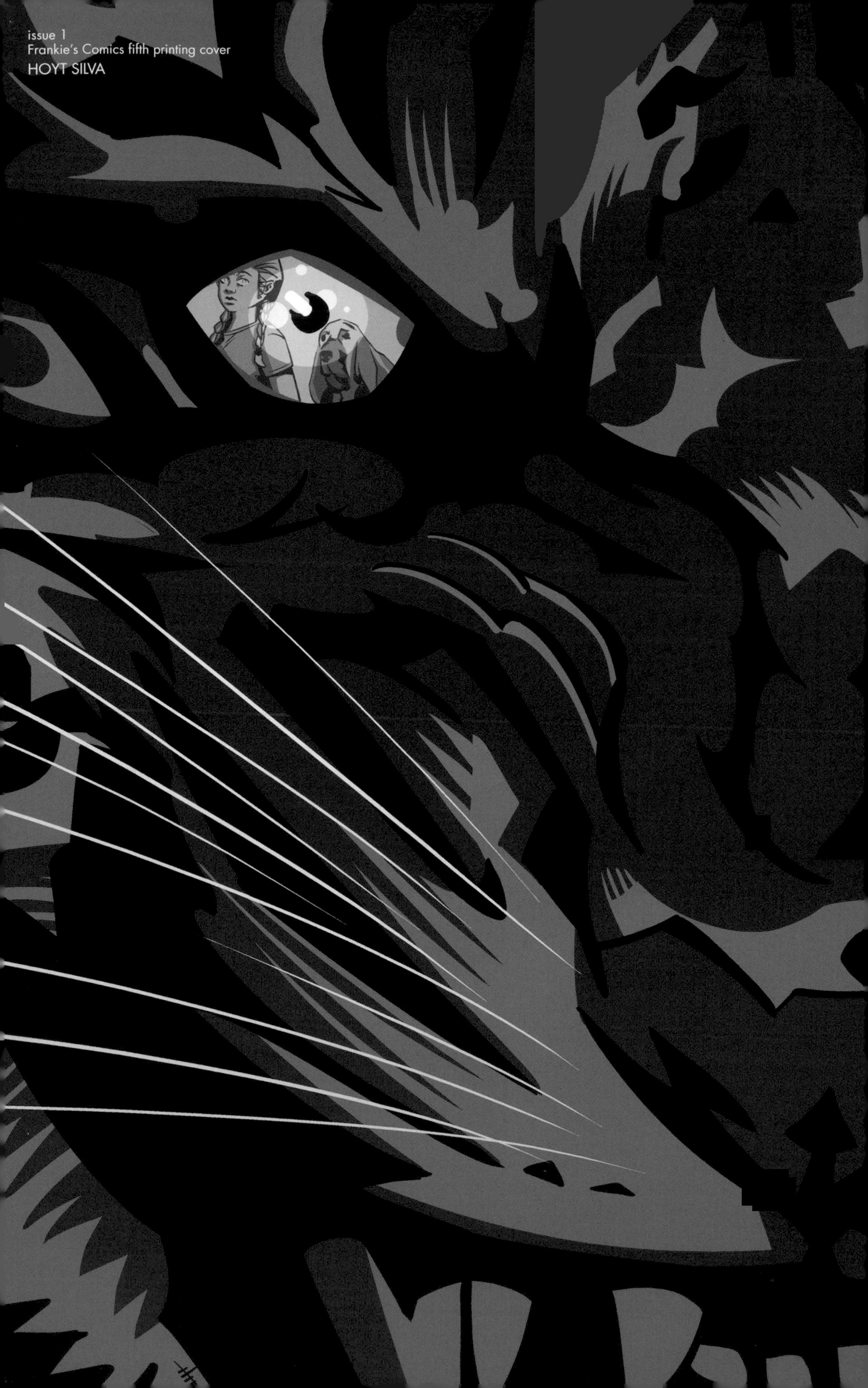

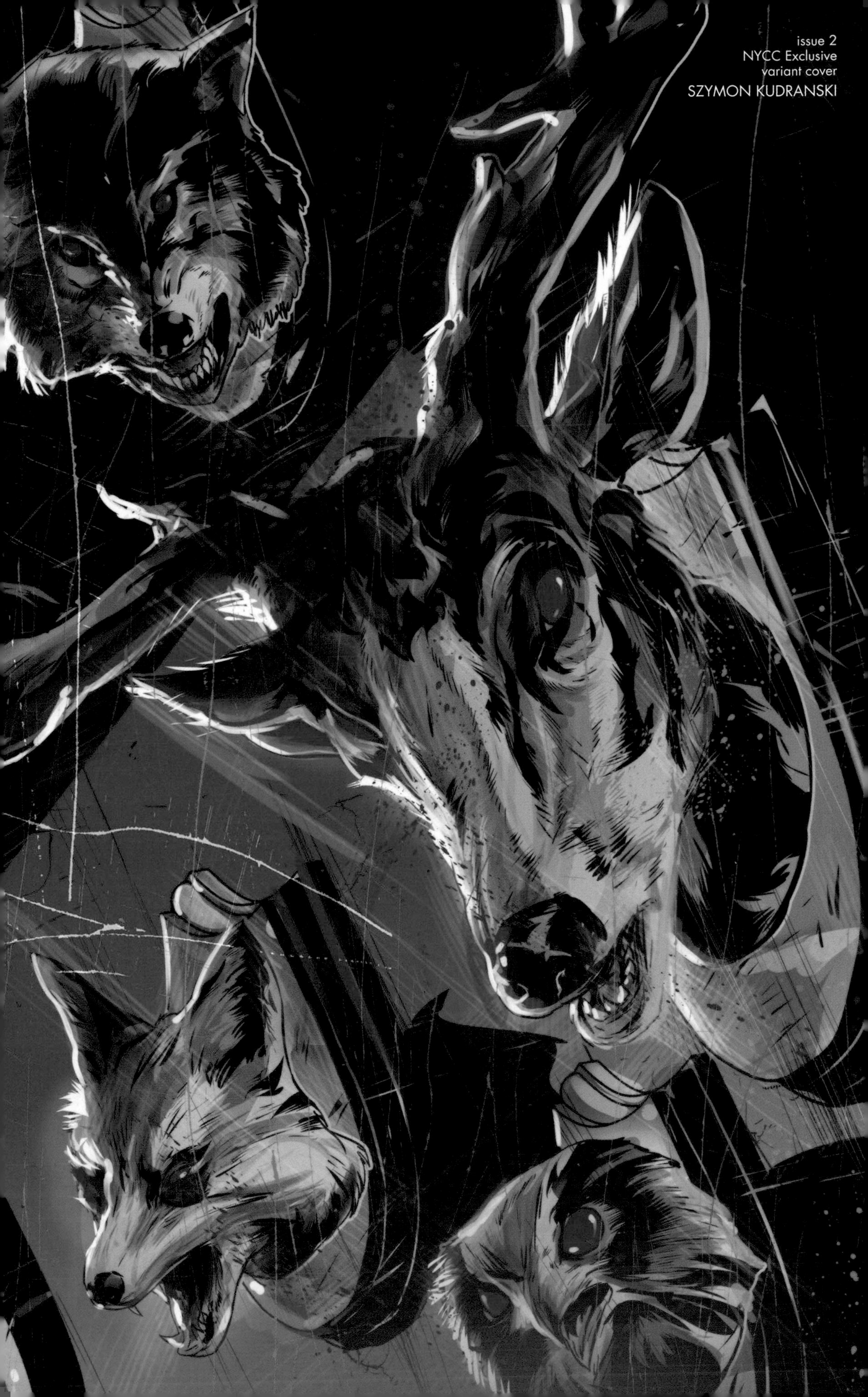

issue 2
NYCC Exclusive
variant cover
SZYMON KUDRANSKI

issue 2
Frankie's Comics variant cover
KYLE STRAHM &
GREG SMALLWOOD

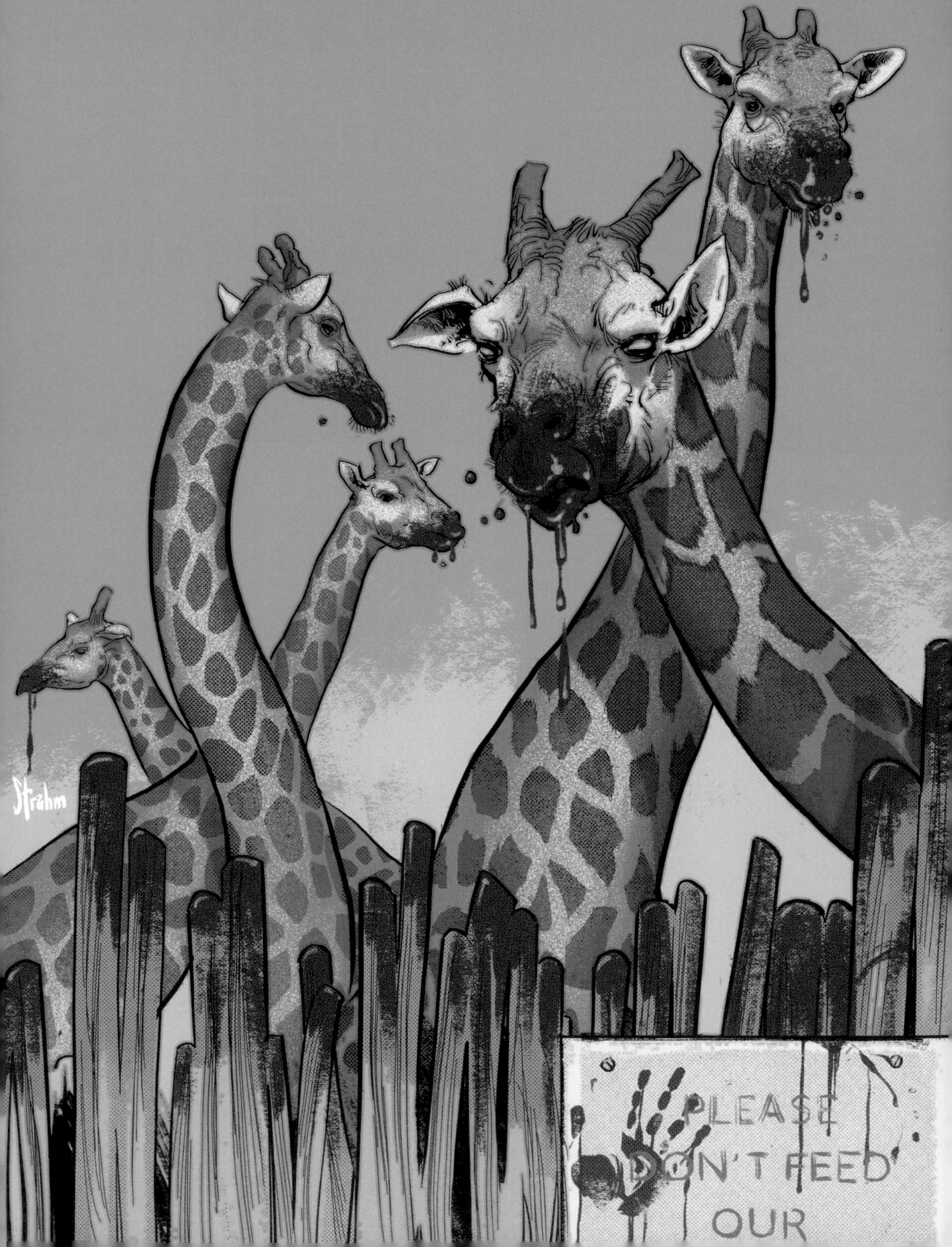
Strahm
PLEASE
DON'T FEED
OUR

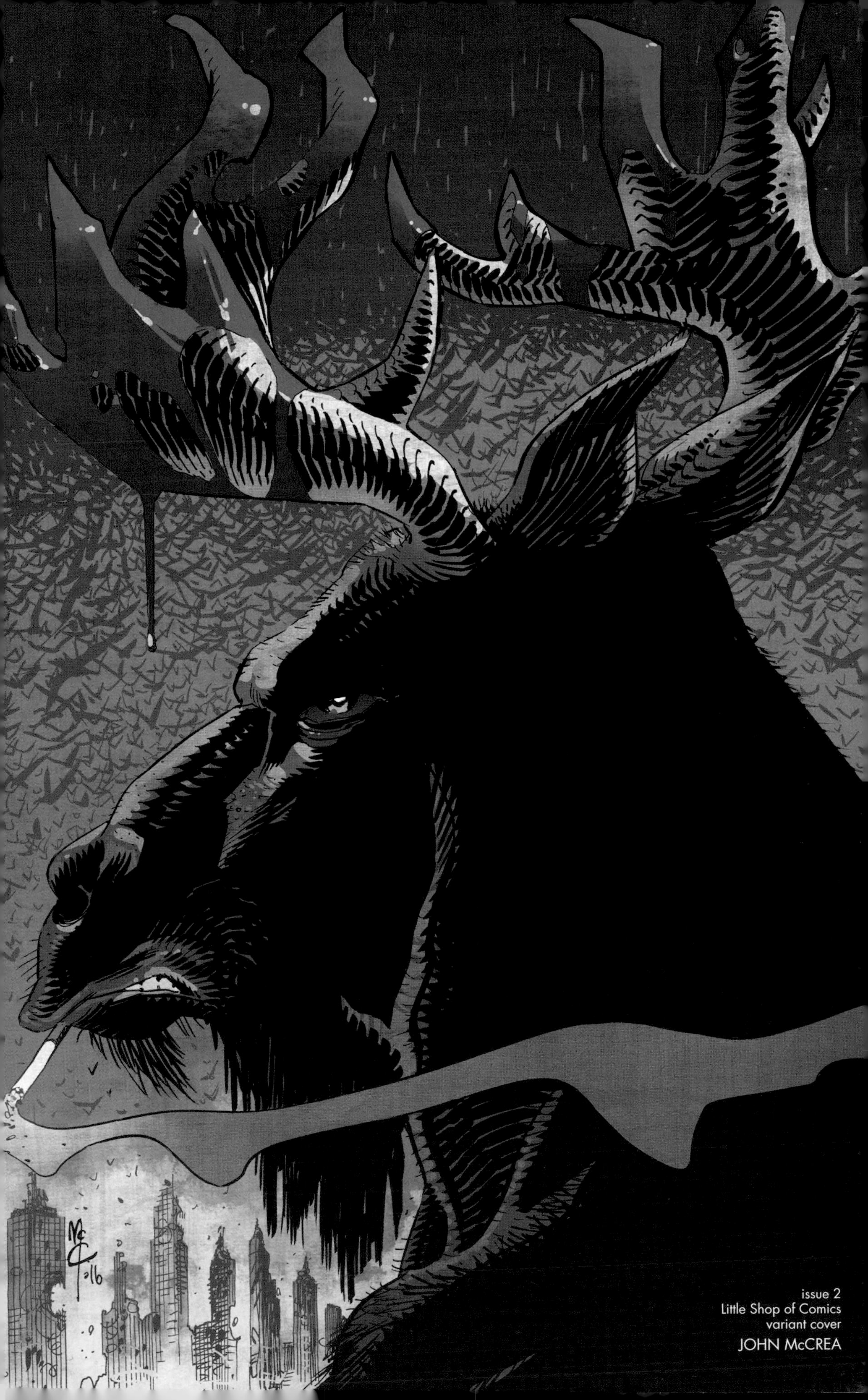

issue 2
Little Shop of Comics
variant cover
JOHN McCREA

issue 2
The Comic Mint variant cover
KELSEY SHANNON

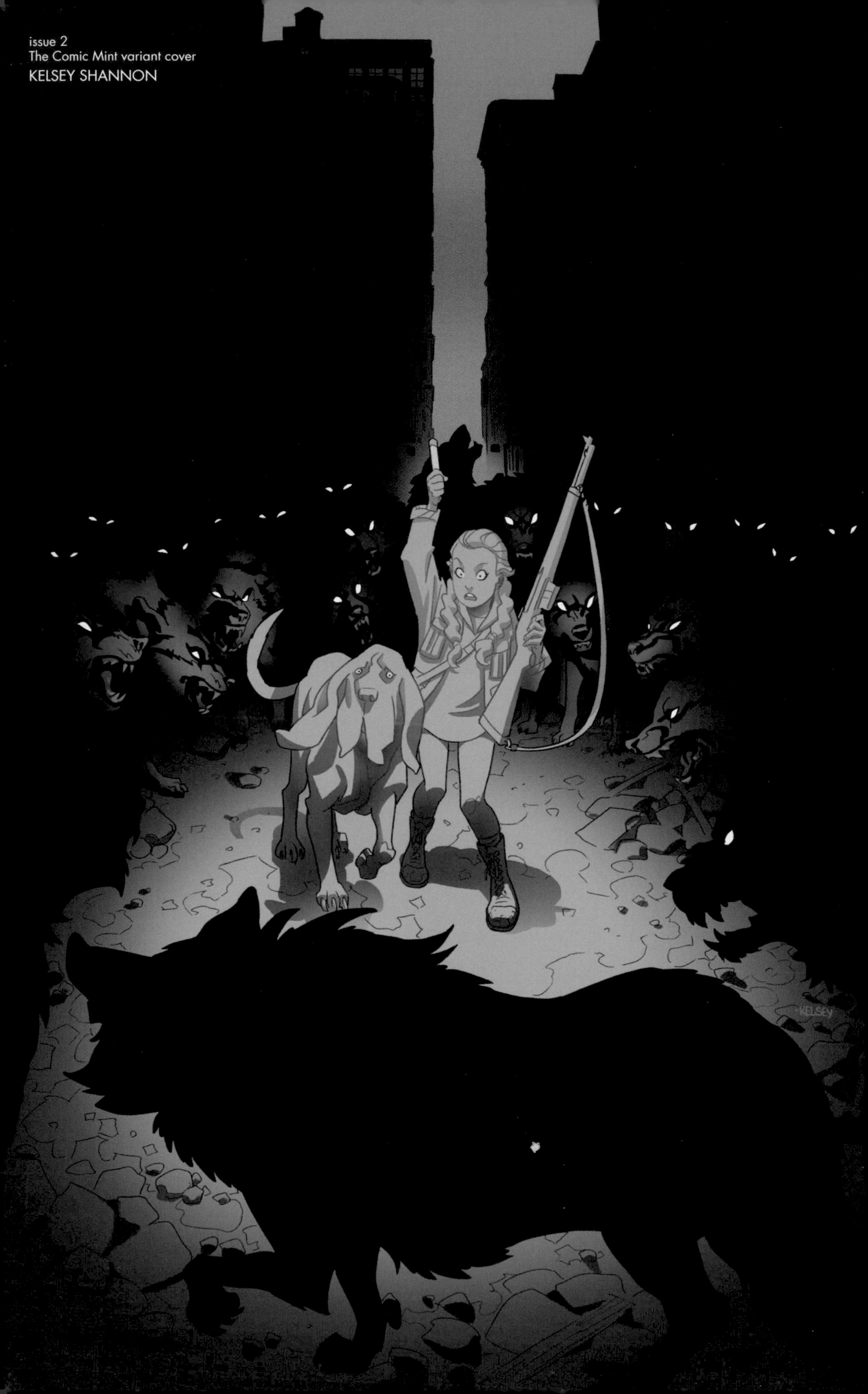
KELSEY

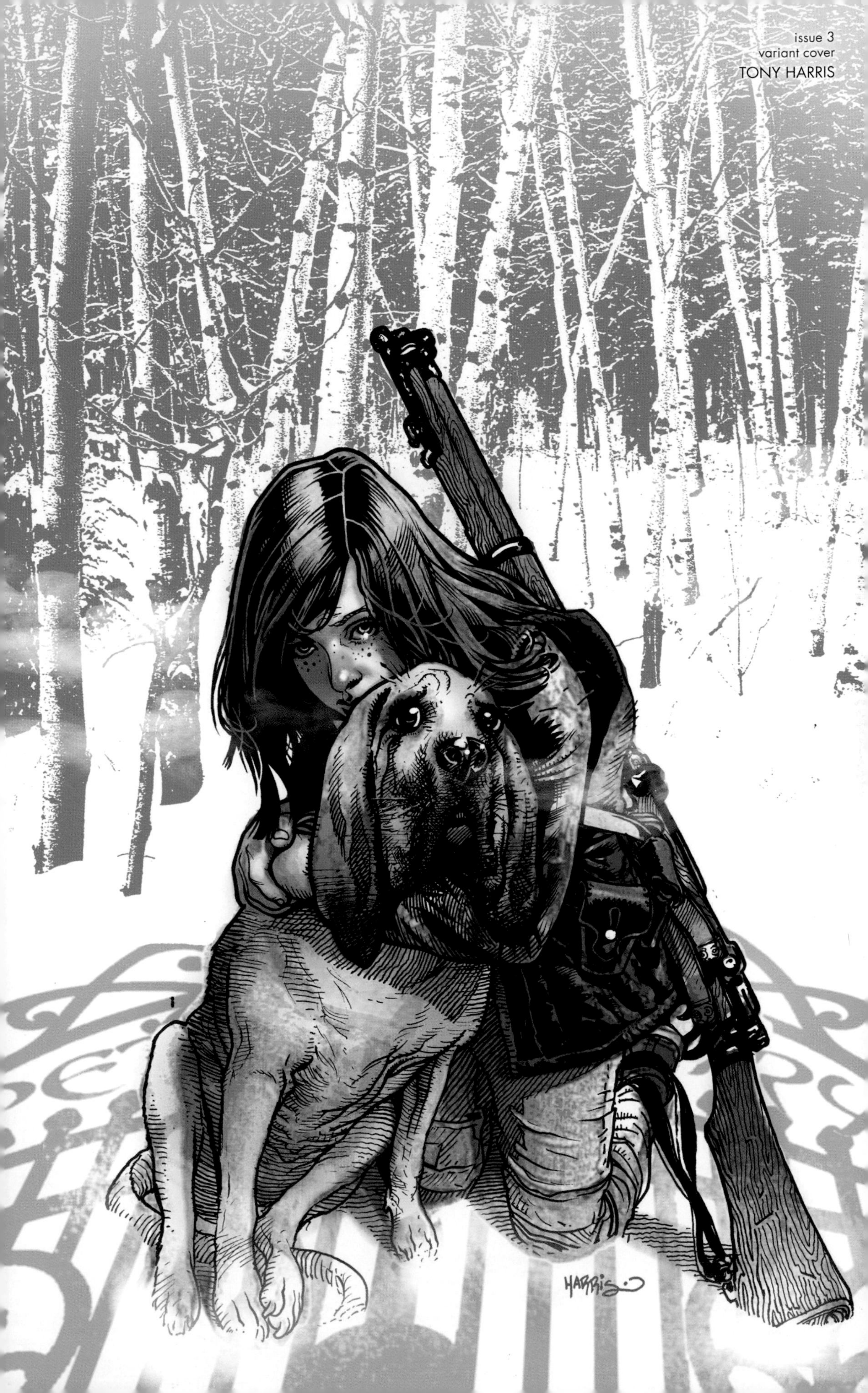
HARRIS
issue 3
variant cover
TONY HARRIS

issue 3
Frankie's Comics variant cover
KYLE STRAHM &
GREG SMALLWOOD

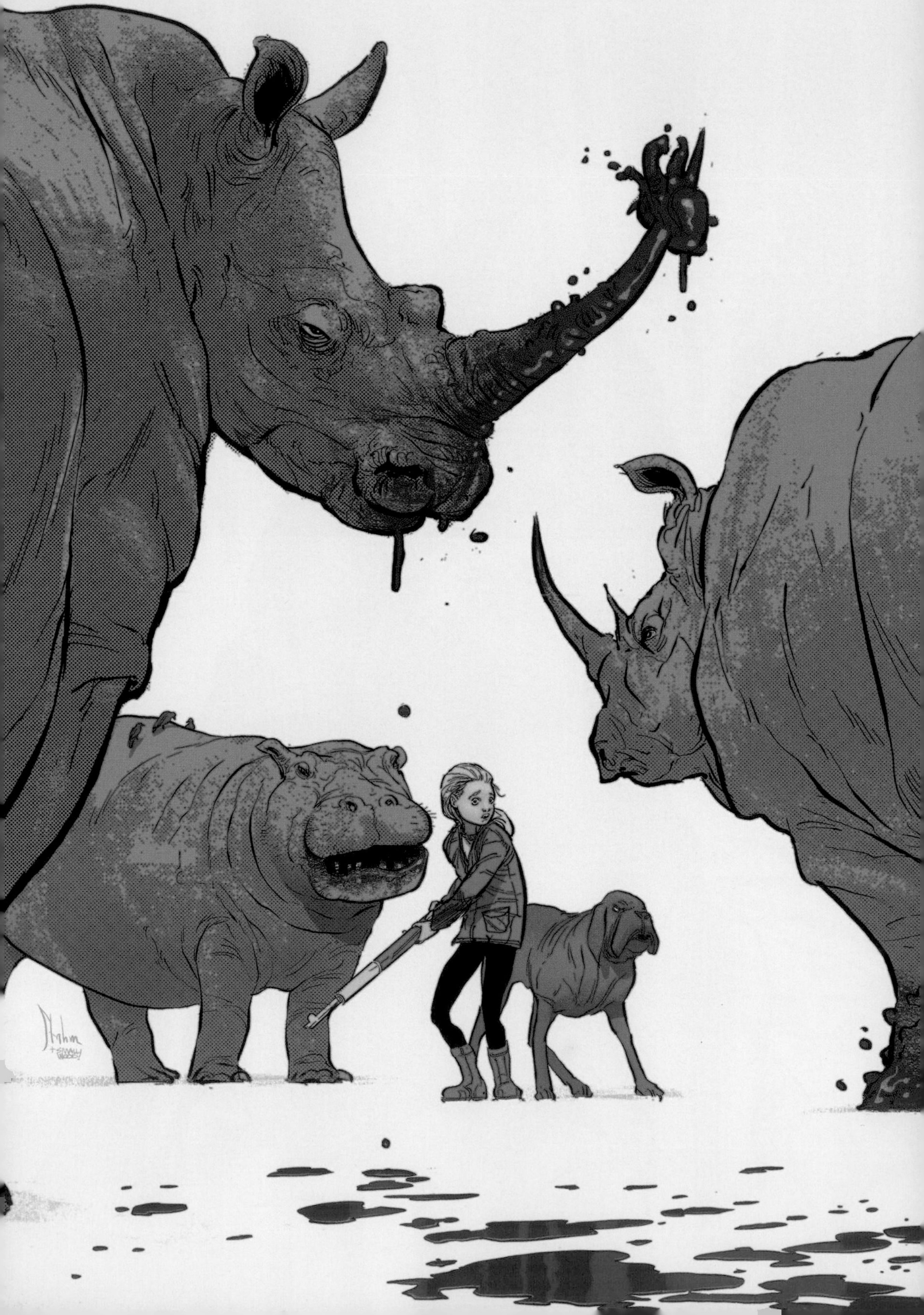

issue 3
MM Comics variant cover
KELSEY SHANNON

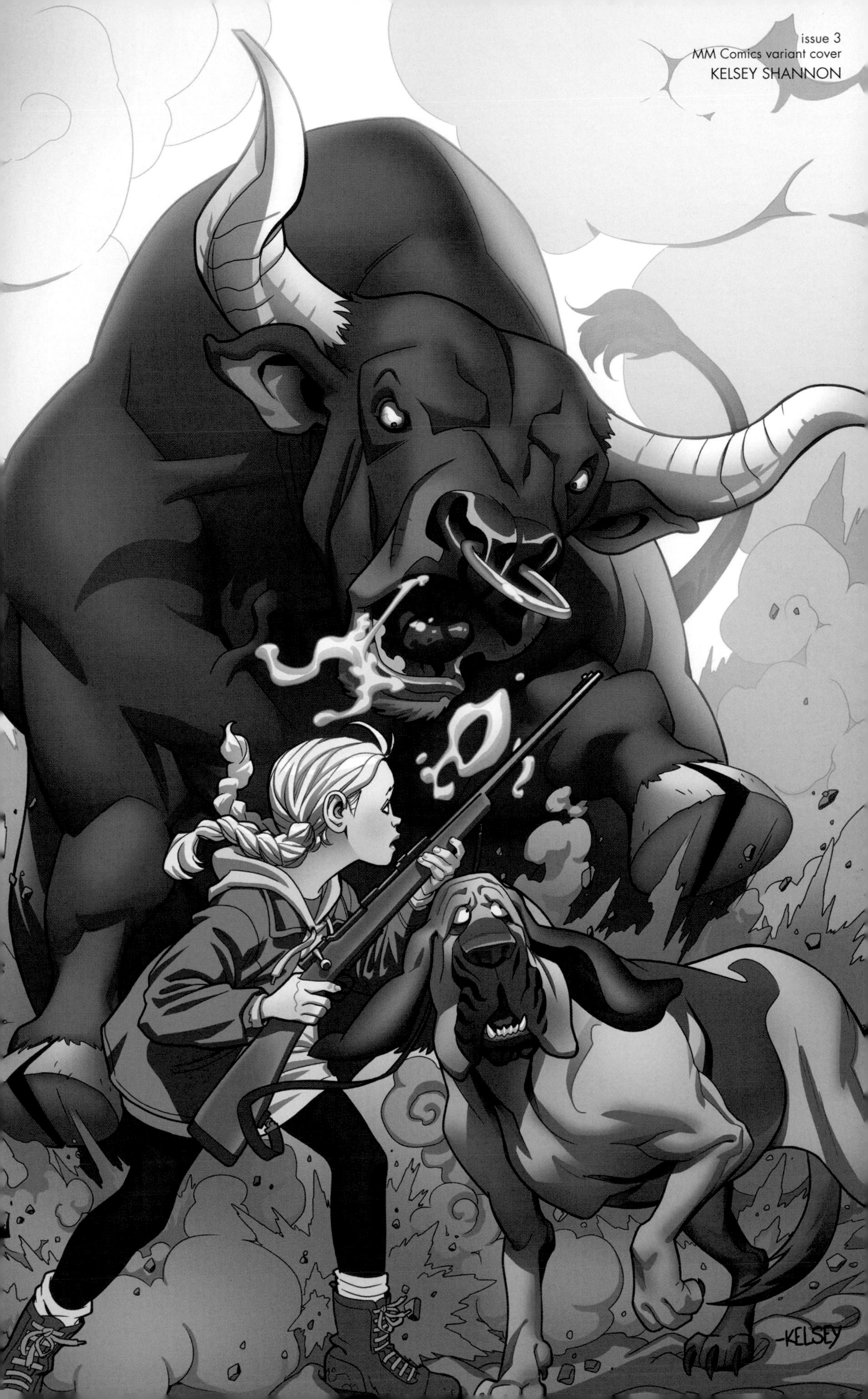
-KELSEY

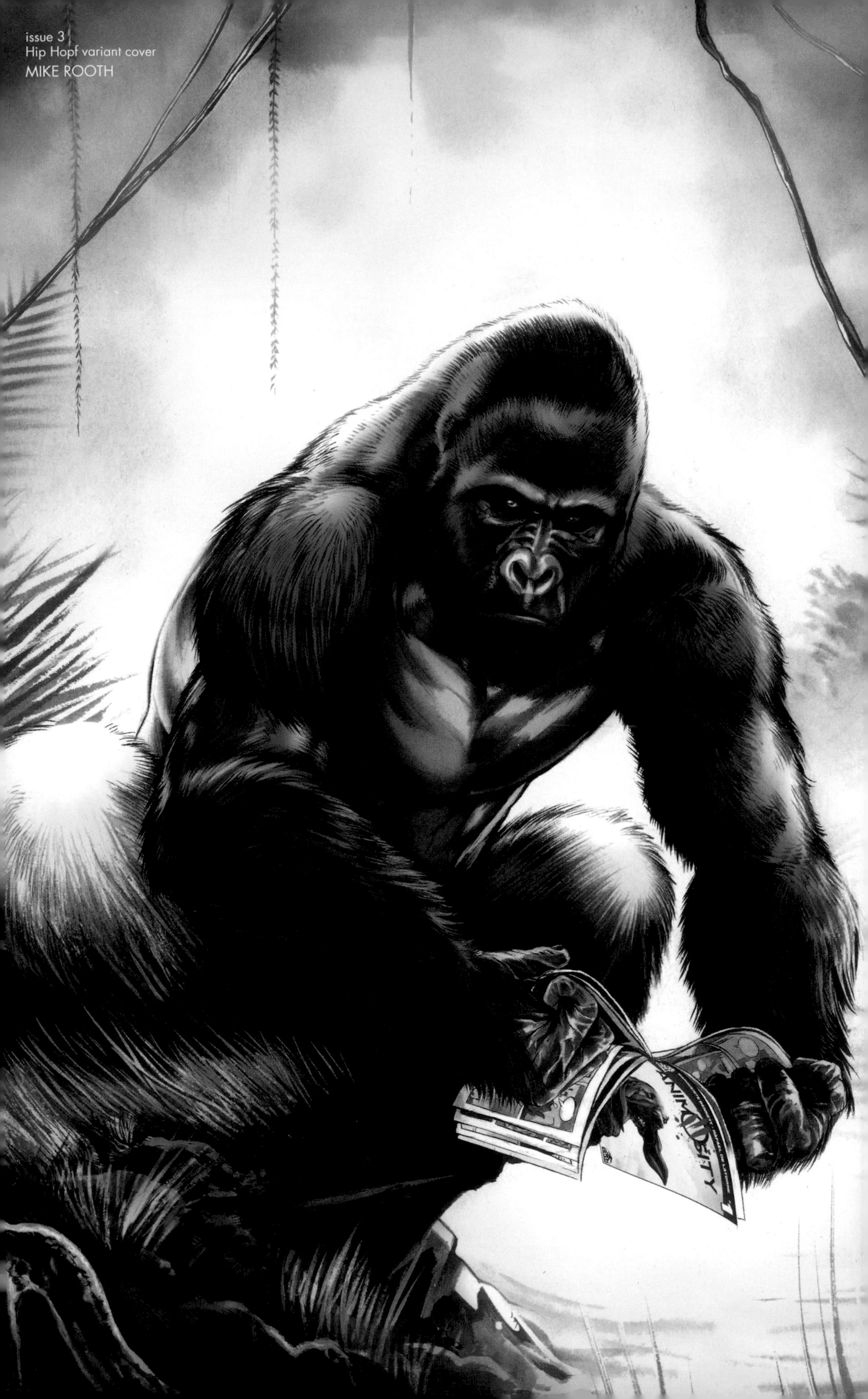

issue 3
Hip Hopf variant cover
MIKE ROOTH

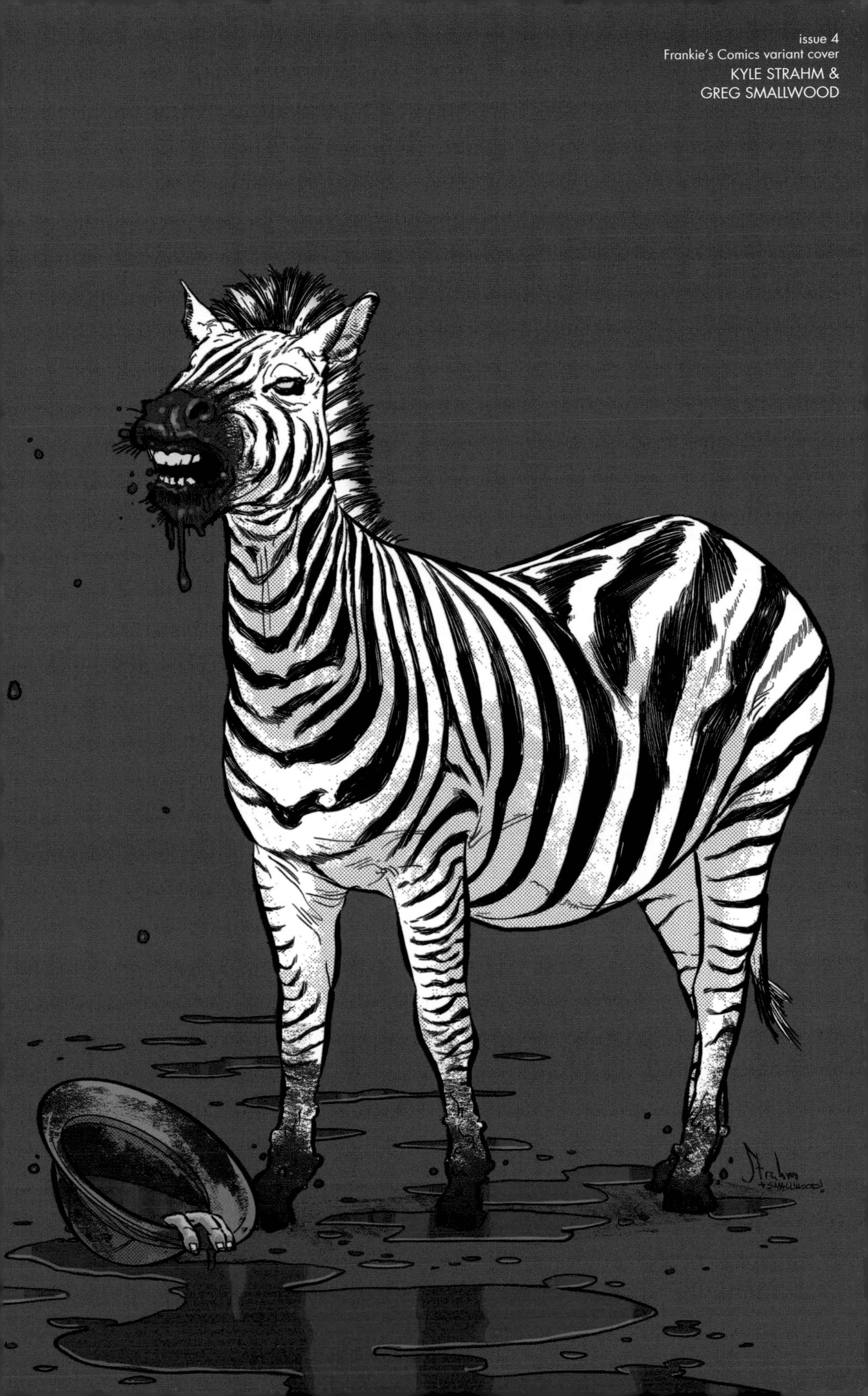

issue 4
Frankie's Comics variant cover
KYLE STRAHM &
GREG SMALLWOOD

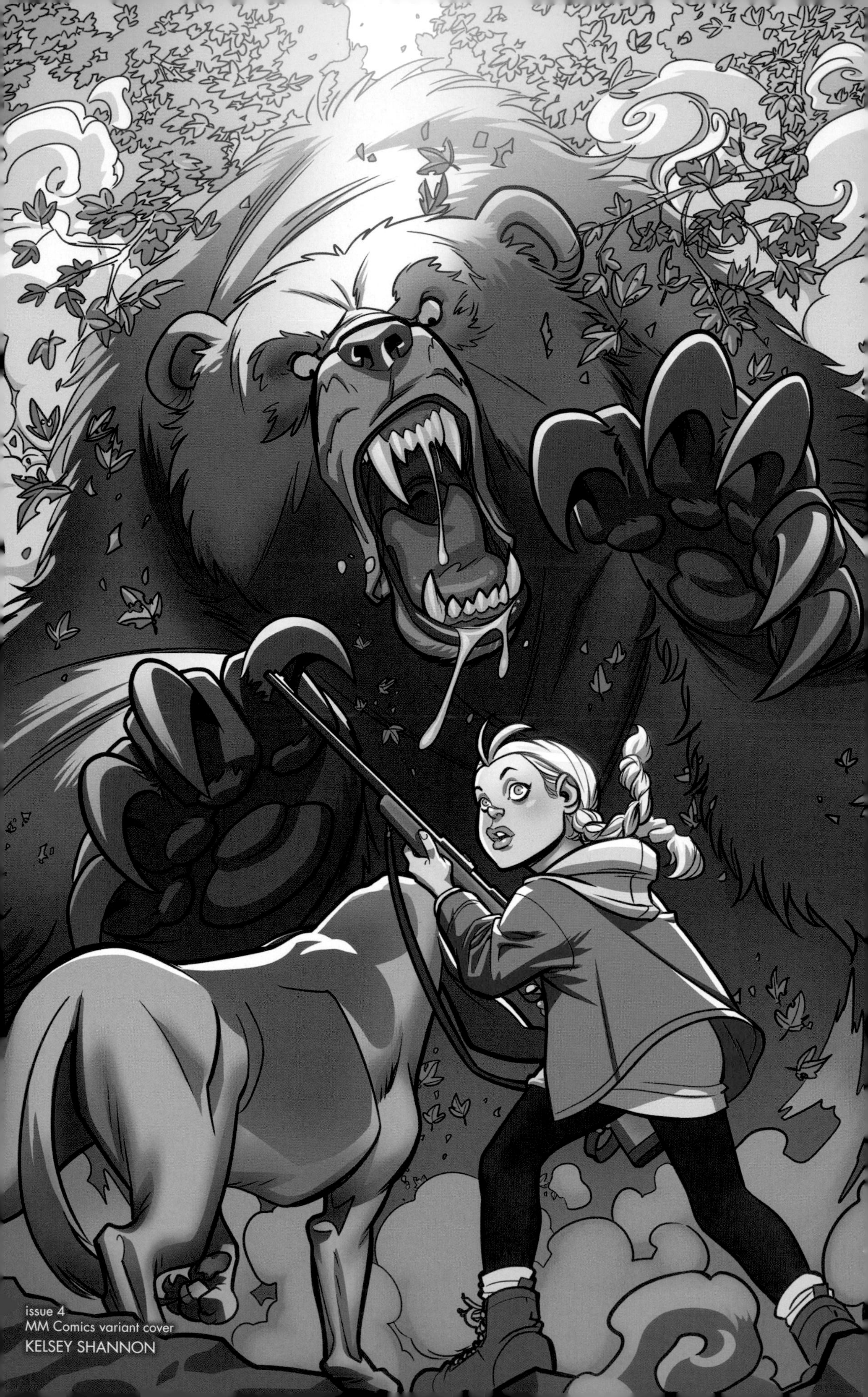

issue 4
MM Comics variant cover
KELSEY SHANNON

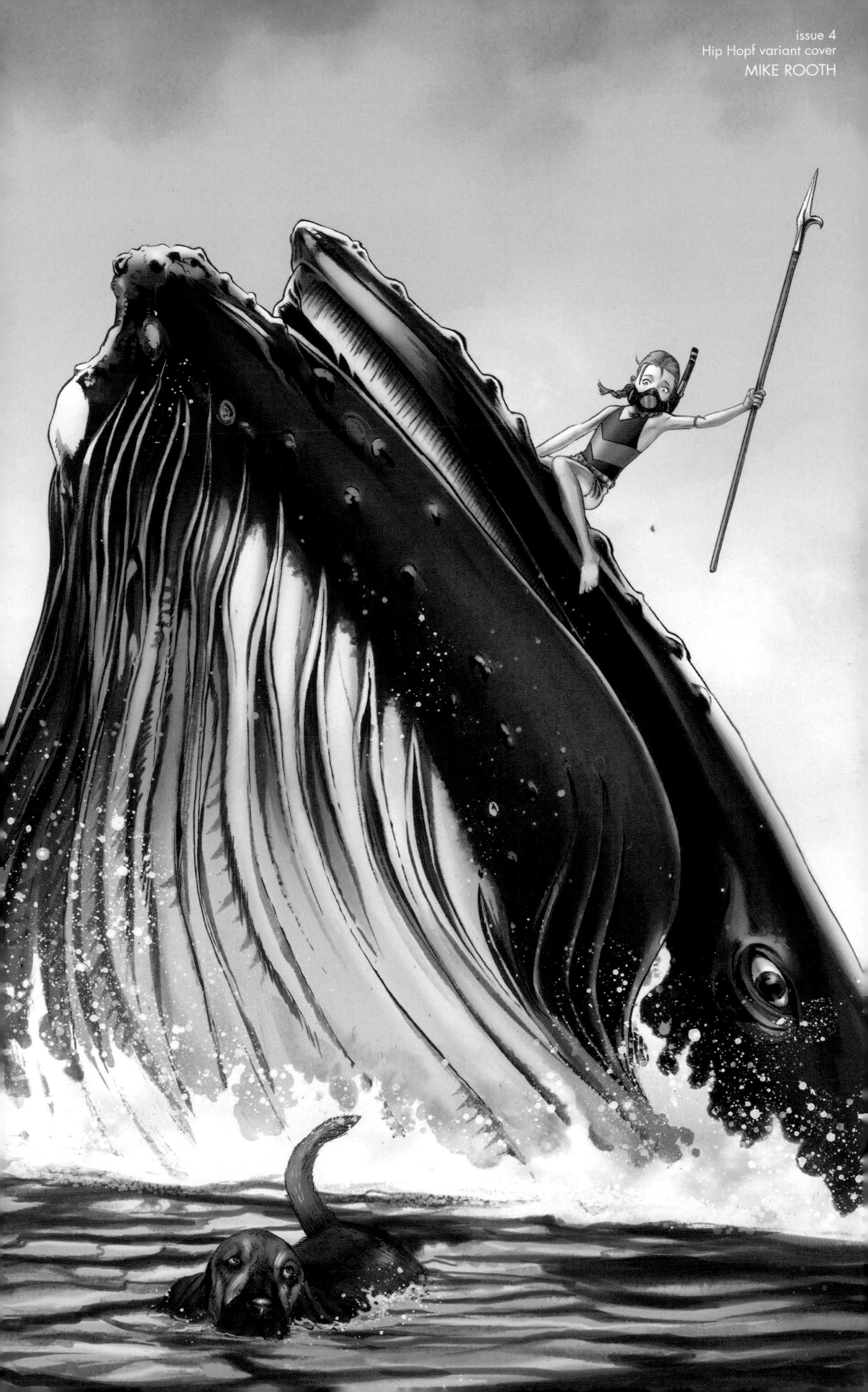

issue 4
Hip Hopf variant cover
MIKE ROOTH

THE RISE
variant cover
BRIAN STELFREEZE

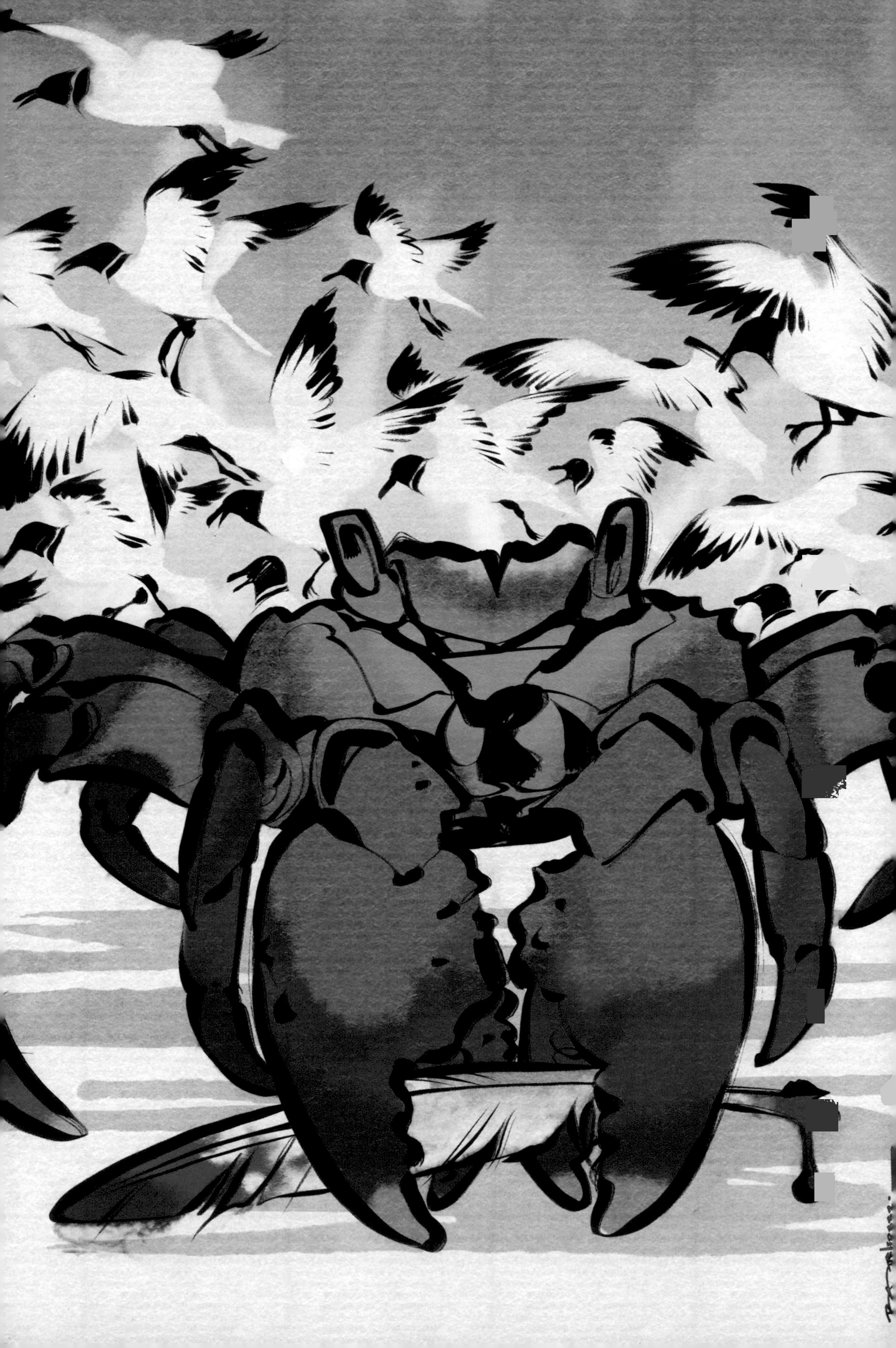

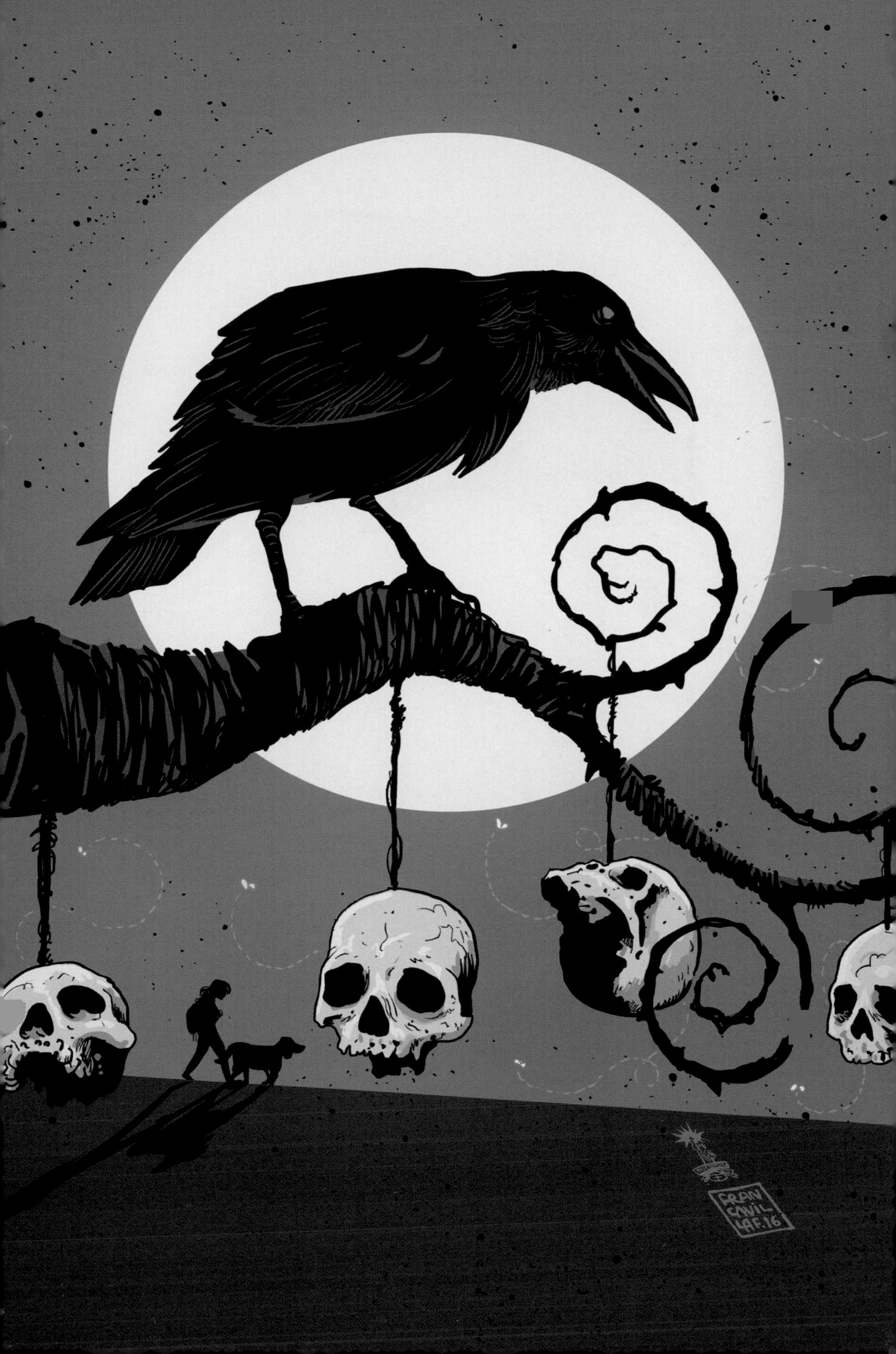

THE RISE
Frankie's Comics variant cover
FRANCESCO FRANCAVILLA

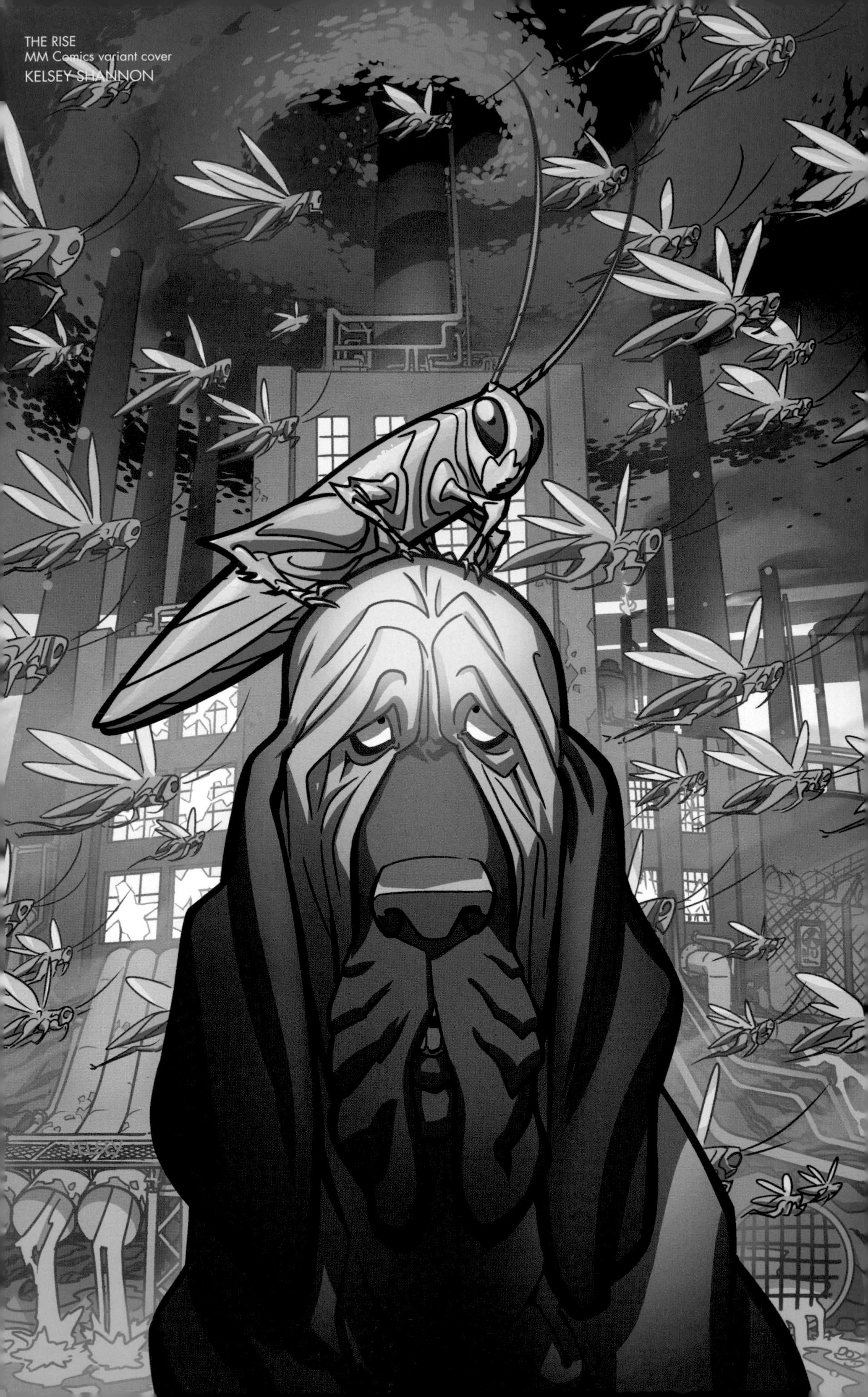

THE RISE
MM Comics variant cover
KELSEY SHANNON

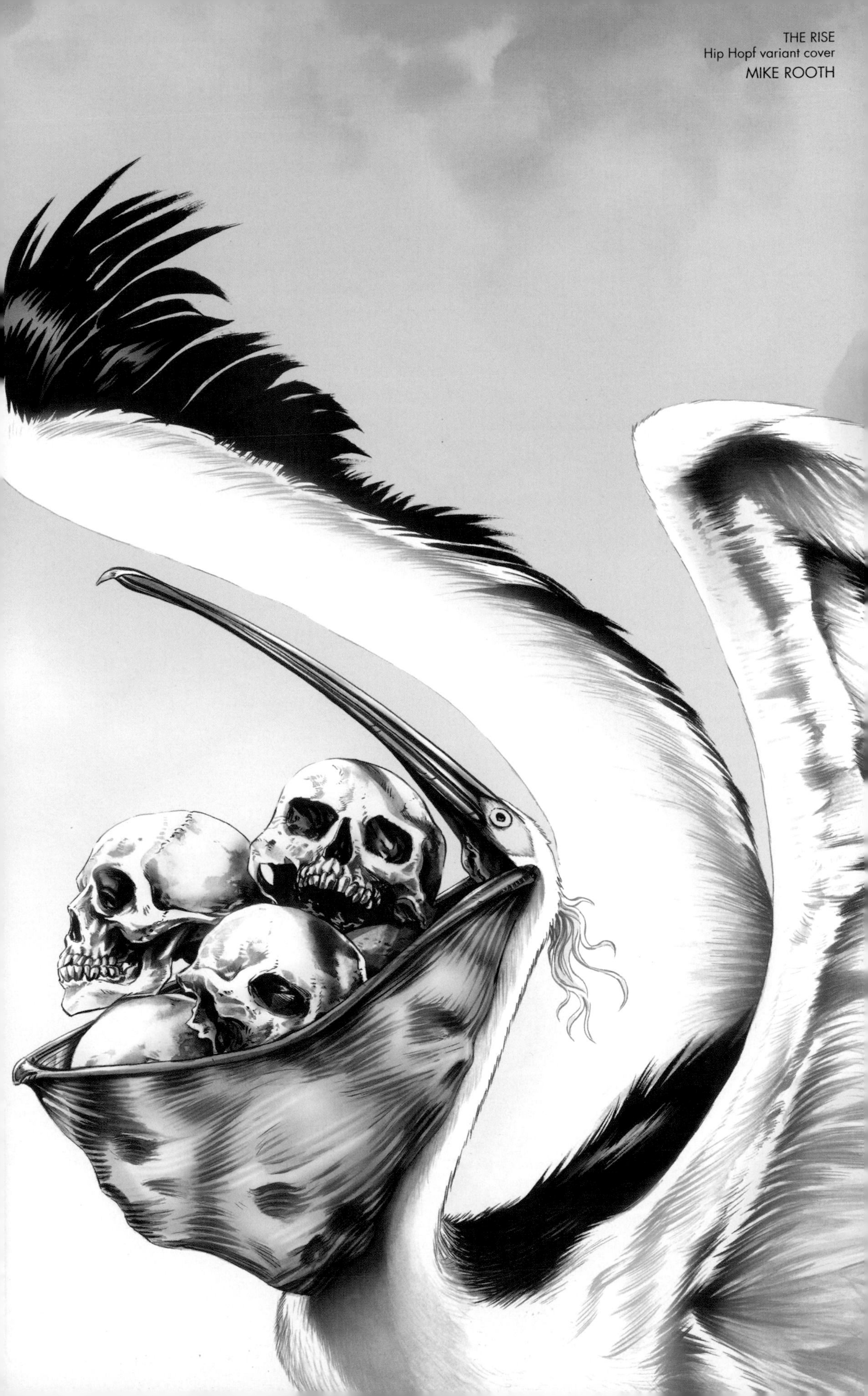

THE RISE
Hip Hopf variant cover
MIKE ROOTH

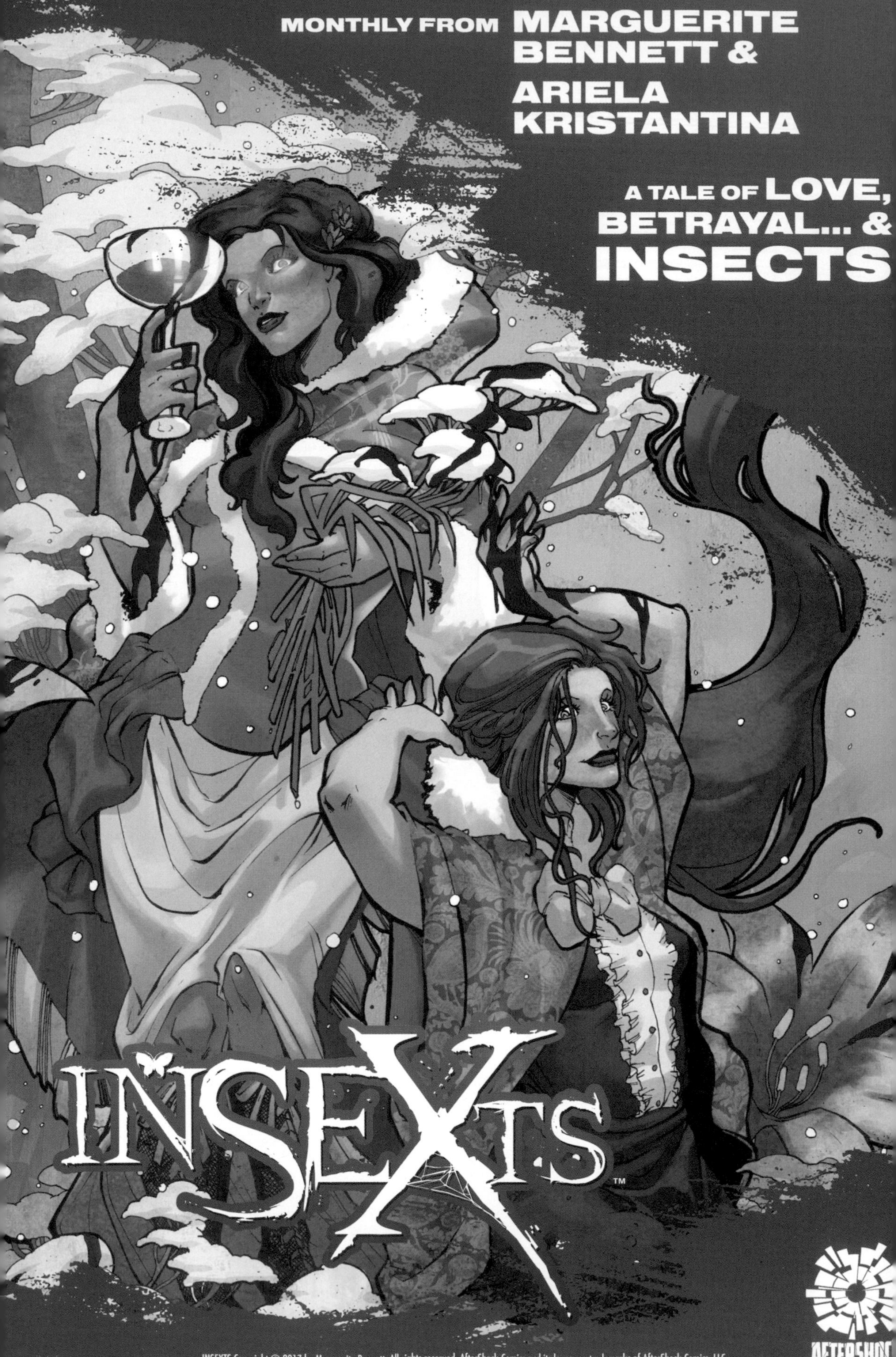
MONTHLY FROM MARGUERITE BENNETT & ARIELA KRISTANTINA
A TALE OF LOVE, BETRAYAL... & INSECTS
INSEXTS™
AFTERSHOCK

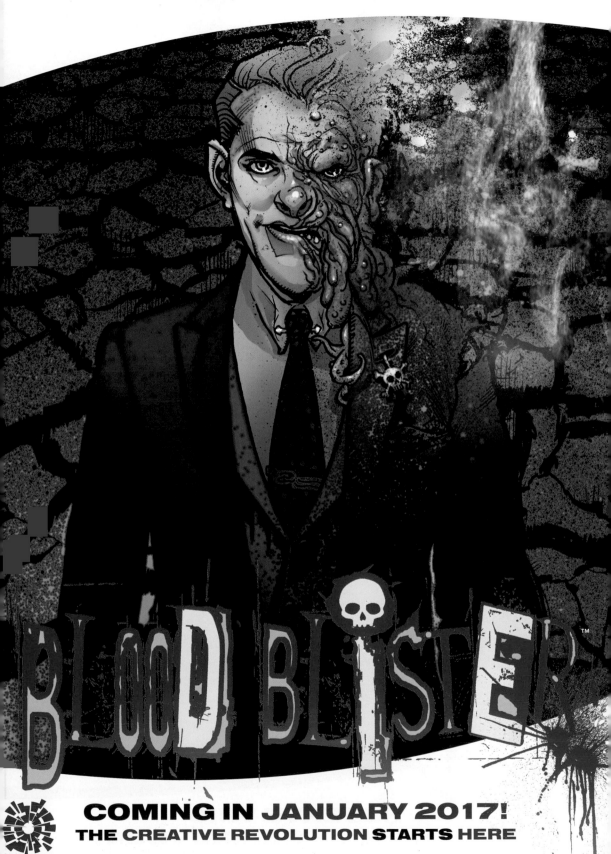

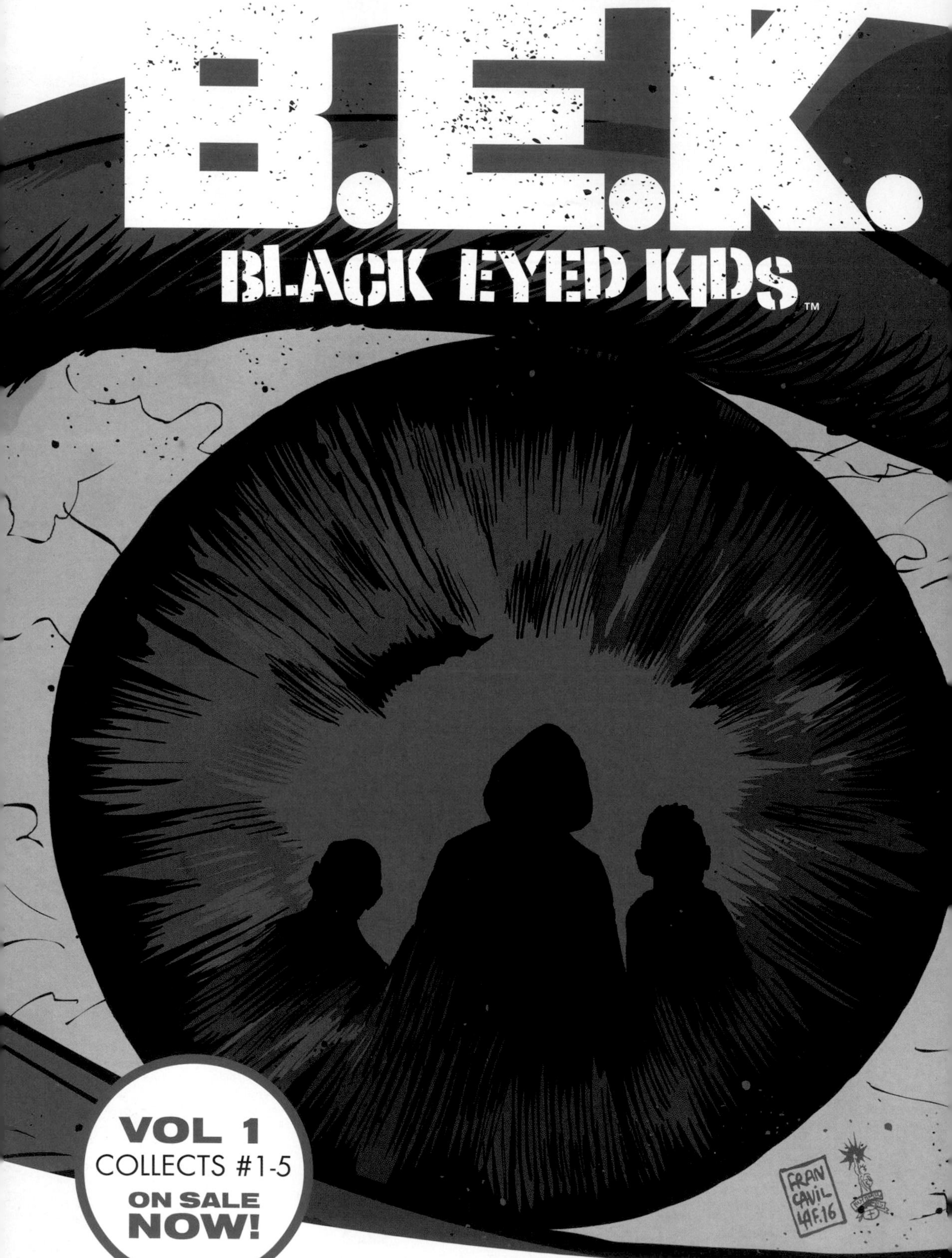
B.E.K.
BLACK EYED KIDS™
VOL 1
COLLECTS #1-5
ON SALE NOW!